THE IMPERIAL
SEASON

THE IMPERIAL SEASON

America's Capital in the Time of
the First Ambassadors, 1893–1918

WILLIAM SEALE

Smithsonian Books
Washington, DC

This book may be purchased for educational, business, or sales promotional use. For information, please write: Special Markets Department, Smithsonian Books, P. O. Box 37012, MRC 513, Washington, DC 20013

Published by Smithsonian Books
Director: Carolyn Gleason
Production Editor: Christina Wiginton
Editorial Assistants: Jane Gardner and Ashley Montague

Edited by Robin Whitaker
Designed by Brian Barth

Library of Congress Cataloging-in-Publication

Seale, William.
The imperial season : America's capital in the time of the first ambassadors, 1893–1918 / William Seale.
        pages cm
    Summary: "America's Capital in the Time of the First Ambassadors, 1893–1918"— Provided by publisher.
    Includes bibliographical references.
    ISBN 978-1-58834-391-8 (hardback)
    1. Washington (D.C.)—History—19th century. 2. Washington (D.C.)—History— 20th century. 3. Diplomats—Washington (D.C.) I. Title.

F199.S396 2013
975.3'04—dc23
                                                        2013023611

CONTENTS

To Maria Downs

PREFACE

This book begins in the capital of the United States in 1893 and ends there in 1918. During that quarter century the nation claimed a position of equality among the great powers for the first time in its history.

World power, if yet untested, presented a wholly new context for the United States. Reverberation from the sudden rise shook Washington long before it had much influence over the rest of the country. The character of official life and diplomacy transformed, and work started toward replacing Washington's provinciality and symbolic shortcomings. Change came not with a single stroke but by many innovations that altered situations from what they had been. The old American capital seemed suddenly a new place.

Those who lived through the change, and even helped create it, were a varied lot. Some were merely powerful, some were merely talented, and some were merely rich, but all were overwhelmingly self-confident, and all considered themselves visionary. None lacked objectives. Most were builders on one level or another, the most ambitious broadcasting the nation's new glory through public architecture and fine houses—inspired by Paris and Rome, London and Vienna, Berlin and Budapest, and the other capitals across Europe—that through the nineteenth century had been remodeled and extended to neoclassical magnificence. What they built still defines the heart of Washington today: the monuments and great civic buildings on the Mall as well as the mansions on the avenues that were designed as private houses but today serve as embassies.

The capital's age-old appeal of politics joined the city's social delights. Ambassadors from the ancient kingdoms of Europe crowned the diplomatic core in America's century-old New World democracy. The State Department, which shared its headquarters with the Navy and War Departments next door to the White House, was the hub of an ever-growing wheel of American diplomats, with spokes reaching over the world. Both business and pleasure attracted a busy winter community of people devoted to goals too numerous to categorize. Even some reformers appeared. Like all the rest, they saw the capital as a place to get what they wanted. Altogether, the era saw a sweep of diverse winds, borrowed traditions, and ideas that reshaped capital life.

This book, I hope, revives the era and its spirit, visiting the various human forces that gave life to what I call the "Imperial Season." The word *imperial* in the book title comes from America's overseas expansionist impulse of the late nineteenth and early twentieth centuries that paralleled movements of longer duration in Europe. *Season* in the title is borrowed from the social period known as "the season," which occurred in many cities of that time. Long ago the season was simply a loosely defined period of good times in winter after the crops were in, business was done, and it was good to relax and play. Washington knew it as the few months between December and spring, when Congress was in session and hospitality was notable. I recycle the word to stand for the whole quarter century, as an episode in American history, thus the Imperial Season.

Some of the characters you are likely to know well already, such as Presidents Cleveland, McKinley, Theodore Roosevelt, Taft, and Wilson. Others you may remember a little about, for instance, Secretary of State John Hay; John Sherman, politician and brother of the more famous general William T. Sherman; and the powerful volunteer leader of the Red Cross, Mabel Boardman. More, however, you probably do not know at all, such as the hostess Mary Scott Townsend, the diplomat Alvey Adee, and the glamorous feminist Inez Milholland. A few individuals you may have forgotten for a moment, such as the bombastic congressman Joe Cannon, the seafaring philosopher Captain Mahan, and the dreamer and builder of great fairs and city gates Daniel P. Burnham.

I have crafted this history as I saw fit. Some figures you may expect to find have been omitted. Usually these people were excluded because they did not serve my descriptive purpose, or, for all they might have promised, when weighed in the context of the whole story, their presence was merely repetitious of others who do appear. Personal letters and diaries have provided the main sources, in combination with public records of the Department of State and to a lesser extent those of the Departments of the Interior and the Army. Especially rich sources are the published memoirs, which, for the most part, I dug out of the great anonymity of used books for a few dollars each. Nearly all of them were written after World War I by people looking back on the Imperial Season as a time already remote and glowing in their minds as having been special. Countess Cassini's, the last written, was published in 1962 and provides a charming account of a young girl's life in diplomatic Washington at the season's peak. You will find reference to all of these in the notes and bibliography.

I wish to thank friends and colleagues for help and advice over the decade and more of research and writing: Charles M. Harris, James M. Goode, Joel Treese, Bonnie M. Hart, Will Seale, Marcia M. Anderson, Frederick J. Lindstrom, Anna J. Cook, Stephen Plotkin, Fiona Griffin, Liz Argentieri, Nenette Arroyo, Bruce R. Kirby, Annita Andrick, Karen Mark, James E. Holland, Lydia Barker Tederick, Carol Johnson, Molly Kudner, Mildred Elmore, James B. Renberg, Jeff Bridgers, Antoinette J. Lee, Jennifer

Brathoved, Shane Hunt, Gary S. Scott, William Bushong, Ruth Lincoln Kaye, Amy Verone, Barbara M. Kirkconnell, Ellen McCallister Clark, Susan Raposa, Maria Downs, Valerie Sallis, C. Ford Peatross, Susan G. Everitt, of the Charles B. Everitt Book Agency, and, by no means least, Lucinda S. Seale.

At Smithsonian Books I thank Carolyn Gleason, director, Christina Wiginton, Matt Litts, Kathleen Stanley, and Jane Gardner. Thanks to Robin Whitaker for her thoughtful and comprehensive editing. I also wish to remember Caroline Newman gratefully for her early interest in the manuscript.

William Seale

PROLOGUE
The First Ambassador

G reat Britain's ambassador-designate could easily have walked across the lawn from the State Department to the White House next door, but on one particular important day—and few in his life had been this important—Sir Julian Pauncefote agreed to travel in a carriage. He knew as well as anyone else that ceremony for most Americans was confined to courthouse and church. Nonetheless, they loved foreign show. Even if a crowd of spectators had gathered to see this procession, it would have provided only glimpses of sunshine sparkling a bit on the golden trimmings of the candidate's uniform, discerned through the windows of the regulation State Department coach that carried Sir Julian and two other officials with him up the gravel driveway from Pennsylvania Avenue.

Beneath the shelter of the famous columned portico, neither Pauncefote nor his two companions moved to alight right away, although a uniformed White House footman stood by to open the carriage door. Exact punctuality was mandatory for diplomats. The hundred or so guests and officials admitted inside to witness the ceremony also waited for the hour of eleven.

It was April 11, 1893. Sir Julian already had served Britain in the Washington diplomatic community for nearly four years as the queen's minister plenipotentiary and extraordinary. His elevation to ambassador might have come nearly a year earlier, but Britain waited for the U.S. Congress to approve an American ambassador to St. James's before the Foreign Office in London felt free to send such a high official of its own to Washington. All the ins and outs that had come together two weeks before awaited only the morning's presidential approval to be finalized. When the ceremony was over, Pauncefote would become the first foreign ambassador stationed in the United States of America. Excitement among the people invited that morning was clear enough, but the guests from the diplomatic corps were surprised that no cheering spectators had collected among everyday citizens on the street.[1] It would have been different in Europe.

When State Department officials followed the rules and customs of international diplomacy carefully, even a brief ceremony, simple on the surface, was not simple in any other dimension. In this case the ceremony had to honor tradition, yet take into account a more informal "American" character. The third assistant secretary of state was in charge. His name was Alvey Augustus Adee. Alvey Adee's stated listing on the federal payroll seemed almost meaningless, considering the extent of his responsibilities. A simple job description could never have covered his work, which at his high level in the State Department was more independent and diverse than similar positions in any other department in the federal government. Among the many aspects of diplomacy he mastered were the ceremonial procedures of foreign courts, in which he was especially well-versed. Now that an ambassador was in Washington, the extent of Adee's knowledge was more useful than academic. And if the ceremonies he devised were even to suggest the grandeur that surrounded foreign monarchs, the ire of Congress would surely fall hard upon the department. Adee was an artist at delicately peeling away princely features—no bowing, long addresses, or patterned marches—yet preserving the basics of the diplomatic forms intact. The Adee style in designing the reception of the ambassador, based upon a casual presentation of credentials started by President Jefferson some ninety years before, created a form that morning that was used from then on in the accreditation of ambassadors to the United States.[2]

The third assistant secretary had approved the guest list with the president, selected the luncheon menu, helped pick the musical scores (although he was deaf), and ordered palms and flowers dollied in from the conservatory to complete a festal background. He typed the words that President Grover Cleveland was to speak. Adee's hand was in all the details.[3]

In the hall, John Philip Sousa tuned the red-jacketed Marine Band. Guests had entered in double lines, gently urged on by ushers. The curtains were drawn to block the daylight, giving the interior over to a shower of hard, cold electric light from overhead. The muscled hulk of President Cleveland crossed the hall from the elevator, hustled along by his secretary and close friend, the newspaper man Dan Lamont. Both obeyed patiently as Adee positioned them on X marks he had chalked on the carpet.

At last about half a dozen queer-looking old White House clocks dinged, clanged, and gonged together, announcing the hour of eleven. Now the ceremony commenced. Secretary of State Walter Q. Gresham, Pauncefote, and the British embassy secretary, Cecil Spring-Rice, entered the front door, walking rapidly. On the eleventh chime they passed through Tiffany's colored-glass screen, then to the Blue Room, where the silent audience stood soldierlike around the walls. Pauncefote had followed a similar procedure when he presented his credentials as minister plenipotentiary. The ceremony revised for ambassadorial status was stiffer, shorter, and more tightly orchestrated. Sir Julian wore not a mere business suit, as a foreign minister would have, but the uniform of a full-rank ambassador. The stately black-velvet suit, more quaint than handsome, was tailored with knee breeches and short coat. In the familiar White House portrait hanging on the wall, George Washington was represented in similar costume, an unadorned diplomatic suit current a century before. The most obvious difference between the two suits was that the ambassador's was enriched with pounds of gold bullion and gilt buttons. He must have looked wonderfully foreign to the American guests. With pride the heavy-set Sir Julian, white-headed in his early sixties, displayed at his side the silver presentation sword sent to him by Queen Victoria upon his rise to ambassador. A flock of ribboned medals pinned on his coat marked milestones of honor in more than twenty years in service to the crown.[4]

The secretaries took two steps back, and president and ambassador addressed each other point blank, first the ambassador, who gave brief, eloquent remarks from memory, after which Lamont handed the president Adee's paper, and Cleveland read his response in his detached monotone, squinting over a pince-nez. When the two shook hands, Adee signaled Sousa, and "The Blue Danube" waltz sanctified the moment. The company moved, rumbling en masse, to luncheon in the state dining room down the hall.

After lunch was over, President Cleveland rose from the table—his presidential privilege was to depart first—more than ready to return to the office upstairs. He nodded presidentially to all those down the table and disappeared into the elevator. The ambassador departed as he had come, in the plain black State Department coach, hardly the gilded vehicle that would have transported him in nearly every other capital in the world, but it rolled him swiftly home to the legation, which during the ceremony had officially become the Embassy of Great Britain.

Quietly, symbolically, the White House ceremony marked the beginning of a new age for the mighty North American democracy. The presence of Ambassador Pauncefote in Washington established a way for the greatest power on earth to have immediate and definitive interactions with the American president on the scene, without consulting his Foreign Office in London. If this was big news in London, Paris, Berlin, all over Europe, it aroused little interest in America. Diplomacy was a subject distant to Americans. They really didn't understand it. The accreditation of Sir Julian passed by them barely noticed.

Britain's ambassador was soon followed by ambassadors from other major powers that sought closer association with a rich and strong America.[5] The "sleeping giant," as the European press liked to call the United States, represented to them all a resource in reserve, even if they were not prepared to recognize America as their political equal. The American warehouse of strength was especially important to the British, for they, like every other kingdom in Europe, closely watched the technological buildup of the weapons of war, notably in Germany and Austria-Hungary.

Americans' concerns remained elsewhere. Apart from that small number who were sufficiently well-heeled and inclined to travel abroad, the vast majority, as a general rule, seem to have dismissed Europe as decadent and archaic. After the Pauncefote ceremony, a reporter from the Washington *Evening Star*, lingering outside the White House door, witnessed an innocent example of this amused contempt: a group of congressmen "from the West" paused to watch the president's young wife, Frances, alight from her carriage. Just as she did, the Italian minister, Baron de Fava, swept before her with a deep bow and kissed her hand. The congressmen "nearly fell off the porch" laughing.[6]

America was a world power before most Americans realized it. Only those in Washington, the capital, took to the idea at once. The perception was not deep but was inspiring. People came from everywhere to turn the city into a stage for great things, acting as players to light that stage with beguiling fantasies of life in a world power.

How this all came to pass over the twenty-five years after Sir Julian's ceremony occupies the following pages.

ONE

The Capital of the Sleeping Giant

In 1893 Washington offered little of the glory an experienced ambassador like Sir Julian Pauncefote might have expected of a national capital.[1] After a century in existence, the District of Columbia was no small place by American standards, having some 210,000 citizens;[2] however, more of a city had been intended than was actually built by then.

The visionary plan drawn up by Major Pierre Charles L'Enfant and approved by George Washington in the last decade of the eighteenth century had been honored in some of the construction since, but the city as conceived was unfinished. Long, straight streets of a stately, even a ceremonial, character linked the public places and diagonally pierced an everyday grid intended for neighborhoods of houses, stores, churches, and the workaday life of citizens. This distribution of parts, in a sense, has prevailed in Washington. By the 1890s most of the permanent residents had settled in the capital because they were beholden to the government as employees, contractors, and lobbyists.

The capital presented groves of shade trees and vacant lots. As for the buildings, no dominant style unified them, unless it was that of the expressionless red-brick row house that formed the monotonous neighborhoods built off the avenues. Public buildings varied in style from the early classical edifices of local stone, dressed and painted white, built in the generation of the Founding Fathers, to later structures of brick and stone in various forms that bespoke their eras, especially the Prussian grandeur of the Treasury Building and the Patent Office commenced by Andrew Jackson's time, and more so the heavy granite and red brick in the period of growth in the government following the Civil War. Europeans called the public architecture provincial.

The one dominating feature of the capital was the house of Congress, the Capitol, which could be seen from every part of the city. Congress kept its lofty, iron-domed house painted bright white, never allowing a bit of rust or a splotch of mildew, and while the elected officials might have battled within it over the cost of the paint bucket by bucket, to the world outside they presented a unified front in the protection and total possession of their building. It was the only building in Washington that proclaimed "seat of government."

The architecture of the Capitol as built had been inspired by neoclassical motifs popular at the time. Later on, when the building was greatly enlarged to add functional space, the architecture was altered to honor the aesthetics of proportion. Completion of the original Capitol in about 1820 was followed around thirty years later by the addition of very large side wings, which created a monotonously heavy and horizontal building. To correct this, the Capitol was given its signature dome. The new element, with its single, triumphant, upward thrust lightened the look of the building. It was purely a decorative feature and accomplished the goal stunningly by bringing balance to the whole.

Civil War soldiers passing through had been so moved at seeing the rise of the fresh, new dome during their hard fight that they called it the symbol of the Union they had interrupted their lives to preserve. The dome's simple structure—a skin of cast-iron plates laid over a hoopskirt skeleton of the same material—made some see the dome as a sham, a flimsy confection, even though little criticism was made of its structural model, the iron dome of Saint Isaac's Cathedral, built a little earlier in St. Petersburg, Russia. The light weight of the iron compared with heavy masonry made it possible to preserve the historical walls of the original Capitol. No building in the nation was more immediately recognizable than the Capitol. It was the foremost architectural emblem of the democratic American society.

From the Capitol's halls, verbal wars stormed ever-furious; waves of political power crashed and flowed from that building, rippling to the farthest corners of the town, then rolling on through the rest of the nation into every house and every life. In spite of this, by 1893 it had addressed the broader world very little.

George Washington's new capital had been established in approximately the center of the nation as he knew it. Furthermore, it was built beside the Potomac River, upon which a sailing ship could travel three hundred miles from the sea. The capital was to be both the economic and the governmental center. The Louisiana Purchase precluded the economic promise of that idea by opening the Mississippi River to commerce; the steamboat dealt the *coup de grâce*. All that was left for the capital was the political role. By 1893 the city it proudly surveyed was a comfortable relic. Its heart was the government, and that alone set it apart.

The Georgian "Executive Mansion," as the White House was officially known, with the incongruous added portico poking out on the north side and another on the south, had the need for remodeling or replacement written all over it. Americans, however, loved the old house that George Washington had built and where the Great Emancipator had lived. The president's house, like other buildings of early-day Washington, had been joined by new structures decade after decade, each reflecting the ideas of architecture current in its time. The public buildings and public streets fell under the jurisdiction of the Army Corps of Engineers, which had been put in charge by President Grant nearly a quarter century before the first ambassador came to town. Jealously guarding their authority, the corps maintained the capital's buildings and the city's streets neatly and efficiently, drawing money from Congress with ease for any projects they cared to undertake.

If a visitor to Washington wanted to see the capital city, it was possible in the 1890s to tour it all on foot, including most of the residential districts. If done energetically, the process would probably have taken a full day; for slow walkers, two. No one was likely to want to see it all. In terms of its network of small communities, Washington seemed like New York or Boston or Chicago but not at all like those cities otherwise. The capital was wholly without a pronounced, overriding urban quality. The best way to see Washington was on a bicycle. Many people in Washington rode bikes; visitors rented them. Swaying among pedestrians and horses and carriages on weekends, the two-wheeled, pedaled vehicles were so plentiful, numbering in the hundreds, that Washington was sometimes called a "bicycle town," like Cleveland.

Alvey Adee, the diplomat who planned the first ambassadorial ceremony at the White House, was the best-known bicyclist in Washington. Several days a week he rode his bicycle aggressively over the capital streets. He had his reason for doing this, beyond the fashionable cycling craze. When as a young man he suffered a bout of life-threatening illness, he determined that come what may he would build his physical stamina to as near perfection as he could. Lean and healthy at the age of forty, he had not surrendered regular, vigorous workouts, usually on his bicycle, but varied now and then by rowing his canoe on the Potomac, a sport he liked to share with his not-so-athletic friend John Hay.[3]

No one was better dressed than Adee for all occasions, including bike riding. Newspaper clippings picture him beside his bike, wearing knickers with black stockings, jacket, vest, white shirt open at the collar, scarf, and the serious rider's tight, brimless hat with drop-down goggles. The third secretary of state also took evident pride in his bike, keeping it polished, greased, and in perfect order. He had owned this bicycle for years, placing it in his affections on a par with his best birding rifle, camera, and favorite volume of Shakespeare. Adee kept the bike with him at work, and when he was ready to ride, one of his State Department messengers and aides, usually Eddie Savoy, a tall, authoritative black man, carried the bicycle from its stash inside, down the long steps, to the street. Savoy could clock his boss's reappearance on his watch—precisely one hour, at which time the messenger stood waiting to return the vehicle to its place inside.[4]

Although he was an easy-going man on foot, Adee took a mad delight in speed that sometimes made him a menace on his bicycle. Pedestrians instinctively stepped aside as he flew along, bent over the handlebars. But his daring was not extreme. Rain might not stop him, but he did not cycle in a thunderstorm, with its threat of

Alvey A. Adee, ca. 1902. *Records of the Department of State,*
U.S. National Archives.

lightning, or in icy conditions. He once suffered a broken rib for dodging a dog, and he was embarrassed when the mishap was reported in the press. In summer he pedaled through Europe for about a month to six weeks, covering as much as a thousand miles, he claimed, with time out for photography and socializing at the embassies.[5]

In Washington on a fair day the path of Adee's ride was likely to provide a sketch of what the city was like before all the changes of the next quarter century took place. The capital was unique among American cities. Adee varied his ride, but his route usually included the heart of the capital. Close to his office, where he began his ride, was the central area, including principal public buildings, main commercial streets, better residential areas, and the Mall. In the vicinity of the White House were the major mansions that might be expected in a capital. For instance, W. W. Corcoran's Italian villa shared with the president a view of Lafayette Park, only from its opposite side. But Corcoran, a Mexican War millionaire, art patron, and philanthropist, died in 1888, and even though his family stayed on for a while, by 1893 the shuttered windows and the peeling paint were criss-crossed by vines, because the perfectionist Corcoran was no longer there to remove them.

The Corcoran house stood roughly in the middle of a six- or seven-block neighborhood of other important houses, large and not so large, centered by Lafayette Park. It would seem the most stable of neighborhoods because of the presence of the White House and executive offices, but in 1867 the Army Corps of Engineers had firmly decided to replace the White House as the president's residence with a larger house on Rock Creek. By the early 1890s, the surrounding houses, like the Corcoran house, had been in a slow decline in prestige and condition for more than twenty years.

Old houses facing the square had become rooming houses or clubs. The Senator Scott house, facing the park on the west, was still occupied, but the only daughter, Mrs. Townsend, had unrolled plans for a new, more modern house out on

Massachusetts Avenue, well removed from this old part of town. Around the corner, facing the State, War, and Navy Building, was the art gallery Corcoran had given to mankind. Next door the old-fashioned houses of the Blair and Lee families held on, filled with heirloom treasures consciously assembled. As many another house has perpetuated a family's glory well beyond its virile generation, Blair House has preserved the name Blair.

Other houses woven into Washington history had not fared so well. They were little noticed, but it was hard not to pause before two. At the edge of the neighborhood, the once-handsome Van Ness house, where the celebrities of the early republic had mingled, had fallen into use as a beer garden, the former park in back laid out as a race track. Circus and theater posters papered its garden walls. A few blocks away, the Tayloe family from Virginia still owned the Octagon but had cut it up into apartments. This was the house where President Madison had signed the peace treaty that in 1815 ended America's last war with Great Britain.

Adee might have been able to point out twenty houses at most in the general area that could be singled out as better than the usual found in American cities of the time. Most Washington houses were relatively ordinary, even the large ones. An exception was the double house of stone and brick at the northern head of Lafayette Park, two designed as one. This was one of the three houses in Washington designed by H. H. Richardson, the leading architect of the time. The tall, romantic double house served as the Washington residences of John Hay, a man of the world, and Henry Adams, the historian. Adee knew these houses better than the others, being a friend of both occupants, but especially of Hay.

More typical of prosperous Washington were houses of relative middling size, having public rooms that served as a parlor and dining room, perhaps a library, and the rest of the rooms as private bedroom spaces. In 1893 such houses were still being built, as they had been for all the years since the Civil War: houses with small porches or stoops, wide windows, and heavy cornices and fairly well filling the lots upon which they were built. Washington lots were not generous in size. Most houses could allow for a patch of front yard, with a walk of concrete or tile to the front steps, and grass or flowers planted along each side. The scant backyard was largely taken up by a back building, which might be a stable, servants' house and wash house, or a building maintained as a rented "alley house," opening from the alley behind.

A good house built of light stone at 1019 Fifteenth Street, three blocks from Lafayette Park, was the home of Adee, his brother, David Graham Adee, his brother's wife, Ellen, and their three children. A look beyond the heavy oak and glass doorway revealed that the six formed a busy household, a close family circle. The bachelor Adee was "Nunc" to the children, and he saw them born and grow up beneath the same roof. He had moved in with David and Ellen Adee twenty years previously when he returned sick from Europe. He was a physical wreck, or perhaps his problem was a nervous breakdown. It is not certain what was wrong, but he was lovingly nursed back to health.

John Hay, then working briefly at the State Department, had helped him get on at State when he had recovered enough to work, and Adee then bought the stone house with David and Ellen. His library was housed in a room to itself, with thousands of books of poetry, fiction, religion, and Shakespeare in every form, from full-length books to play scripts. Many of his books were in foreign languages, notably Spanish and French. He had bound series of the *Century, Scribner's*, and the *Atlantic Monthly*, all venues for which he wrote from time to time and in which his brother published poems.[6]

David Adee had his collections as well. He was a distinguished Supreme Court reporter for several newspapers and magazines, as well as a poet. Add his books to Adee's, and theirs was a house full. The Adee domestic circle was admired by all who were privileged to enter it. Their and their neighbors' contentedness was of a sort that spread far and wide in Washington, where most such prestigious households were based upon a government position, not a bad salary at all, and one somewhat protected for more than a decade by the Civil Service Act.

From ten or twelve blocks of ample upscale houses like Adee's, with similarly comfortable occupants, the city grid gave onto the plain brick houses of lesser government workers. More Washington's norm, they were invariably narrow, with mean plans and small rooms. More often than not they were row houses. There were some semi-attached houses and a few solitary houses that stood up in lines like shoeboxes set vertical, awaiting companions that would be built against each bare, windowless side. Many of the houses like Adee's are gone today, along with numerous of the simpler row houses. Age has given those that survive a certain cachet, but in their time they could not have been more unremarkable.

As Adee zipped along, the row houses can only have formed a reddish blur in his peripheral vision, so similar were they all to a traveled eye like his. So much about what he passed on his bike expressed sameness: linen window shades with dangling tassels or little pull rings hoisted all at the same halfway level, lace curtains hanging straight inside them, a fancy oil lamp in practically every window, walks swept, rocking chairs lined up in perfect order on the porches, when there were porches, and when there were not, then flowerpots on the steps, planted seasonally and turned upside down in winter so as not to crack from freezing.[7]

Even modest Washington houses functioned primarily through the labors of black men and women servants or perhaps part-time workers, as did the hotels and businesses that required a domestic staff. Although inventions such as washing machines and electric lights lessened the need for so many employees, it was still a hand-operated era, and very much of the hand work in the capital was supplied by African Americans. Within that context some found good jobs; for others life was insecure. These last sort lived task by task, day by day, in stark contrast to the well-paid black federal employees, who were nearly always classed as government "laborers" and "messengers," as well as the whites, who were nearly always classed as "clerks."

African Americans composed nearly one-third of the capital's population. Not all of them lived segregated from whites, yet most were. The reason was both racial and economic. Whole communities of poor black people—city records do not suggest the number until later—thrived in the alleys behind the houses that faced the streets, a building custom that had existed in Washington from the first. Out in public, away from home, life was not so segregated. Visitors from the South were surprised to find in a self-styled "southern" town, as Washington was, relatively little racial discrimination in public places and none at all in the lunchrooms and restrooms of government buildings. Otherwise the town was segregated indeed, including noninvitational receptions at the White House. Even prominent African Americans rarely appeared there for fear of being sent away by the police, along with the ragged poor, prostitutes, and panhandlers who tried to test the extent of democratic admission at the palace.

Located in convenient proximity to work and supplies, the alley houses, later to be derided as "alley slums," were small houses of wood or brick lining the narrow alleyways. Some were built on independent parcels behind the houses that fronted the street; some parcels were not detached from the original town lot that faced the street. Various alley houses were adapted stables or coach houses or barns; the better ones originated as actual houses that were built as outbuildings to houses long replaced, dating perhaps many years back. Many of the houses were well-constructed of wood, two-stories, with one apartment up and one down, a stair outside. The photographic record reveals that few were maintained well, showing worn whitewash and ramshackle structure; however, most of the photographs were essays made for or by reformers who wanted the alley houses out of the way. Alley pavements were of stone or brickbats; they had wheel-worn slices through them that filled with rainwater and bred mosquitoes. At one time the alley houses had been occupied by both blacks and whites, but by 1893 nearly all of the some forty thousand occupants were black.

In these backstreet villages, the home industries of their occupants flourished from block to block: washing and ironing women, day laborers, porters, seamstresses, cobblers, boot blacks, bootleggers, woodworkers, and tinkerers. Where black Washington was concerned, the alleys were a contrast to the distant, coveted, well-kept neighborhoods where the well-to-do "colored" homeowners lived in their own social milieu. That community of black professionals, landlords, federal employees, and businessmen wanted no part of alleys.[8]

Congress had already begun the end of the alley houses with an ordinance in 1892, prohibiting issuance of new building permits for small houses there. When a quarter century later the assault on the alley houses accelerated, the massive removal that followed took away the good and the bad. The demolition was motivated primarily by a wish to rid center city of the dirty alleys and their ramshackle houses along with the poor who lived there, in spite of well-advertised claims otherwise.[9]

A significant part of Washington's white population occupied rented rooms in boardinghouses. One couldn't tell a single-family house from a house in which rooms were let. Numerous private houses took in boarders, particularly Capitol Hill row houses built for the purpose of serving from six to perhaps twelve or so residents. The entire household shared one bathroom. Keeping house was much more a task than it is today. In that context the boardinghouses were a fine convenience for busy people. The hosts typically offered a midday meal. Tenants could invite guests to eat, for whom they paid extra.

Adee certainly dined at many a boardinghouse table, as had most men and many women in Washington. The food, usually plain, was described as being quite good, served family-style, the hospitality homelike. Each house had its special clientele, not least the "foreign" houses, restricted to tenants who spoke the same mother tongue, most of them employees of the legations.

A snow-white reputation was important to a boardinghouse, especially to those serving single people and particularly to the ones admitting only female residents. Rules were strictly observed; men did not go past the dining room or parlor in a women's boardinghouse, and the same applied to women in men's quarters. A few of the houses were notorious mills for news stories about girls from the country taking wrong turns. Some boardinghouses were closed by the Metropolitan Police.

Members of Congress often resided in boardinghouses. Wives were often left behind to tend the children and the farm, so an elected official was as likely as not to share a boardinghouse bed with a colleague. A few members of Congress could afford to rent or purchase houses or even live in hotels such as the Arlington or the Willard, but to save money most chose boardinghouses. Others lived on a higher scale. The old Confederate general Joseph Wheeler, a U.S. senator from Alabama, was willing to rent a fine house in Washington during the season from December to March, but outside those months he moved to a boardinghouse.

Washington was unmistakably a capital, if revealed only in the character of the small businesses that crowded its streets. In number far beyond what prospered in most towns were the confectioners, hoteliers, restaurateurs, caterers, tailors of suits and uniforms, dressmakers, suppliers of livery and renters of evening clothes, hairdressers, florists, and renters of carriages and furniture. These were the entrepreneurs of ephemeral enterprises common to capitals, where so many people are in town temporarily and have reason to make an impression on short notice. In that sense Washington, Paris, St. Petersburg, and Vienna were not really dissimilar, except in size.

Public halls above stores were available to rent for meetings. Fine hotels—the Willard, the National, the Arlington—welcomed crowds when Congress was in session. Many other hotels offered less in prestige. Some businesses closed June 15 until mid-September, because not much went on in Washington during that time. Street doors along the sidewalks gave access to second-, third-, and fourth-floor offices of lawyers, correspondents, and countless lobbyists. Modern offices in the newer buildings were served by elevators, yet the old offices above the commercial rows remained busy, even as the inconvenience of their stairs rendered them steadily less usable. Clara Barton's Civil War office, abandoned in 1865, still contained her papers and effects in 1893, forgotten. And this trove would not be discovered for nearly one hundred more years.[10]

Through this capital city Alvey Adee rode his bicycle. "The Bicycle is really a great thing," he said to a news reporter. "Last vacation I covered 1800 miles on my wheel. I think there is nothing to equal a bicycle for wholesome all around physical exercise. . . . When the roads are good, the weather pleasant, and there is no wind I can do 60 or 70 miles a day without fatigue."[11] No place in the city was more popular with cyclists than the shady groves of the Mall, the ceremonial grounds of the capital. In close proximity to the government buildings, the Mall was a lovely outdoor place to walk, picnic, ride a horse, or promenade in a carriage. For bike riders the Mall provided a graveled "run" from the Capitol to the Washington Monument. If Adee picked his time well, his path through the Mall on a weekday was likely to be fairly well clear.

Thick naturalistic plantings of trees on the Mall had grown to beautiful maturity, to the credit of General Grant, who was president when Adee moved to Washington in the 1870s. Grant had sponsored the introduction of sixty thousand trees of mostly native species on the Mall, embellishing it on a human scale as a parklike place, while eradicating the grand, open sweep George Washington had intended. But the Mall of Washington's vision had more glaring intrusions than Grant's trees. Commerce also was all too evident. The tracks of the Baltimore & Potomac Railroad entered from the south and crossed to the depot a few blocks from the base of Capitol Hill, passing through a seeming fairgrounds of railroad sheds protruding 130 feet into the Mall. The arched and towered station, one of the busiest places in the capital, loomed like a giant samovar, with steam puffing through its arches and skylights. Angled across the Mall from the station, on the south, the Smithsonian Institution Building asserted its castlelike red sandstone mass into the Mall, a sermonic headquarters for the government's cultured stepchild, bequeathed by an Englishman.

The last official government building going west on the Mall was the highly decorative red-brick Department of Agriculture Building, completed in the "Renaissance" style just after the Civil War. It called to mind old chateaux in the romances of Dumas *père* with windows of various shapes and soaring roofs of slate. Built on the Mall proper by the government, the building's particular pride was the formal garden that extended before it, stretching even farther into the Mall, a much attended seasonal

Baltimore & Potomac Railroad depot, a Victorian intrusion on the Mall, ca. 1895. *James M. Goode Collection, Washington, D.C.*

exhibition of floral abundance, already alive in April with daffodils and other spring flowers blooming among the boxwood borders and iron urns.

The Washington Monument stood a short distance west of Agriculture's garden, mounted on the knoll thrown up for it. The singular obelisk soared above everything, rivaling the distant dome. Striking simplicity set the monument apart; any decorations added to it would have been superfluous. No one regretted that the original plan had been reduced from a colonnaded design to the unadorned stone shaft. Adee had very likely planned and orchestrated the monument's dedication nine years before, in 1884, which followed thirty-six years in construction. At that time the monument was the western termination of the Mall and its groves. Marshland had extended beyond that point all the way to the river.

The Army Corps of Engineers had begun the process of filling these watery, mosquito-infested lowlands not long after the Civil War. By the year in question, 1893, with the corps' work nearly finished, a muddy sprawl linked the Washington Monument to the Potomac. The watery marsh with its reeds was gone. Tiber Creek was effectively gone, although still today it continues its fierce rush to the river underground, beneath a masonry vault. The land was filled along the river and where the Lincoln Memorial would eventually stand. The corp's landfilling was accelerated in the early 1890s when the commission to honor the four hundredth anniversary of Columbus's discovery of the New World decided to consider Washington as the place for a grand, celebratory world's fair. A coterie in Washington, including top corps officials, saw the proposed world's fair as the golden opportunity to stimulate a renaissance of the city, a means of obtaining fine buildings that would be paid for by someone else and could be converted to governmental use when the fair was over. A generous appropriation from a most interested Congress hurried completion of the landfill, where the fair was to be built. As it turned out, even while the politicking was at high fever, Chicago won the fair's designation.[12]

The most Washington would gain from the world's fair, which its promoters had worked so hard to obtain, was a bizarre souvenir, a hollowed-out giant redwood tree, cut down in Tulare, California, displayed at the Chicago fair, and eventually shipped to Washington. It had been quite an attraction, this tree of a thousand years, with circular stairs and windows carved into it. The tree was ultimately taken to the Mall as an overlook pavilion for the Agriculture Department's gardens.

Meanwhile ideas for what to do with the flat, totally bare, plain at the western end of the Mall were many. The empty site was perfect for major buildings. In the spring of 1893, to venture with Adee on his bike or on foot into the newly filled land was to follow pounded-down work roads into a meadowlike area the corps had planted with grass to keep the topsoil from blowing away. Many went there to wander, some to imagine futures for the new area, with the handsome waterfront created by jetties and piles of retaining rocks. But the Army Corps of Engineers made it clear to all that the challenge was the corps'. Officers of the corps insisted that they would be the ones to develop the filled land, just as they had created it.

By the year of the first ambassador, the corps had established its vision of the ambitious improvements to be made. The engineers believed that Washington was on its way to being a great world capital. Officers in the corps entertained a dream that Washington might one day become a capital as fine as the capitals in Europe. They worked toward this but did not begin with the filled land. Their excitement in 1893 was in the nearing completion of a new and monumental building at the opposite end of the Mall. It was a piece of splendid architecture that was as richly conceived as any in Paris or Rome and rivaled the Capitol, even if secondary to it. This was the new Library of Congress, rising across the street east of the Capitol. The building already dazzled the eye and glorified the Army Corps of Engineers.

The corpsmen considered the remarkable building a pilot project for even greater works to come, and the Library of Congress had their hearts, their energy, and not least their pride proving them gifted monument builders. It had been love at first sight. Once they saw the library drawn on paper, they pushed the architects away and

The Library of Congress during construction, 1893. *Library of Congress, Prints and Photos Division.*

called the project their own. The chilly gray granite walls were rising in 1893, and the giant form already defined itself against the eastern sky. Anyone who knew anything about architecture, or, like Adee, knew the great civic architecture in Europe, plainly saw that the inspiration for the exterior was the Paris Opera. Maybe it would outstrip the opera when the engineers finished with their elaborations. Engineers dominated the planning; engineers added ever richer details of marble, mosaic, statuary, and fountains to the original idea. It was the sort of building the corps had hoped the world's fair might bring to Washington.[13]

Washington was built to be a city of ceremony, but spectacles had been almost nonexistent through its first century's history. For instance, the emperor of Brazil and a prince from Afghanistan had visited President Grant without parades.[14] However, inaugural parades and military reviews had been held. And no one who attended the two-day march of the Grand Army of the Republic at the close of the Civil War could forget it. Also, before that, Lafayette's visit in 1824 had been a national carnival, attracting huge crowds, as had the visit of the Prince of Wales in 1860. But none before and few since have attracted the public adulation accorded the visit of an infanta of Spain in 1893. Perhaps the context was in part the interest with which Americans followed Cuba's growing unrest over Spanish rule. However it may have been, the visit of the princess generated a high level of excitement and comment that the first ambassador, only a month before, had not.

She came to Washington as part of her participation in the 1893 World's Columbian Exposition, which opened in Chicago that spring.[15] President Cleveland was to dedicate the fair officially, and the special guest, Princess Eulalia of Spain, was to shed monarchial glory on the event. Americans, for all their democratic ideals, dearly loved royalty as a great curiosity and had seen very little of it. The State Department was to have a role in public presentations at the fair, which called for Adee's involvement. The delicate task of receiving royalty would have been simplified had the Spanish officials participated in the planning. But the Foreign Office in Madrid informed the secretary of state, "The government of Spain confides to the discretion of the President the terms and manner of receiving the Infantes."[16] Every detail of her visit then fell upon Adee.

The twenty-nine-year-old Princess Eulalia was the aunt of the boy king, Alfonso XIII, and her visit had created great interest months before she stepped onto American soil. Adee never wrote down how he approached his planning, or his notes have not survived, but precedent was slim. Great visits were so few as to have accumulated no archive. It was clear early on that the infanta was going to draw crowds. The State Department suggested that she stop in Washington before proceeding to Chicago, perhaps an idea of Adee's or less likely of Secretary of State Walter Q. Gresham's, as a means of establishing the ascendancy of the president in his capital.

To the Spanish government in Madrid, the Washington visit of the popular infanta seemed an excellent idea. Difficulties between Spain, Britain, and the United States and the unrest in Cuba made a visit of friendship by royals seem a good way to improve public opinion. The royal party included such celebrities as the Duke of Arcos, dubiously billed as a direct descendant of the Florida explorer Ponce de Leon. Eulalia, whose name was well known to followers of royalty, was the daughter of the notorious queen mother, Isabella II, whose romances and political intrigues had made Spanish history one of the riveting royal melodramas of the era.

Adee had known various members of the Spanish royal family over the years. When he worked as secretary to the American minister to Spain, it had been Eulalia's late brother, King Alfonso XII, who had invited Adee to photograph an ancient royal corpse exhumed at the Escorial, creating a prized image that he hung framed in his house back home. Eulalia had been born at the palace in Madrid, daughter of Queen Isabella II and King Francis. At three she had been taken along on her family's desperate flight from political upheaval to Paris, where her father died; at ten she returned to Spain when the monarchy was restored. At twenty-two she was given in marriage to her first cousin, Prince Antonio de Orléans y Borbón, the fourth Duke of Galliera.

Adee wove the official details of the state visit together into a program—military escorts, dinners, accommodations, public appearances, and ceremonies. The planning took research, conferences with the Spanish legation in Washington, and a series of memoranda detailing the responsibilities of each agency. Adee appointed an American aide for each of the royals. This was the first large public event of an international character that had presented the State Department with quite so strong an impact. The visit of the Prince of Wales in 1860 had been a big event, yes, but the prince had been officially incognito, so the planned program was small. Emperor Dom Pedro of Brazil had come to see President Grant twenty-three years before, but in comparison to what Adee faced now that was a quiet social visit. Years later Princess Eulalia would recall the tight organization with which the Americans had governed her visit.

The infanta's trip was spiced with contention before it even took place. Her government scheduled a stop for her in Havana on the way to the United States, meaning to show goodwill but underestimating how angry Americans were becoming over the Spanish treatment of Cubans. The Spanish saw that she was heavily guarded in Cuba, lest she be kidnapped by revolutionaries.[17] When she arrived in New York, far larger crowds turned out than expected, mingling popular enthusiasts of royalty with those protesting Spanish oppression in Cuba. Controversy followed the infanta through the United States, increasing the numbers who came to see her.

On May 19, 1893, Third Secretary Adee was working full tilt in the early morning humidity. Princess Eulalia was to arrive with her party that afternoon. It was a public event. Sir Julian's quiet reception as ambassador, a month in the past, was a simple thing indeed compared with this. In late afternoon the royal train was to arrive at the B&P depot. A large crowd had assembled by four and was impatient in the heat. Two troops of United States cavalry appeared, but when the train was delayed indefinitely and the captain's men began fainting, he marched his troops back to the shade trees at Fort Myer, across the Potomac. At the Department of State a succession of telegrams advised Adee that the train, although still behind schedule, would arrive between eight-thirty and nine. When this was announced outside the station, a confluence of people advanced into the cooler interior and left thousands spread out into the street. They edged to the tracks for a closer look. Several railroad porters tried to clear a path for a red carpet runner, and the crowd became angry and disorderly.

When informed of the situation, Adee did not hesitate to have the chief of the Metropolitan Police raise rope barriers. The presence of uniformed police threatened bold people into docility. It was about dark when officials began to arrive in their carriages with wives and children, fascinated to see a princess and, less so, a descendant of Columbus. The third secretary, part of the official welcoming party, joined the group of men cordoned off at the red carpet, where the train was to stop. He had determined that it was inappropriate for the president to attend, but he did bring Cleveland's silver-mounted carriage-and-four for the use of the princess.

The crowd swelled to huge numbers. The prize was all the more desirable for being late. From Fort Myer, in the cooler air of evening, the mounted troops returned, including the famous African American "Fighting Ninth." Suddenly the train rolled in from the dark as if puffed from a silver cloud. The steps were put up, and the princess appeared. She was young, with big brown eyes and a bright, ready smile. Her conquest of the spectators was instant. Escorted by the welcoming party to the carriage, she was taken in great state down Pennsylvania Avenue to the Treasury Building, accompanied by the troops. Crowds along the way watched the windows of the coach in silent enchantment as the face of the princess flickered in and out of view in pools of gaslight shed by the streetlamps and the windows of the buildings. Her procession rounded Lafayette Park, paused respectfully in front of the White House, and then turned to the nearby Arlington Hotel, where the flag of Spain floated in electric light atop the building, denoting a royal residence.[18]

For the rest of the Washington visit Adee was absolved from worrying about trains. Everything was close at hand. Sir Julian entertained the party, placing velvet-draped thrones in the embassy ballroom, before which the princess and Prince Antonio received the guests, who came forward singly, from a long line that rambled through the house. Washington had never experienced anything like this before. Some guests nodded, some strutted self-consciously, some looked away in embarrassment, and those few in the know bowed low. Lady Pauncefote wore a court train (a detachable panel three yards from shoulder to hem) in gray satin. The "little mouse of a woman," as the press reported, curtseyed the most authentically of all, and when she rose, mindful not to turn her back on royalty, moved her train with her foot effortlessly and swept away.[19]

At the White House reception the whole world seemed to turn out. Thousands pressed to the iron fence; enthusiastic males scaled the elm trees and President Jackson's equestrian statue in Lafayette Park, and some spectators climbed to the roofs. Windows of adjacent buildings were filled with people. Metropolitan Police cleared a passage wide enough for a carriage in the streets. That day it was not an unruly crowd, nor one, it seems, that was particularly upset over Cuba; this crowd was fixed upon the royals. The princess arrived in the president's carriage and stood for a moment on the north portico. Inside, a large number of invited guests waited, a mixture of political figures and, as was a White House custom, people selected from a list of Washington locals. Any invitations to private dinners or parties extended to the princess were intercepted by Adee, and all had been declined.

In the Blue Room, which had been made into a summerhouse of roses and sweet peas, President Cleveland bent protectively toward his young wife as the receiving line opened. Frances Cleveland's celebrated "English cream" complexion was framed in a high-waisted gown of white cotton mull poured over by a cascade of colonial lace that covered evidence of her pregnancy. She wore no jewelry but her wedding band, in contrast to the princess, who wore diamonds and pearls "as large as marbles" in strands that reached the floor. After a visit with the president and first lady, the princess was taken back to the north portico so that the crowd could have a better look.

An old woman outside the fence waved a white handkerchief and led three cheers in Spanish. The princess melted her audience by acknowledging this with "the prettiest of smiles."[20]

Washington's erratic weather proved Adee's only tormentor. This he could not control with a note signed AAA or a snap of his ear trumpet. The night of the state dinner that followed the reception began steaming hot, then turned into a storm. The temperature dropped and winds howled, tearing the red carpet from the front steps of the White House and rattling the windows fearfully. This was the worst of it. Adee had planned a number of drives, so that the princess might be seen by the public and at the same time tour the city. The drives were announced in the press in advance. With her party she hurried down the steps of the hotel into an open carriage and followed the prescribed routes with spectators all along the way. When her carriage rounded a corner at one point, someone knowledgeable called out, "Hats off," and all the male spectators obliged.

Thus the American capital experienced its first full-scale visit of state. The Washington *Evening Star* assumed innocently that "the exact procedure which, in the history of this government, has always distinguished the reception of foreign dignitaries has been adhered to in every particular."[21] Princess Eulalia spent a week in Washington. On her last evening she and her party visited the Library of Congress, tracing clean-swept wooden paths the engineers had prepared. The royals were driven in open carriages from the library across the street to the Capitol, where on the west terrace they all stood together and watched the sun set over the city.

TWO
Men of Distinction

Washington's permanent population meant nothing to most Americans. The capital's dramas that concerned the nation were played out not by those who lived there but by elected transients who swarmed to the capital on official business. This vital hierarchy was topped by the president, who by tradition had to live for his term in the house that Congress provided. Members of Congress were free to come and go as business allowed. The justices of the Supreme Court were expected to remain largely in town, like the president. Those individuals of executive, legislature, and judiciary, primed and fueled, struck the sparks that ignited the machinery of government.

One particular stratum of people who were a feature of Washington, in fact universal to capitals, was that transient population of well-heeled wayfarers, intruders in the city of positions and jobs. Living half in the capital while keeping their roots elsewhere, they were people who could arrange their lives as they wished. In the late nineteenth century, with the increasing public works of the Army Corps of Engineers and the rising splendor of the diplomatic community, the appeal of the American capital rose, and activity in Washington foreshadowed a new golden age of which those on the spot might partake.

Two conspicuous members of this class were John Hay, an author and celebrity for having been Lincoln's secretary and by marriage a gentleman of leisure, and his neighbor Henry Adams, the hard-working, world-traveling historian. The capital had a history that significantly touched the life of each of these men. In the mid-1890s, they stood a part of the capital scene and still well apart from it. But before the decade was spent, John Hay's life would carry the story when he sprang suddenly from a life of independence into the absorbing role of statesman. He was to mirror the transition of the American nation into an international power.

They were the closest of friends, Hay and Adams, and well-known figures in town, two men of middle age, small of stature, Adams heavy-set, Hay less so, walking side by side along the streets, taking their day's exercise. Their walk was as much their custom as the bike ride of their friend Adee was to him. Talking incessantly, their comments fit together like a puzzle; they reacted to everything they saw, the commonest observation a springboard to clever essays. An eavesdropper might judge them complete snobs. But to know them better was to understand the depth and breadth of their interests. Covering perhaps half a dozen blocks, they returned home soon enough to the double house that overlooked Lafayette Park. This looming, gloomy building was a monument to their friendship. Henry Adams built and occupied the west house that faced the park, while Hay and his family occupied the much larger eastern section, facing Sixteenth Street across from Saint John's Episcopal Church.

Born in the same year, 1838, John Hay and Henry Adams were from different backgrounds and experiences but had grown up to be very much alike. Adams was descended from the father and son Adams presidents, the first, John Adams, Founding Father and second president of the United States, first to occupy the White House; the second, John Quincy Adams, Henry Adams's grandfather, sixth president and member of Congress for twenty years after that. Hay came from the middle class, the son of an Indiana entrepreneurial medical doctor who dabbled in running newspapers, and though John Hay was close to his family and given a good education by his parents, the distinction associated with his name came entirely from Hay himself, not from his ancestors.

John Hay and Henry Adams's celebrated double house on Lafayette Square. *Library of Congress, Prints and Photos Division.*

Although Adams, when not traveling, was usually in Washington, he never sank his roots very deep. He moved into the house following the suicide of his wife, Clover, one of those tragedies of mental illness that seemed explained by grief over her father's death. The stoic, sharp-tongued Adams battled with the pain of separation from her for the rest of his life. A chunky, fleshy man, he appeared lethargic, but no one who read his histories and law essays was likely to call him lazy. It was true, however, that even most people who owned his books probably had not read them, so had to judge by what they saw and heard. If he wished to incur local favor, it was not evidenced in the way he unrelentingly mocked every individual and every strata of the national capital.

He and Clover and John Hay and his wife, Clara, commissioned the great Henry Hobson Richardson, whom Adams had tutored at Harvard, to build their two houses to look like one. The site across Lafayette Park from the White House had been, in the early 1880s, about as near perfect a bit of ground as one could find in the capital. They paid the astonishing price of seventy thousand dollars for the double lot, a challenge for Adams, but no sacrifice for Hay. The Adamses kept close watch during the building process, vigilantly blocking Richardson's efforts to make expensive changes as he saw the house take shape. Hay, who maintained a residence at home in Cleveland, was rarely in town, so Richardson had in him a dream client and could do as he pleased, make any changes he wished. The architect, who had known Henry Adams well as a fellow student at Harvard, concerned himself little with budgets and was annoyed by the clients' intrusion into his work as one might be annoyed by mosquitoes. When, after the building was done, Adams told Richardson he found Hay's house the better of the two, Richardson sniffed that Hay had left him "entirely untrammeled by restrictions wise or otherwise."[1]

Adams had not moved to Washington simply to pass the time. He was one of many scholars and writers in the city as well as the best known. His decision to write a book on America as it existed in 1800, a hinge year, he believed, when Jefferson defeated John Adams in the presidential election, kept him tied most of the year to Washington. The historian had left a teaching post at Harvard to move near the documentary sources in government papers, which, in the absence of any national archives, were opened up to him in the files of the various departmental offices. He wrote his books from these papers, assisted originally in research by Clover, then by various assistants. Part of the 1800 study was published privately in 1884, the year Clover died and the year Henry moved into the new house.

Henry Adams was a familiar caller at the Department of State, where a scholarly Adee was sympathetic to his purpose and bestowed favors. The Departments of Treasury, War, and Navy opened their doors to Adams. Congress gave access to "Professor Adams" to poke through the stuffed boxes of documents that filled the attic, cellar vaults, and offices, all awaiting comfortable storage when the Library of Congress was completed. For access to congressional records, Adams's former student and Harvard's first PhD in history, Senator Henry Cabot Lodge, provided a latchstring that might be pulled whenever necessary. The mid-1890s found Adams settled in his womanless house, amid a profusion of books and souvenirs for about six months a year. The other six months he traveled. It worked well for him.

Adams's neighbor John Milton Hay did not have to live with so ancestor-rich a personal heritage. His youth had been blessed with luck and with a natural ability to make useful friends and push ahead. Hay's life had been profoundly influenced, indeed had fired off like a rocket, in the four years he spent as secretary to President Lincoln.

In Springfield, at about the time of Lincoln's election, Hay had become close friends with a fellow writer and book lover, George Nicolay, a German-born news-paperman who, when Hay met him, was headed to Washington to serve as Lincoln's secretary. Having nothing better to do after his graduation from Brown University and bored reading law in Springfield, Hay was a bit at loose ends, but with his penchant for being in the right place at the right time, he passed idle hours with his chum at Lincoln's campaign headquarters. As the packing was taking place to go to Washington, Nicolay convinced Lincoln to take Hay along, and Hay put his law books aside without hesitation. He and Nicolay shared a room in the White House and bought meal tickets at the Willard Hotel.

Lincoln's trust in Hay and Nicolay grew quickly with their performance of sensitive missions of observation and communication for the president. Hay was granted the military title "colonel," which would be attached to him at times for the rest of his life. White House experiences honed his ability to deal with high-placed people. The two secretaries and their mentor climbed Brady's stairs to sit for a photograph that became well known: Nicolay on Lincoln's right, tall, lanky, and rather like a grave-looking owl; Hay on Lincoln's left, a shorter figure, age twenty-three, making a cocky stance, still boyish, and not so serious.

Hay left Lincoln's office early in 1865, just prior to the president's death, to see the world in the diplomatic service. He found employment as secretary to his friend General Daniel E. Sickles, the American minister to Spain. Sickles, a war hero, had lost one leg on the battlefield of Gettysburg and, grounded by his handicap, had befriended Lincoln's secretaries during the war, spending many an hour lounging on the sofa in their White House office chatting, glorying, as Hay put it, "in the broad sunshine of fame and popular favor." When the office was too busy for him, he hobbled down the hall on his crutch to sit with Mrs. Lincoln, who found him amusing.[2]

It was while working at the Spanish legation in Madrid that the twenty-six-year-old Hay met Alvey Adee, who was four years Hay's junior and an assistant legation secretary at the time. There was a personal background to Alvey Adee's appointment to that position. His uncle, the celebrated Manhattan trial lawyer David Graham, assisted by Edwin M. Stanton, then a lesser light, saved Sickles from the near certainty of hanging for shooting his wife's lover, the son of Francis Scott Key, author of "The Star-Spangled Banner." The murder, which took place in broad daylight on Lafayette Square, was followed by a sensational trial. David Graham turned public favor away from the famous man's amorous son to a wronged husband avenging the violation of his marital sanctity. Saved from the gallows, a grateful Sickles later was happy to employ in his Spanish legation the bright, deaf nephew of his lawyer.

Intellectual companionship led to a lifelong friendship between Hay and Adee. They enjoyed nearly constant association and made frequent trips together. In the hours after work, they collaborated on essays and stories for amusement. Hay, who insisted that Adee was a greater literary talent than he, wrote from Spain to an American friend that Adee "makes nice verse. . . . He can twitter like a young Tennyson and Maunder like old Browning in a stile it would do your heart good to hear." While in Spain Adee published a dark, supernatural tale called "Life's Magnet" in the American monthly *Putnam's Magazine*, a story that is still today a classic of the horror genre. "The plot is mine," wrote Hay at the time, "the execution my young friend Adee's. . . . I confess I was greatly tickled with it. He wrote it after fifteen minutes dictation from me as to the general run of the old story."[3]

Both went on to write books and many articles. Hay's stories in the Hoosier dialect of his Indiana childhood became popular in the nostalgic years of the 1870s, and his *Pike County Ballads*, his best-known book, has been favorably compared with the western stories of Bret Harte and the New Orleans tales of George W. Cable, who in the 1870s and 1880s shared with Mark Twain the most acclaim for depicting regional American characters. While in Spain, Hay wrote a book of a different sort, *Castillian Days*, which was well received in the United States but not to the extent of his Indiana stories.[4]

Hay left the diplomatic service to pursue his writing in America, where he joined the staff of the *New York Tribune* as a special features writer. The art of the journalist came easily to him. His letters and diary are no different in style from his essays and articles, and none of it seems labored, but light, as though the language flowed to the paper and never had to suffer strikeouts or erasures. Hay's life went somewhat that way. Perhaps he might have joined the pantheon of American writers, but he was lazy by nature and, if offered a choice between any two of life's cushions, would always select the softest. Observing wealth and luxury all around him, he became opposed to the idea of sacrificing comfort in favor of his pen.

Witty and good looking enough, the smart, dandified young man began following rich pleasure seekers to their retreats. At Saratoga he met a full-figured, personable young lady, ten years his junior, named Clara Stone. She was from Cleveland. Her doting father was Amasa Stone, who, for railroad companies, built hundreds of miles of rails and also a unique type of railroad bridge that he had patented. Stone poured his profits into steel mills and banks in Ohio and various other parts of the Midwest.

A very rich man, he readily welcomed such a remarkable young man as Hay into the family circle.

John Hay and Clara Stone were married in 1874. The groom was thirty-four. Hay may not have married for money, but it is unlikely that he would have married without it. Clara Stone was smitten. When Hay's friends teased him about courting the fat girl, he took the blows good naturedly. The Hays began married life in New York, where he remained with the *Tribune*, but after about a year were lured back to Cleveland, where Amasa Stone built them a fine "family"-type house next door to his and Mrs. Stone's and awaited grandchildren. Four children were born to the Hays, two boys and two girls. Hay, employed by his father-in-law, wrote from his office to Adee: "I do nothing but read and yawn in the long intervals of work, an occupation that fits me like a glove."[5]

He returned to Washington to serve President Hayes as assistant secretary of state, which was when he was able to help Adee get on the payroll. One could live in Washington without making a community commitment. Hay liked that very much, but the job bored him. Back in Ohio he was also miserable, for many board meetings and civic obligations of Mr. Stone fell to him. He was exhausted with public responsibility. He did take the time to write a novel about Cleveland, *The Breadwinners*, an unpretentious story, published anonymously, about what the title suggests. The sudden death of Amasa Stone in 1883 removed the main obstacle to Hay's leaving Cleveland. Although he and Clara retained their Cleveland house, in 1885 they returned to Washington, where they built their part of the double house and dug in to stay.

Hay at last found in Washington a place that suited him, one with an ebb and flow of residents, one where he did not have to account for himself, one where he could dwell and not dwell at the same time and still enjoy the social status he wanted—most of all perhaps, a place where he could park his family while he traveled. Clara found Washington a compatible town where the children might grow up. She knew her husband's restlessness. Indeed, time would show that it was Clara who gave the marriage its strength. Her generosity in standing aside, freeing him to do as he wished, was not usual in a wife who held the purse strings. By withholding funds she could have clipped his wings. But as time had shaped things, her money was not the binding dynamic. It was her solid character that made her husband strong. Not until success came to Hay through personal achievement was he to understand what Clara had meant to him all along.

Money fit John Hay well. For the next twenty years—the balance of his life—he followed an annual cycle of traveling half the year. Sometimes Clara went along, others he was alone, but for half of the year the Hays remained together as a family in Washington. One activity his wife demanded of him was that Hay continue membership on the Cleveland boards of directors and building committees that had meant something to her philanthropic father. Hay did take an interest in Republican politics, feeling that he had been part of the party since its beginning. His association with Lincoln and the wide acquaintance that had resulted sustained his importance within the party. Yet he kept to the wings of the political stage, and those in control of the party were not certain about his seriousness. Henry Adams often said that as far as international affairs were concerned, Hay was the brightest light among the Republicans, but Adams's view was colored by friendship and was not universal or much noticed.[6]

Hay moved among his avocations, forming himself as a man of the world in a country where there were few who could be so-called. Ever witty and charming, he carried on a stream of talk in company but was not a blowhard; he seldom lacked for an anecdote or a commentary on some novel, poem, news item, crowned head, or orator. He loved people and collected friends and acquaintances as eagerly as some others collected books, pictures, porcelains, or bronzes. His ever-growing repertoire of stories of people he had met and places he had visited were the gold nuggets in his narratives. An eloquent and courteous man, he had a way of saying the appropriate thing when called upon. In private his acerbic side sometimes took over so surprisingly that he seemed not to be the same man. Theodore Roosevelt blamed Hay's biting sarcasm upon the influence of some of his literary friends, notably the novelist Henry James, whom Roosevelt found an obnoxious snob.[7]

Hay gathered his intimates over cigars and drinks in his lofty library, where the fire that burned logs in the inglenook was reflected in the room's dark paneling, polished brass, and red marble. The general arrangement with late afternoon guests was that they drop by at the close of day. The company, usually only men, was likely to include a wide variety of temporary Washingtonians, notably diplomats such as Lord Pauncefote, Baron de Fava, and one of Hay's favorites, the Chinese minister Yang Yu. Lodge was a regular, and Henry Adams was always there when in town, the one who held back when others left, accepting an unspoken dinner invitation. He was at Hay's house every time the tablecloth was unrolled, nestling affectionately into the family life denied him personally. Hay's children called him uncle and ran and kissed him.

The frequent dinners held when Hay was home were devised by Hay, not Clara, who quietly managed the details. Guests were at table for hours, ate good food, and enjoyed it and the clever conversation, led always by Hay, with a sort of Greek chorus by Adams. On New Year's Day, several hundred people dressed to the nines drifted across Lafayette Park to Hay's house for a good time after enduring the afternoon labor of a reception at the White House. All the fantastic trappings of the diplomats—ostrich feathers, epaulettes, gold buttons, ladies' trains hoisted up over the left arm—crowded in with the dark suits and simpler costume of everyone else, all moving through the high, dark-beamed rooms and along the broad, rippling staircase that rose beneath a colored-glass window. The dropping-in went on into the night, the table replenished by liveried African American servants, the wine and whiskey punch flowing freely. Foreign languages spiced the conversations, Americans trying French,

Italians trying their English. Here and there women guests stylishly dramatized new freedoms by boldly expressing opinion and even occasionally lighting cigarettes.

~

When the first ambassador appeared, Washington was suffering the panic of 1893, like everyplace else in the country. Even though the capital's pain was not the match of that in other cities, the city's good luck did not lessen the great scar that the panic left on the entire decade of the 1890s, weakening political alliances and creating new agendas. "The state of depression here is astonishing," wrote one Washington diplomat describing the nation in 1894, "and there is really small hope of improvement. There are said to be a million men out of work. The U.S. troops are busy [stopping strikes] in several states and the railroads are occupied by armed bodies of men. A coal famine is imminent."[8]

Unrest was certainly one source of the panic, if not its entire cause. Unemployed workers gathered by the thousands following one Jacob Coxey from Ohio to Washington in a protest march, and imitations of "Coxey's Army" emerged in various other parts of the country, all protesting the economic situation. In the midst of a nation so troubled, Washington was still fairly tranquil, with regular federal salaries forming a sort of ballast for the storm-tossed economy. Excursion trains loaded up for the Chicago World's Fair. Shops did not close in any notable number. No one was jumping out of windows. Financial hardship was the constant subject of political talk and most other talk.

Senator John Sherman, ca. 1895. *Library of Congress, Prints and Photos Division.*

Of the elected officials who came to Washington during the sessions of Congress, no two politicians were more feared and respected than Senator John Sherman, of Ohio, and Representative Joseph Cannon, from Illinois. Their type could be found in the corridors and chambers of state capitols. The Congress had varying degrees of Cannons and Shermans in its membership, all with ambition, but few with the expertise and savvy that set these two apart.

Powerful names in their respective legislative bodies, Sherman and Cannon, in their similarities and contrasts, ably represented the sort

Congressman Joseph Cannon, ca. 1898. *Library of Congress, Prints & Photos Division.*

of place the U.S. Congress, with its hundreds of members, was in the 1890s. Cannon was southern by the instance of his birth in North Carolina but wholly midwestern by adoption and sensitivity. Sherman, brother of the Civil War general, was a native of Ohio. Each man was the object of cartoonists' delight; each was followed daily by mobs of petitioners. Politically both were Republican, but more than mere party men, they were also both realists. They represented long years of service in Congress, of going home to stump, deal, and stand elections, and of returning for the opening session.

Joseph Gurney Cannon, lean and rawboned, seemed from published photographs that he ought to be tall but was not. He always looked a little scruffy in his ready-made suits, chewing a saliva-soaked cigar that was likely to be unlighted. He was gruff, but except in his rare dark moods, a grin was never far away. A reporter for the *New York World* painted him in words: from the "Methodist cut of his gray beard and the Presbyterian length of his upper lip" to his "forget me not eyes," the energetic Cannon was in "no hurry to sit down."[9] The sentimentality that lurked behind the tough expression was not as well hidden as he might have thought.

His secretary of twenty years, L. White Busbey, recalled that Cannon and many others of his generation brought with them to Washington "the flavor of the soil and the tang of the farm, and their speech was racy of the land." Cannon's "wild and wooly" remarks and stories traveled over road, rail, river, and probably by telegraph far beyond his state of Illinois and his high-domed Washington workplace. He was serious about statesmanship, although he would have sneered at the application of that word to him. He recognized that politics had a carnival side, and in this he was more than willing to play his part. The public liked him as they always like an official who puts on a good show. At times he made them rock with laughter.[10]

During a political career of forty years, Cannon stood for election to the House of Representatives twenty-three times. Some of his contests resulted in defeat. In his early years he was both elected and defeated repeatedly. By 1898, however, he was there for a long stretch, and his power in the Republican-dominated House was formidable. For much of the decade, the House was under the thumb of Thomas Brackett Reed, of Maine, who was Speaker during three of the six sessions. Through the 1890s Cannon's power grew gradually in committees, particularly when he became the chair of Ways and Means. In an introspective mood, "Uncle Joe" Cannon wrote, "I am one of the great army of mediocrity which constitutes the majority. I have made little effort to separate myself from that majority, and it has not been difficult for me to keep in sympathy with the average citizen, for I have always belonged to that class. All my experiences have been as an average man."[11]

John Sherman, in the Senate, was no less a man of the people but dramatized that identity in an entirely different way. He was tailored, polished, and dignified in appearance, not scrappy at all, almost professorial. Like Cannon he created his public persona from self and situation. Sherman appeared cold and distant. He had a quick mind and a temper well under control. Constituents in Ohio respected his ability as a senator but found it unnecessary to love him. Thirteen years older than Cannon almost to the day, Sherman reached his seventies in the 1890s and could reflect upon more than thirty successful years in the U.S. Senate, having taken his seat in the first year of the Civil War. Because of his patronage and ability at organizing, a whole group of Ohio men rose into being the most potent political force in Washington in the last decades of the nineteenth century. Constituents had followed Sherman to the capital to broker power, including the Andersons of Cincinnati, the Boardmans of Cleveland, and many more.

Although Uncle Joe Cannon had no higher ambition than the Congress, John Sherman wanted more. Sherman looked to greener pastures. He had left the Senate only once, to serve President Hayes, his fellow Ohioan, as secretary of the treasury. In that office Sherman was noted for several achievements but celebrated for only one: He ordered the first telephone the government ever installed, although he could only call home or the president or his neighbor Alexander Graham Bell from it. Yet it exemplified his acceptance of innovation, and he liked to tell about it.

When Sherman returned to the Senate to take the place of James A. Garfield, who had stepped down upon his election to the presidency, he was never again content as "Senator Sherman." He tried unsuccessfully to secure the Republican nomination for the presidency. When that failed, he continued to long for a place in the cabinet, focusing at last upon the most prestigious appointment, secretary of state. By the later 1890s, as head of the Senate Foreign Affairs Committee, his presidential aspirations relaxed somewhat, but ambition gnawed inside him for that particular appointment to the cabinet.

Where he belonged was in the Senate, although no one could have made him understand it. Few in that body were as well qualified as he for the work or as adept at carrying it out. Years of legislative experience, beginning with the fiscal challenges Congress faced during the Civil War, had made him deft at designing compromises, particularly in financial matters. He was a fine debater, of relatively few words, and an able maneuverer behind the scenes. Sherman could pull apart most jumbled legislation and revise it to clarity as well as urgency. "His forte," reported the *Baltimore American*, "was more in the cool analysis of a proposition, appealing to the judgement rather than the emotions."[12] The political dukedom of John Sherman consisted of a network spread over Ohio, which he controlled from Washington. Unlike most of his colleagues, who eagerly awaited the close of session and their departure from the train depot, Sherman never wished to go home to Ohio. Washington was his field of labor and home to his heart.

The most powerful man in the Sherman organization was the rich Cleveland wholesale merchant and coal magnate Mark Hanna, who happened also to have been an old friend of Amasa Stone and had known Clara Stone Hay affectionately all her life. Bored with the day-to-day management of his business fortune, Hanna made politics his avocation. Cleveland was a key city in the nation in the latter years of the nineteenth century. It had produced many millionaires, not least John D. Rockefeller, and represented an effective concentration of political power on the national scene. Hanna had his political views, some of them contradictory, but essentially he felt that the country should follow the route most beneficial to business. To his thinking, prosperous businesses meant well-paying jobs and plenty of them. Yet the more involved he became in politics, the more he lent his ear to the views of labor, which he came to believe also deserved a voice.

Hanna, no philosopher, loved the mechanics of politics. Sherman took him to the field and set him free like a bird dog in training, and through natural intelligence and instinct, Hanna developed extraordinary and innovative skills in promoting candidates and communicating for them. There is a near-modern ring to his techniques of informing the public and shaping opinion through media. A good stage manager, Hanna became a king maker. He had a loud, although oddly intimate away about him, a bully's manner in taking over, which lingered from the days of his climbing to the top in industry. But also he had a genial manner while he was tilting the playing field in the direction he desired. Hanna had hoped to place John Sherman in the presidency and supported his nomination several times on the Republican ticket. Only in the mid-1890s, after failing repeatedly with Sherman, did he take his gifts to another candidate, William McKinley.

Cannon's political machine was less complex than Sherman's, and he ran it out-right. He and his wife, Mary, lived simply in rooms rented in a modest downtown hotel with a dining room. Sherman bought a fine house at 1321 K Street, in Adee's neighborhood and a few blocks from Hay, improved it elegantly in 1893 for him-self, his wife, Margaret, and their beloved niece Mary, who was like a daughter to them. Invitations to their dinner parties were prized. Their entertaining was always formal, and they took pains to assemble interesting company. The Shermans "went out in society," as it was phrased then, where he was received as a senior statesman. In this social side to the man, Sherman was quite unlike Cannon, whose appearance at a dinner or reception was a surprise, not only because he rarely went out, but also because he never responded to invitations; nonetheless, even without an invitation, if he wished to attend a function, he might do so.

William McKinley, of Ohio, was to figure in the lives of both Cannon and Sher-man but in different ways. McKinley, though only fifty in 1893, was closer in age to Cannon, who had also known him longer than Sherman had. McKinley was some-what like each of the older men, maybe like Cannon on the inside and Sherman on the outside, but that comparison is more apparent at first glance than on close inspection. McKinley was indeed a strong politician in his own right, no matter the importance of Hanna in his political rise.

With Sherman, McKinley always maintained a distance, out of deference to Sher-man's age and admirable record of experience. Sherman saw in McKinley ambitions that conflicted with his own. When Hanna put Sherman aside in selecting his presiden-tial players and turned to McKinley, Sherman found it an almost unbearable confirma-tion of what he had feared all along. Still, on the surface his and McKinley's relationship remained cordial and civilized, for they had to work together continually on political matters of mutual interest in Washington and back home in Ohio. Sherman extolled the younger rival when he introduced his speeches and praised him in print.

As a young man at the beginning of the Civil War, McKinley had entered the Twenty-Third Regiment, Ohio Volunteer Infantry, while Sherman and Cannon spent the war years in the Capitol. Mustered out as a brevet major, McKinley, known ever after as "Major McKinley" or simply "the Major," opened a law practice in Canton, Ohio. He began his political career there as the prosecuting attorney for Stark County. In Canton he married well, his bride, Ida Saxon, a pretty blonde from a family with money and position in the state. At once strong-willed and charming, she seemed the perfect wife for a public man. Their contented private life would turn to personal, bit-ter sorrow with the deaths of their two young daughters. Mrs. McKinley, who never absorbed the loss, rather limped along beside her beloved husband and clung to him as his political star climbed.

McKinley served six terms in the House, going to Washington at the same time as President Hayes, his former commanding officer. He was defeated in the Democrats'

1890 assault on Republican management of the economy. Under Mark Hanna's tutelage back home, he aimed again for public office and was immediately elected governor of Ohio. McKinley was a much easier man than Sherman to sell to the public. He had a handsome, prosperous appearance in middle age and a self-certain composure combined with a warm and friendly demeanor that made people like him instantly. It was often remarked that he looked like Napoleon, only an Anglo-Saxon version. He dressed fastidiously, in a dignified manner befitting his status as a public man. Strong of expression, courteous of manner, McKinley was a special sort of American-style gentleman. Like Cannon, he had the common touch, which to a politician is worth a bushel of shamrocks; yet like Sherman, he seemed reflective and thoughtful. Like both, he was ruthlessly ambitious.

McKinley continued to live in Canton with Ida, who was probably very shrewd—or at least one is left with that impression of her—but she was a withdrawn woman who hid out with maladies actual and imagined. At last she was diagnosed with epilepsy. Husband and wife were devoted to each other. Onlookers, particularly women, missed neither the tender way in which the Major doted upon Ida nor her tender responses. McKinley was a man people felt they knew personally, even those whose paths would never cross his except in the ballot box. He was an easy, first-class product for Mark Hanna to market.

As a member of the House, McKinley had been successful in his career, if not a match of Sherman and Cannon. He was a candidate, informally and rather timidly, for Speaker of the House in 1889, and Tom Reed of Maine, who did become Speaker instead, was angry that the Ohioan had dared oppose him. McKinley wisely sidestepped confrontations with so clever a politician and so formidable a bully. No one wanted to be lashed by Reed's sarcasm from the rostrum or, worse, have it recounted in the papers. Speaker Reed's general popularity was great. Fellow pedestrians stood by admiringly as he took has daily stroll from the Capitol to the rented guest house of the Arlington Hotel, where he lived, near Lafayette Park.

It might have been better for Reed had he lost the speakership to the upstart McKinley. Then perhaps he would not be remembered as one who had outlived his time. Hindsight would show that Reed remained in office too long and should have quit with praise, instead of departing despised. Few Speakers in American history have so dominated the House of Representatives. He reorganized it, changed some of the traditions, and kept it in turmoil. However it might have turned out otherwise, Reed did win, and one of his first appointments, to everyone's surprise, was McKinley, whom he made chair of the powerful House Ways and Means Committee. This is exactly where McKinley wanted to be.

McKinley, now well-placed, styled himself a patriotic protectionist of American manufacturers. He had taken center stage as champion of business and battled a full year for passage of the 1890 protective tariff named for him. That act of Congress would not be celebrated for long, but its favoritism to large corporations and manufacturers would tag the Republican Party from then on as the party of the rich and privileged. The bitter taste of this label turned public opinion against Republicans in the presidential election of 1892 and brought the Democrat Grover Cleveland to the presidency. Alas for him, the economy collapsed in his first few months in office in the national crisis that came to be known as the panic of 1893. That spring, when Sir Julian Pauncefote took office, a dark cloud of blame was already forming over the Democrats. Republicans escaped damage, although if anyone was responsible for the panic of 1893, it was they.

Representative McKinley, meanwhile, was a temporary fatality of his tariff. In the summer of 1890 Sherman divided his time stumping for Cannon in Illinois and McKinley in Ohio. Both lost. Determined to keep McKinley in the public eye, Hanna organized the successful campaign that made him governor of Ohio. This required paying off McKinley's substantial debts, for he too was a victim of the panic. John Hay was among the contributors, along with other rich Republicans. Governor for two terms, until January 1896, McKinley was fit and ready to run for president in that year's election.

Joe Cannon ran for the House again in 1892. Both McKinley and Sherman worked hard for him, albeit his campaign was in Illinois, not Ohio, and he won. It was an election that sent a large number of Democrats to the House, so this Republican victory in Illinois was singular, drawing warm congratulations from Speaker Reed. Cannon was to remain in Congress for twenty years longer, then suffer another interval of defeat, to return and serve eight years after that.

Long stretches of concentrated work campaigning created a bond among Sherman, Cannon, and McKinley that had not existed before. They traveled in summer heat. A scene remembered from their travels is the three of them stripped to their underwear, napping on beds in a hotel room awaiting the next event, windows open, the air stirred by electric fans, a pitcher of ice on the dresser. Both beside and sometimes slipping apart from "Czar" Reed and the hostile Democrats, the three fueled the Republicans in the House and Senate, themselves forming a sort of bridge between the two chambers. In Washington, political interactions were accompanied by convivial evenings among colleagues beneath dangling lightbulbs in the Capitol's vaulted cellars, whiskey passed around. Politicians also took long walks, pausing for talks under the elms and oaks on the Mall; stood amid steam and coal dust in the B&P depot, with two, three, four men collecting there to talk; huddled in a detached corner at a party or at a church gathering, making connections, stretching the network.

Not one of these three politicians gave a minute's thought to diplomats or foreign lands or, for that matter, to art or architecture. It was money they liked and the advantage money gave them in keeping people voting for them. Theirs was a hard, workaday world in politics, assisting and monitoring the nation's movement through time, pulling, stretching, transforming it sometimes, in the course of making what they labeled improvements. They threaded their way through forces legal and human to achieve what they wanted and still keep politically afloat. Of the three, only Joe Cannon was happy with what he already had.

~

John Hay's marriage had given him ready access to the important Ohio Republican contingency in the national capital and thereby a measure of political power through them. It would be difficult to call Hay political, and some of his contemporaries might have broken out in laughter at the idea. Henry Adams described Hay's political side in this way: "Hay belonged to the New York school—like Abram Hewitt, [William M.] Evarts, W. C. Whitney, Samuel J. Tilden—men who played the game for ambition or amusement, and played it, as a rule, much better than the professionals, but whose aims were considerably larger than those of the usual player, who felt no great love for the cheap drudgery of the work." With the Republican Party, Hay was "one of themselves; they asked his services and took his money. . . . but they never needed him to equivalent office."[13] In other words, they respected his views and his advice but most of all wanted his money.

The accumulation of political power seems to have been far from Hay's mind. Some of his influence among politicians, however, was a by-product of his unobstructed access to any people he wished to see. There was always the idea that he might make a tool of this enviable blessing. While he may have lacked the family background usually associated with social contact, wealth and natural charm oiled his ascent among people of the upper class. His "artful" writing also gave him ready entrée. Mark Twain was among his good friends, as were the learned William Dean Howells and the young tycoon Jay Gould, both charming companions on long, conversational walks. Hay and Clara accompanied Andrew and Louise Carnegie on their honeymoon trip to Scotland.

Queen Victoria knew Hay by sight, which was no mean accolade, especially for a man without official position. A list of lofty friends and acquaintances of Hay in America and Europe, especially Britain, would have been very long. But the advantage of having money, not his friends, was mostly what built his self-confidence. He could order up on the spur of the moment a beautiful tea or dinner party in his hotel, send flowers in abundance, stay for weeks and even months in the finest hostelries, or enhance his presence in a foreign place in a thousand other ways. He wrote to Adee: "My work is merely the care of investments, which are so safe they require no care."[14] The world was, it would appear, quite his oyster. For all the poor health he occasionally suffered, he was a busy man of leisure.

Yet Hay, like most such people, occasionally suffered insecurity. He knew well that his independence was based upon Clara's money, and he feared what might happen if he ever found himself without it. This deep uncertainty took possession of him for a period in the summer of 1893, while he was traveling in Europe. News reports on the early stages of what was to be the panic of that year convinced him that his financial security was threatened. In nervous alarm, he boarded the next ship home, boiling over with anxiety, railing out loud to his fellow passengers against Democrats and their labor strikes, which he was convinced had sunk the economy. When he learned on his arrival in New York that his money was intact and all else was well, he straightened up, dropped the subject, and returned to Europe at once to resume his season of travel.

As John Hay, Joe Cannon, John Sherman, and William McKinley continued their pursuits and the 1890s wore on, international events of long standing began to jell and would entwine them all in a web. Since the 1870s American businessmen had kept an avaricious eye on foreign lands that might serve U.S. interests. Sugar-rich Cuba, a possession of Spain since Columbus's time, had long been attractive to Americans as an asset the United States would be wise to control. Most people could not conceive of the annexation of Cuba by the United States, but the few who did had been volatile over the past sixty years in making it their goal. The interest was stronger than ever in the late nineteenth century and well-soaked in moralistic syrup. John Hay had visited Cuba as a young man and knew the stringency of Spanish governance elsewhere, which led him to believe that Cubans lived under such excessive oppression that they deserved the blessings of American liberty, to be granted under some sort of protectorate. It was not an uncommon view to those who had spent any time at all on the island.

Amid such personalities and their beliefs, the coals of internationalism gradually began to glow in Washington. The idea of capturing and possessing a foreign domain that was in proximity to the United States was not new. A bonanza had come with the Mexican War fifty years before, stretching the nation to the Pacific Ocean. With the advent of coal-fueled ships, American commercial interests saw a need for fueling stations and warehouse ports in the Pacific, to house and distribute the heavy coal supplies needed for trade with Asia. Almost any body of land relatively close at hand or along trade routes was open game if it seemed useful to America's expanding sea trade.

Cuba, a tantalizing ninety miles away and about half the size of England, was close and the most conveniently located foreign shore for the shipping industry. The idea of controlling the Spanish colony was not new to Americans. Jefferson had encouraged the annexation of Cuba not long after the heady triumph of the diplomats' purchasing the Louisiana Territory. Filibustering expeditions through the nineteenth century had actually landed in Cuba, notably that of the ill-fated Narciso López just before the Civil War. The bullet and sword, if not the garotte, awaited all callers.

The panic of 1893 and repeal of the McKinley tariff the following year ended the prosperity Cuba had enjoyed from selling sugar duty-free to the United States. Revolution soon exploded in Cuba, where poverty and even starvation had become rampant. Spain's suppression of the insurgents was violent and swift. Thousands of troops sailed from Spain to join those already stationed in Cuba. The garrote, firing squad, whip, and tortures almost inconceivable were the instruments of official reaction. Refugees poured into the United States with tales of horror. Invasionary filibustering schemes to free Cuba by force popped up along the Atlantic and Gulf coasts. American entrepreneurs and to a great extent the politicians they helped fund saw territorial opportunity in the chaos.

President Cleveland opposed the annexation of any foreign lands to the United States, be it Hawaii or Cuba or Santo Domingo. He scolded the business interests for setting their sights on this goal and condemned them for stalking the halls of Congress seeking political support for it. Upon going to office for the second time in 1893, Cleveland quickly destroyed the process then underway for bringing the Hawaiian Islands under the American flag, although he did recognize in the following year that the Hawaiian republic, through which American sugar interests invested in the islands, had replaced the monarchy. Deposed Queen Liliuokalani soon appeared on Cleveland's doorstep in Washington to lobby for the restoration of her crown. As for Cuba, Americans had no overwhelming desire to actually own the island, but controlling it seemed more desirable than ever. Intervention for humanitarian reasons soon fit and sweetened the idea beautifully. The press now supported the interested businessmen, with whom the publishers naturally identified. Emotional news reports described Spanish injustice in Cuba, and according to firsthand accounts from correspondents on the scene in Cuba, a lot of what they published in the so-called yellow press, though strongly biased, was true.

In the 1890s interest was aroused among thinkers who were considering the future of America. The astonishing advance of war technology and the building physical power of European nations brought questions of how America's national security could be best maintained. A revival of expansionism appeared. The West had been won by 1890, so new frontiers beckoned over the ocean. But how could the United States hold its own if it became geographically strung out beyond its shores? By what right did Americans take over places that historically they had no right to at all?

One man seemed to have the obvious answer, and the effect of his message was profound. Captain Alfred Thayer Mahan was a somewhat familiar figure in Washington as an off-and-on resident of the capital. He moved in high circles. A quiet man, he was known to be learned and an able writer as well as a skilled sailor. He created attention everywhere after his book *The Influence of Sea Power Upon History, 1660–1783*, published in 1890, made a mighty impact in its justification of American expansion.[15] Advocates of annexing new American territory offshore pointed to his book as a philosophical basis for their most visionary plans.

Mahan's thesis was intellectual, stirring, and commonsense all at once, with an impact that lost little of its punch for forty years. Proclaiming overseas expansion as a necessary feature of any nation's power, Mahan used history to prove to the satisfaction of most of his readers that whoever ruled the seas ruled the earth. He supported the missionary's sensitivities to the humanitarian aspects of expansion, as well as the commercial aspirations of the businessman. The Admiralty in Britain praised the book. Kaiser Wilhelm II called it gospel and quoted it in his speeches. Theodore Roosevelt, the young Civil Service commissioner, adopted Mahan's ideas and kept them close to his heart.

Few books have had so profound an effect upon the course of history in their own time. It is unlikely that Mahan's views planted ideas in his followers as much as they supplied a supporting philosophy to ideas his followers already had. Especially to Americans it seemed to light the way to a place at the world table. *The Influence of Sea Power Upon History* was a tight and compelling narrative, and it and Mahan's other naval books showed that prowess at sea had built and sustained the great nations that dominated the world. He made his points dramatically: "The surest way to maintain peace is to occupy a position of menace."[16] With a careful synthesis of the best current naval histories, Mahan told the story of sea power from the reign of Louis XIV in France to the Treaty of Paris, which ended the American Revolution. He gave special attention to Britain's rise at sea.

Mahan attached little significance to America's historically notable place in commercial shipping, believing that Americans had too long neglected the value of raw naval sea power for its own sake. Now he offered a mandate that the United States build a great navy in anticipation of its future in the theaters of the world. Whatever it took to achieve this must be done. Building ships and acquiring fueling stations were mere details. The United States was not really safe until it could master the ocean. The notion was not entirely new to either the navy or the Congress, which in 1883 had appropriated large amounts of money to build three steel naval cruisers, the first ships commissioned since the Civil War. Through the balance of the 1880s the Department of the Navy, under Secretary William C. Whitney, had undergone an enlargement and reorganization that included the establishment of the Naval War College, at Newport, Rhode Island.

Mahan's formula for international greatness, however, promoted the idea of America's future power by defining a direct route to achieving it. For all the echoes his views would make through the century to come, Mahan's *Influence of Sea Power* helped unite the crassly commercial political viewpoints of the business interests with the urgency of national security. The international context encouraged his concepts, for outside America's gates the whole world seemed troubled and afraid. Networks of mutual protection woven at the Congress of Vienna in 1815, after Napoleon's defeat, still lived in diplomatic concept but were vulnerable to the chauvinism that had come to characterize the most powerful nations. Newspapers were filled with unsettling reports of conflicts in the colonies held by Europe, as well as crumbling alliances between kingdoms in Europe, class unrest that was lingering from the eighteenth century and had been intensified by industrialization, revolutions in the Mediterranean countries, war in Asia, and assassinations in Europe. America, so distant from it all, might well imagine that mayhem would spread like a wave and inevitably reach its shores. Mahan's views came just in time.

By 1896 the situation in Cuba was the dominating topic in the American press. Tabloid news reporting gained a unified voice with that of the regular news nationwide, crying for intervention against Spain to rescue the Cubans. Americans kept traveling to Cuba as always, although warned that sometimes there was gunfighting in the streets of Havana and Santiago. In Florida, Tampa and Jacksonville were filling up with refugees, while many others fleeing Cuba died in the attempt to escape. Spain rejected President Cleveland's offer to mediate between the Cubans and Spain. Although Cuba was the major international issue before the American public, it was not the only one. In late 1895 President Cleveland stirred a controversy between Great Britain and the United States into serious ill feelings by displaying anger at England's challenge to Venezuela over ownership of a supposedly common frontier. It was an old issue that had originated in the early nineteenth century, before the Monroe Doctrine, in Dutch Guiana's ambiguous concession of several South American provinces to Britain. Venezuela, involved at the time with achieving independence from Spain, did not protest until after it had achieved that independence in 1830. Then Venezuela denounced the validity of Britain's then longtime claim to part of the frontier.

The issue lingered with little more happening for nearly seventy years. Discovery of gold in the disputed area in the 1880s made a solution desirable. America now called up the Monroe Doctrine to keep Britain out. During Cleveland's first administration, Secretary of State Thomas Bayard suggested that the United States sponsor an arbitration between Britain and Venezuela before hostilities broke out. The British Foreign Office simply ignored the request, making no response at all. The silence became insulting as it lengthened, but the matter hovered, still unsettled, until it became useful to the Republicans in the presidential campaign of 1896.

When he returned to the White House in 1893, after the four-year absence, Grover Cleveland still smarted from the British snub. He took a stand on his own that had the diplomatic impact of an earthquake. The president of the United States delivered a message—a diplomatic "note" or commentary—threatening to take the "Venezuelan matter" in hand personally. He ordered Great Britain to submit to the proposed arbitration at once, assuring the British government that if this was not done and Britain actually occupied the territory, he would uphold the Monroe Doctrine by force. Adee wrote the draft of the president's note. Letters and drafts surrounding this document do not survive. They might indicate how much or how little Cleveland altered of what Adee had written, but it can be assumed that the president rewrote the note, because the language was anything but diplomatic and lacks Adee's subtlety with words. Reading it over, one suspects Adee shrank from the undiplomatic tone of the finished text.

With the Venezuelan note President Cleveland performed a seminal act in American diplomacy and indeed in American history. He opened a window on the future. No American president had ever spoken so boldly to the world, much less to the country then acknowledged as the greatest power in the world. In so doing, Cleveland served notice to all nations that the United States was a world power able and willing to attend to its own interests.

News of the president's note flashed through the diplomatic community in Washington like lightning. Politicians on both sides of the Atlantic were astonished when they read it. But Cleveland had only begun. He demanded from Congress the money to fund any military action he saw fit to initiate. Congress refused, in part because a majority was uncomfortable with the note, but more so because in granting the money the lawmakers would be giving the president power they had no intention of granting. As it turned out, a boundary commission was appointed by the United States to encourage Great Britain and Venezuela to cooperate through arbitration. Tension relaxed a bit. While the attentions of Congress turned elsewhere, the diplomatic world continued to look in wonder upon the United States, which, heretofore, had been relatively moderate in all responses. And the problem itself remained unsolved. In the presidential contest of 1896 it would lie on the political table, begging for a solution.

As it turned out, this situation swept John Hay into public life. He took his annual trip abroad in 1896, departing as customary in the spring, although a little earlier than usual. In London he found his friend Henry White (known as Harry), the diplomat from Baltimore. White and his wife, Daisy, were living on their own in England for a while. Since he had stepped down as secretary to the American legation upon Cleveland's election, White was standing by, hoping to return to St. James if there was a Republican victory in '96. His encyclopedic knowledge of the diplomatic scene in Britain quickly informed Hay on the British side of the Venezuelan situation.

Hay checked into his usual rooms at Brown's Hotel. Sending his cards around town, he soon found his mailbox filled with invitations. He sent his valet out with invitations of his own to dinners he planned to hold at the hotel. Mingling with his English friends, Hay considered the opinion against Grover Cleveland and quickly assessed that he was in a prime position to do some good for his Republican friends back home. There is no evidence that he had ever taken such a lead before or that it was authorized officially, but now, perhaps for pure gamesmanship, he undertook to do what he might about the United States, Britain, and Venezuela. Without portfolio or instruction, simply as a gentleman traveling abroad, he set to work.

Hay began talking pointedly in places where it counted. He praised McKinley, the Republican candidate for the presidency, as a man of reason and peace. At dinners, country weekends, club luncheons, golf or tennis matches, nearly anywhere he might find himself, he struck up conversations about American and British relations. Important people listened. Hay had assumed the role of unofficial ambassador.

He kept his course with increasing vigor and obvious fascination. A firm objective quickly formed in his mind: to convince key figures in British politics that McKinley was going to win in 1896 and that he did not share Cleveland's hostility toward Britain. It was therefore highly desirable for England to settle the Venezuelan issue before McKinley took office, so that McKinley would not have to take the issue as Cleveland left it. To Clara Hay, John Hay wrote to describe one evening in London: "After dinner, in the smoking room, I sat between Lord [George Nathaniel] Curzon and [Joseph] Chamberlain, and had some very interesting talk with each of them. My talk with Chamberlain was especially important. I was urging him to have the Venezuela question settled before McKinley came in."[17]

Sir William Harcourt and Arthur J. Balfour wanted to speak with him at the House of Commons. "So we went to Harcourt's room (he has a room to himself as leader of the [Liberal] Opposition) and saw him and Balfour [Liberal majority leader] for a few minutes. It turned out . . . both were anxious to talk about Venezuela." Hay wrote that he and Harcourt "had a talk of an hour of great interest and importance. He thinks the Venezuelan matter ought to be settled now."[18] Lincoln's former assistant secretary now wrote carefully crafted on-the-scene letters to the American newspapers, describing the situation as he found it in England. His long-dormant abilities as a journalist revived in the urgency his letters conveyed. Details about personalities he encountered heightened public interest. McKinley should be elected, he wrote again and again, for he was the only man who would keep the United States out of war with Britain. Hay emerged from the episode not only a political figure but also a statesman in his own right.

He returned home in August before the fall election to find politics in turmoil and himself seen in an entirely new light by his fellow Republicans. His accomplishment for his party and McKinley's campaign was inestimable. He found everyone into politics and talking about Republicans. Even on the tranquil crossing, American politics was the overriding theme in all conversations. Dyed-in-the-wool Democrats were vowing to cast their votes for McKinley. Hay was amazed. The Ohio governor had won the nomination that summer in St. Louis. It seemed to the Republicans that McKinley would beat Cleveland with ease.

But Cleveland was not to be McKinley's rival. The Democratic convention suddenly turned support to William Jennings Bryan, an unknown thirty-six-year-old from Nebraska. He captured the nomination with a spellbinding oration on the powerful, populist platform of rich versus poor. Bryan denounced the gold standard as favoring the rich and called for a silver standard, which would increase the quantity of money for everyone. In a clear, sonorous baritone he cried out to millions from platforms across the nation, "You shall not press down upon the brow of labor this crown of thorns," he boomed. "You shall not crucify mankind upon a cross of gold."[19]

Bryan's campaign was far-reaching. The handsome young candidate had a magisterial, yet ever so slightly vulnerable presence that made him an interesting, rather theatrical character for his audiences. In this age, most men running for the presidency still followed the old tradition and made none or very few speeches in their own behalf. Bryan, pursuing his own star, promoted himself in churches, theaters, train stations, and union halls and on courthouse steps. "What a dull and serious campaign we are having," wrote Hay to Henry Adams. "The Boy Orator makes only one speech—but he makes it twice a day. There is no fun in it. He simply reiterates the unquestioned truths that every man who has a clean shirt is a thief and ought to be hanged; that there is no goodness or wisdom except among the illiterate criminal classes; that gold is vile; that silver is lovely and holy. . . . He has succeeded in scaring the Goldbugs out of their five wits."[20]

In no previous campaign had Hay taken such an interest, except Lincoln's, to which he had been peripheral thirty-six years earlier, the year William Jennings Bryan was born. Heretofore Hay had written checks, indeed, but had sat in the shade at the edges of the action, making pithy comments to his friends about those out working in the sun. Invigorated by his busy months in England and the new status to which he had arrived, which made his soul rejoice because he had made it for himself, he actually entered the fray in 1896. Stepping up to the platform in the full light and standing amid fluttering flags, he made speeches in praise of McKinley. Of his wife's Ohio hometown, Hay wrote, "Cleveland has ceased the ennobling pursuit of the dollar . . . and had given itself over to two weeks' debauch of politics. No business is done. . . . Most of my friends think Bryan will be elected and we shall all be hanged to the lampions of Euclid Avenue. I have not yet made up my mind to this."[21]

When Hay went to McKinley's hometown, Canton, the candidate himself honored Hay by meeting him personally at the depot and driving in his buggy, just the two of them, to his home at the corner of Ninth and Market Streets. With the shrewd campaign strategy of Mark Hanna, McKinley was making a special point of remaining at home with Ida, allowing others to do his traveling and speaking for him. Hanna's psychology in this was to make the public see McKinley as already presidential. Thousands traveled to Canton to line up along the street before McKinley's house, where he and perhaps Ida and sometimes a few friends gathered on the front porch, the kindly looking candidate peacefully seated in a rocking chair in the cool shade of geraniums and climbing roses. Drugstores in Canton offered counter specials for visitors. Souvenir flags were sold at the train station; picture postcards were a penny apiece. One could not obtain a room in a boardinghouse or a hotel in Canton as the months approaching November shrank to weeks, then days.

Hay was flattered by his generous reception and wrote to Clara, "[He] took me upstairs and talked for two hours as calmly and secretly as if we were summer boarders in Beverly at a loss for means to kill time." Hay and Adams as well had been intrigued by McKinley's appearance, of which there was much comment also in the newspapers. The candidate seemed to remind people of someone other than who he was. Hay offered his own impression, "I was more struck than ever by his mask. It is a genuine Italian ecclesiastical face of the fifteenth century."[22]

Mark Hanna, after having abandoned Sherman as a candidate, was now determined to win with McKinley. He covered all ports. McKinley was to be perceived by the people of the United States exactly as Hanna wanted. Some political statements would be issued, of course, but let Bryan talk himself into a tangle. McKinley stood by, seeming solid and significant compared with his ecstatic opponent; McKinley didn't need to say much. When he spoke, Canton's son spoke more generally. Everyone knew who he was, so he could speak familiarly of a free Cuba and of friendship with England, America's "mother country." The gold standard had positive advantages to more people than silver could ever provide, and he need not throw out a lot of words explaining why.

Leaving his candidate firmly in place on the front porch in Canton, Hanna launched a master plan for obtaining the presidency that was more exhaustive in its details than any before. With a genius for managing publicity, Hanna deputized agents all over the United States in a McKinley network. A thousand people reported to him. The telegraph lines installed in his headquarters in Cleveland hummed night and day, receiving news, rumors, and warnings and sending out from Hanna's writers "packaged" articles about McKinley for publication. Some were purely human interest pieces, Civil War stories, heroic tales; others were mildly political—never strong doses—assuring that no one forgot the panic of 1893 or the touchy situation President Cleveland had created with England or how passionately the kindly McKinley sympathized with the oppressed Cubans. The stories supplied good, quick reading and were convenient fillers or features for whatever the editors happened to want or need.

McKinley won an easy victory over Bryan in November. A month before McKinley was inaugurated, on March 4, 1897, the British signed a treaty submitting the Venezuelan dispute to arbitration. One of McKinley's first appointments was John Hay as ambassador to Great Britain.

The Hays closed their houses in Cleveland and Washington, and the whole family moved to London. Henry Adams naturally went along but remained only awhile, for it is clear from Hay's letters that the ambassador now kept close to Clara in equal measure to his absence from her in the past. The change in his life had brought a change in theirs, and the joy and good fortune he expressed when describing his wife was something new. He rented an elegant house, Carleton Terrace, because there was no official American embassy residence. Harry White, to be embassy secretary, saw to perfecting the arrangements of the house, employing a butler, a cook, and some eight other servants, as well as purchasing a team of horses to pull the Hays's coach, which they transported with them on the ship from the United States. On May 21, 1897, the ambassador made his first public appearance at the unveiling of a bust of Sir Walter Scott in Westminster Abbey. His address, remembered as one of his finest, defined him to the British as a patrician and a man of letters.

A new day had opened for John Hay, as it soon would for his country. No official was more devoted to his duties than Hay. When he became ambassador, relations were still sensitive between the United States and Great Britain. The American public's historical suspicion of Britain had been stirred up like hot coals. The British public was unhappy over the American threats. Hay was able to smooth it all out by sheer force of personality and intelligence, assuring the British that they and the United States had common interests and a common civilization. It was not a new idea but a theme that would resound ever more loudly in the coming century.

Hay had real work to do for the first time in long years. In most respects the important demands on the ambassador were somewhat akin to his private pursuits, sometimes nearly the same. Social and ceremonial functions were many. His staff of several secretaries and assistants dealt with most situations in which he had to intervene, such as problems between American citizens and British officials, as well as with the myriad other everyday duties that fell on any legation or embassy. Hay had long ago demonstrated that he was disinterested in ordinary things. As ambassador he was no different. An ambassador needed to be free of minor matters and out in the world with open eyes. Hay was a master at this.

He might be asked to arrange a meeting in the guise of a luncheon between an American businessman and one in London. He might decide that he must get to know this or that official or prominent citizen. He certainly had access; Hay was out socially every day. At his residence he held dinner parties and dances, to which he would invite selected diplomats. Weekends he sometimes went to the country, where he leased a house, and the social routine continued there. This sort of life, as well as having the private fortune to support it, was all part of an American ambassador's job. His ties to the British Foreign Office were close, and in many instances the time was a good one to be an American abroad, with prosperity returning and the United States feeling rich again. Corporations were being formed. U.S. gold reserves increased. There was more money everywhere, or so it seemed.

Though the ambassador's time was not entirely his own, he took every opportunity to travel, now nearly always with Clara. Henry Adams wove in and out of the Hays' lives in London, usually appearing from some place on the Continent. He was with John and Clara Hay on a Nile cruise in the winter of 1898 when, as they sat in deck chairs beguiled by the sun setting over the ancient land, news was brought to the ambassador that the American battleship *Maine* had been blown up in Havana Harbor.

THREE
The Pivotal Year 1898

In the Washington diplomatic corps no diplomat was more popular socially than Enrique Dupuy de Lôme, minister plenipotentiary to the United States from the Kingdom of Spain. By the year 1898 he was in his second mission as minister in the Washington legation and stepped to center stage as great events rose around him. He was of medium build and solid looking, according to his pictures, and not fat like many another well-fed, site-bound diplomat. Dark eyed and pale skinned, he had a strikingly aristocratic appearance. According to the papers he looked as much French as he did Spanish, and in fact his forebears had come from France. He was well-groomed—a characteristic of diplomats—with a close-trimmed beard around his chin so thick that it would not have moved in a strong wind, a Louis Napoleon moustache, and jet-black hair waxed down fashionably flat.

In the late 1880s and early '90s, de Lôme had been a late afternoon frequenter of the firesides of Henry Adams and John Hay, where conversation was likely to be in Spanish in his honor. He was also a good friend of Alvey Adee and was seen frequently in the halls of the State Department. De Lôme got around considerably. People in the diplomatic and social circles of Washington liked him. But he never learned to suffer fools lightly, and if he had a devil for a companion in life, that trait was it.

The Spanish legation, like nearly all the rest of the diplomatic headquarters, was both office and residence for de Lôme. It was a hulking red-orange brick house with a porch of Moorish arches across the front. At night bands of stained glass radiated bright colors from the lights within. Set a bit back from Massachusetts Avenue on a grass-planted terrace, the Spanish legation was one of the most imposing of the diplomatic headquarters, standing somewhat apart from the other legations, most of which were on streets nearer the White House. Here, in rooms filled with dark, carved furniture, de Lôme lived with his popular wife and two young sons. Photographs of her show her a pretty matron with a bright smile. She had accompanied her husband on his missions to Japan and Britain and had traveled extensively while in the United States. One reporter at the time wrote that she was "a typical Spanish woman, with

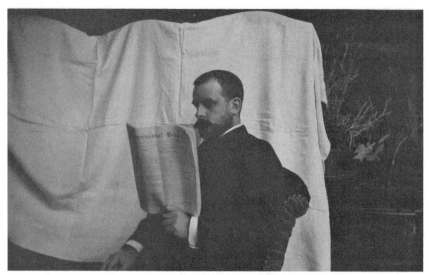

Enrique Dupuy de Lôme, minister of Spain to the United States, 1892–98. *Massachusetts Historical Society, Boston.*

dark penetrating eyes, abundant dark hair, and a tall, well-formed figure."[1] She had been appointed lady-in-waiting and hostess to Princess Eulalia during her American visit. After that the de Lômes went to another legation, departing Washington. The Foreign Office in Madrid took note of de Lôme's success in America.

American popular sensitivities had been building against Spain for several years. Cubans found some covert support in the United States, and by the mid-1890s revolutionaries who had fled to Yankee safety openly sought funds and men with which to return and try to take Cuba. Cleveland's administration, being anti-imperial, gave no quarter to this.

De Lôme's predecessor, Envoy Extraordinary and Minister Plenipotentiary Don Edvardo de Muruaga, had respectfully protested that the State Department should halt filibustering expeditions against Cuba, which were organized in Philadelphia and various cities in Florida, notably Jacksonville. Volunteers to Cuba were openly being recruited in New Orleans. Under neutrality laws, the United States could not harbor such activity. In the winter of 1895, shortly before de Lôme returned to work in Washington to take Don Edvardo's place, vessels lying in Fernandina, Florida, were found filled with arms and supplies bound for Cuba. Secretary Gresham had informed Minister Muruaga in March that this effort had been "apprehended by customs officers."[2] The Spanish minister responded that ships flying British flags were anchored off Havana and the sailors were going ashore.

Muruaga issued his complaints up until the day he departed his post. On May 6, 1895, with the same issues still hot, de Lôme presented his credentials to President

Cleveland at the White House. Secretary Gresham's death soon followed, and Richard Olney, Cleveland's appointment as Gresham's successor and a more seasoned and aggressive diplomat, was at first less inclined to calm any alarm the new Spanish minister might have. He expressed himself in a memorandum soon after taking office. "Sensational articles in the 'Times' and other New York papers," he wrote, "are understood in Madrid to be merely rumors."[3] Having been attorney general, he was acutely aware that the situation was tense, and he assured de Lôme of the efforts Americans were making to thwart filibustering, noting that the Coast Guard had stopped an expedition "fitting out from St. Tammany Parish, Louisiana, to aid in the insurrection now in progress in Cuba."[4]

No sooner did McKinley come to office in 1897 than an upsurge of sympathy came from the public for the plight of the Cuban people in Spain's harsh reaction to the revolt. De Lôme distrusted both McKinley and the Republican Party from the outset, and not without reason. Remarks against Spain by McKinley's secretary of state, John Sherman, were to a diplomat's ears not only hostile but also crudely threatening. Efforts in the Congress to authorize the sale of weapons to Cuban insurgents, halted by Cleveland, percolated again after he was gone, and McKinley was not absolute in his objections. De Lôme's job as minister of Spain became more difficult daily.

By 1897 reports of Cuba's bloody treatment by Spain were sensational fare in the newspapers, fueling American indignation. Where President Cleveland had done little to interfere diplomatically in behalf of the Cubans, President McKinley's minister to Spain, Stewart L. Woodford, did convince the crown to slow the military suppression of Cuba. The American press made little of Woodford's achievement and continued the barrage against Spain.

Reports came to de Lôme describing filibustering expeditions planned in New York, Philadelphia, Jacksonville, Mobile, and New Orleans. Jacksonville, Florida, seems to have been the heart of the filibustering. The minister sent notes continually to the State Department, reporting what he had heard, naming individuals and ships, and demanding action. Adee usually answered him, and the texts of the slips he pinned to de Lôme's correspondence indicate an effort to calm the waters himself, even understanding no doubt that the minister's worries were justified. The inquiries seem to have been turned over immediately to the Secret Service. Most of the expeditions seem to have been concocted by Cuban émigrés, who used their financial connections in the United States for support. De Lôme's frustration mounted as public opinion among the Americans heated up almost to the point of explosion.

When the new year came in 1898, the White House was still hung in black to mourn the death of President McKinley's mother in December. The traditional public reception for New Year's Day, which would have been McKinley's first, was canceled. When the requisite thirty-day mourning period had passed, Secretary of State Sherman pressed for some approximation of the New Year's reception, the first missed since Jefferson's time. McKinley at last agreed to receive on January 19, but when Sherman gave no orders to make ready for this and Adee was thus unable to step forward and plan the event, the president called upon Colonel Theodore Bingham, the public buildings commissioner, to stage the tardy New Year's event. Bingham wanted no advice from Adee. Having seen service as a military attaché in American legations in Europe, Bingham believed he knew how things ought to be done. He loved symbols of state. Now was his chance at the White House.

The event he designed was not like the historical daytime New Year's receptions. It was to take place in the evening. Invitations would be sent, an innovation not tried before. New Year's receptions had always been public. Bingham wanted none of that, even though this reception was a substitute for the regular New Year's event and would be seen as such. Those who might have objected to his plans remained silent, for the president had bypassed the State Department and handed the task entirely to Bingham.

Colonel Bingham was strict and exacting in what he wanted. He responded favorably to people of rank and good blood. He came from a proud and long New England lineage, about which he had published a sizable volume. While he was well liked socially in Washington, he lacked the gentle manner of his predecessor, Colonel Thomas Lincoln Casey, the engaging official who had carried the Library of Congress to completion. Tall and thin, with piercing blue eyes, Theodore Bingham was a loyal official, if a bit overblown in a military way. His subordinates feared him; even his superiors were likely to give him room. Bingham's job was to supervise the public buildings of Washington, which required, he might say, taste as well as political skill and power within his realm.

The corps was at its peak of favor in Washington, for the new Library of Congress (Congressional Library), although not Bingham's project, shed glory on his office and thus also upon the officer in charge of the public buildings. A major and sensitive feature of his job was supervision of the physical White House. It was the live bomb each officer in charge had to carry. For Bingham it was a foot in the door to greater objectives. He was determined to use the position as a platform for engineering the transformation of the American capital into a world-class city.

As for the challenge at hand—the New Year's reception—he sent invitations as a means of culling out the "butchers, cabmen, market and grocery clerks, and the scum of the city," who, to his thinking, appeared all too often at the White House.[5] McKinley would have winced to hear such an unkind comment about his fellow Americans, but he, of course, was well out of range. This is not to say that the receptions were ever "democratic," for they were not in any modern definition of the word. But in their time they were considered so. Known low-life characters were naturally omitted, but otherwise anyone could attend, although they were expected to meet certain standards of dress and conduct and, if not by rule, then certainly in usage, be white people, unless they were diplomats. The tradition was cherished. Bingham's reception illustrates universal truth in the capitals of the world, how a single, even an obscure, official can carry great matters where they were never intended to go.

The scant two thousand invitations reached their destinations. Obviously those who did not receive invitations believed they had been "cut." Six thousand was the usual number in attendance at a New Year's reception. By custom there were no invitations. Callers simply went, stood good naturedly in long lines, and eventually passed into the house, received by a smile and a handshake from the president, a smile and a nod from the first lady, after which they stood about to see who was there, perhaps quenched their thirst at one of the ice water stations (nothing more being served), then departed. The doors were closed promptly at 3:00 P.M. Those who hadn't made it over the threshold were turned away and had to count on coming earlier next time. Portable wooden steps were put up to the East Room windows on the north to encourage early escape. For many people, the reception was a natural part of their New Year's Day; for some, the best event of the year.

The 1898 reception promised to be very interesting because the diplomats were certain to make a full turnout. The Spanish problem had everyone talking about international affairs. Warlike remarks were plentiful. Minister de Lôme had been booed on the street. Idlers watched his house. These threatening outbursts of insolence surely annoyed him, but he also had deeper concerns. His house was guarded, which was rarely the case with Washington legations. Since the appearance of the first ambassador, the Metropolitan Police had patrolled the neighborhoods where diplomats lived, keeping watch over the foreign missions. Threats against de Lôme's life, however, made private guards seem to him a prudent course to protect his family.

Seclusion, however, was not a choice for him. Appearing in public was part of a diplomat's job, safe or not. Within the diplomatic community, including the State Department, the only courtesy guaranteed was between individuals. That de Lôme was the object of public contempt because he represented Spain had no bearing whatsoever among his colleagues. As long as he occupied his position, he was one of them and would be made to feel comfortable. Colonel Bingham must have missed the nuances of this courteous behavior in his years abroad.

On January 19, a raw, windy night, de Lôme walked out of his legation at six to attend the president's reception. A crowd stood on the sidewalk, not disruptive, but noisy. He wore the full diplomatic uniform of Spain: knee breeches and black hose, velvet jacket, cuffs and shoulders heavy embroidered in gold bullion, rows of bright gold buttons, a gold-edged high-standing collar, and medals resplendent upon his chest. Wrapped in a silk cape with high collar, with a ceremonial tricorn hat beneath his arm and a silver dress sword at his side, he climbed into his carriage, manned with coachman and footman, and went to the White House, where duty pleased that he go this bitter night.

The diplomatic corps was always received an hour earlier than the other guests. Entering with the diplomats at the north door, de Lôme gathered among cheery friends in the hot, dry heat of the entrance hall, joining a line that threaded straight ahead to the Blue Room. There President and Mrs. McKinley were receiving to the right of the door. The decorations, an explosion of red, white, and blue, must have chilled de Lôme. Adee's absence from the planning process could not have been more obvious. Colonel Bingham had adorned the Blue Room in a coarse, bellicose way. The Stars and Stripes hung everywhere. Tree branches and vines made a ceiling of greenery from which poked two hundred, maybe more, glaring red, white, and blue lightbulbs. A Spaniard can only have felt in hostile territory here.

When the receiving line closed, President McKinley passed from the room with the tawdry lights into the East Room, seeking out de Lôme. Smiling warmly, McKinley told the Spanish minister he believed matters were going along well and that public opinion was changing in his direction. "You have no occasion to be other than satisfied and confident," he concluded and moved on to other guests. De Lôme absorbed the implications of the studied remark. What the president had really said was that the situation was better but that Spain, by its actions, could quickly turn the current the other way. Minister de Lôme left the White House annoyed by the encounter, and when he called on McKinley weeks later, the president's remarks were about the same.[6]

In his frustration over the general situation, de Lôme allowed himself the very undiplomatic luxury of bringing his personal opinions to the fore. He scorned McKinley as a little-town politician of the sort he saw so numerously in the Capitol. He had first been assigned to Washington during the period of the McKinley tariff, which had been so destructive to Cuba's sugar industry, creating, Spain believed, the troubles that climaxed in the Cuban insurrection. But for de Lôme, trouble of his own making lay ahead. Earlier, in December, he had written informally to a friend and vented his feelings about American attitudes toward Cuba. He was candid, saying that he opposed negotiations with the rebels and resented the Americans' meddling. Of the American president, de Lôme said he was a man who was "weak and a bidder for the admiration of the crowd, besides being a would-be politician who tries to leave a door open behind himself while keeping on good terms with the jingoes of his party."[7]

De Lôme sent the letter to his friend Don José Canalejas, a Spanish newspaperman, using the Washington legation as the return address on the envelope. Spies of the revolution found the letter while searching Canalejas's hotel room. By the time of the White House reception, de Lôme had been told that the letter was missing and must have known that it was only a matter of time before it turned up where he least wanted it to be. In early February, when he learned that it was to appear the next morning on the front page of the *New York Journal*, he telegraphed his resignation to Madrid.

February 10, the day after the *Journal's* scoop, the original letter was brought to the State Department for Adee's analysis. The third secretary read it in disbelief and first judged it a forgery. On a second review, Adee reluctantly conceded that the penmanship was de Lôme's. He took the letter to McKinley, who did no more than to express dismay. The insult called for an apology. Adee worked out the language of the demand and returned to his office to prepare a letter for the American minister in Madrid to present to the queen of Spain. De Lôme and his family were already aboard a train to Canada.

In January 1898 de Lôme had pleaded with McKinley not to yield to pressure to send a battleship to Havana Harbor. What, he asked, would Americans think if Spain were to send a battleship into the harbor of New York? At about the same time, the president was persuaded by General Fitzhugh Lee, the consul-general in Havana and a roaring Confederate vet, that a show of strength was essential to the safety of the substantial number of Americans living in Cuba.

As these negotiations were underway, the sinking of the U.S. battleship *Maine* intervened. It was never determined who was responsible for the explosion that sank the *Maine*. She dropped anchor in Havana Harbor in January 1898, with 350 men aboard. Through the weeks that followed, sailors who went ashore for entertainment met with threats of violence. On the night of February 15, about bedtime, with most of the lights on the *Maine* doused, an explosion tore the vessel apart and sent her to the bottom of the harbor. Two hundred fifty men died on the ship or drowned while trying to swim away. Eight more died in a Havana hospital.

Word of the disaster spread over the American nation through the telegraph, telephone, and newsprint. Papers blazed with news of the "*Maine* Disaster." The Spanish were denounced. Assistant Secretary of the Navy Theodore Roosevelt had no doubt: "The *Maine* was sunk by an act of dirty treachery on the part of the Spaniards."[8] Acting Secretary William R. Day, shocked by the threatening language, denied that anyone on his staff ever made such a remark. Public demonstrations took place in the cities. The verbiage against Spain was fierce.

The day the *Maine* went down, the White House was prepared for another public reception—this one noninvitational—and the details were all in place, from the arranging of the state rooms, stripped of most of their furniture, to the carpet runners that passed from the north door into the Blue Room to serve the receiving line, to the white-covered tables with their pyramids of thick-glass tumblers served by ice water stations along the transverse hall. Newspapers on February 14 informed the public how to participate in the reception, where to enter, where to exit, and where to hang coats. Colonel Bingham, who had usurped Adee's role once again, had not missed a single detail in planning the event and had introduced some valuable shortcuts, such as number cards issued to the coachmen when they arrived and electric enunciator boxes to signal them when it was time to return to the house for their passengers.

Three hours after midnight, with the party long over, the only light in the house was in the telegraph office upstairs, adjacent to the president's office, where Colonel

Ben Montgomery was working the late-night shift at the key. General Fitzhugh Lee's telegraph arrived from Havana announcing the demise of the *Maine*, and Montgomery lost no time slipping down the shadowed corridor to the residential end of the house. In the dark bedroom he shook the president awake. After what seemed only a few moments, McKinley, dressed in a business suit, positioned himself at the end of the long table in the cabinet room and began puffing a Havana cigar.

Congressmen, senators, cabinet members—all climbed the stairs to the room where the president sat. The office staff assembled quickly enough, some thirty men, including John Addison Porter, who held the distinguished position of private secretary, and his first assistant, a tall, dark-haired Knickerbocker named George Bruce Cortelyou. Officials stood before the stone-faced McKinley, who seemed utterly blank to all they said. Cabinet members took their chairs around the table, each man uttering his conviction that war had begun with Spain. Hours passed; more cigars were puffed, until the air was heavy with smoke. The president uttered hardly a word. Ice water was brought in, followed by coffee, biscuits, ham, and eggs. Soon the room smelled of that along with the cigar smoke. McKinley made no effort to talk much, except to shake his head and deny that there was a war.

Finally he dismissed the cabinet. John Sherman remained and talked for awhile, not very usefully. The navy's acting secretary Day was there. Senator Reed appeared for a while and left, his views against a war already well known. Mark Hanna, who had replaced Sherman in the Senate, offered guidance to the president, the man of his making, who listened quietly. The six ambassadors stationed in Washington by Britain, France, Mexico, Italy, Austria-Hungary, and Germany called and urged patience. The ambassadors expressed their certainty that the crisis could be at least reduced to the level of arbitration by diplomatic means. Days went by, and the newspapers boiled with protest and cried for war. In public places McKinley's picture was spit upon and hissed. He and Hanna were burned in effigy. The cry for war seemed universal.

McKinley in a sense barricaded himself in the White House, remaining in constant company with his wife. They discontinued the everyday carriage drives, to the relief of those assigned to protect them. Congressmen and senators were invited to dine at the White House in small groups to tell the president what they thought. McKinley walked with them over the palm-banked paths of the conservatory and listened. Leaders in the Congress opposed war, as did the nation's big businessmen. Most of the other lawmakers, be they Republicans or Democrats, wanted the war. They were reflecting the views of their constituents and pointed to hundreds of prowar petitions that had flooded the Capitol.

On March 3, McKinley decided he was ready to communicate his views to the Spanish. The decision was made to put these in a note, the diplomatic jargon for an official memorandum hand-carried to the Foreign Office of a country by the diplomat assigned to that country. A note could contain any sort of subject matter. In this case, the president's message was wired to the American minister Woodford in Madrid, who took it to the Spanish Foreign Office. Written by Adee, the note was strong, which the president wished, saying that while the sinking of the *Maine* still had to be investigated, the American people were upset, and the "insulting and insincere character of the De Lome letter" had created a very grave condition that would "require the highest wisdom and greatest prudence on both sides to avoid a crisis."[9]

Three days later President McKinley, on a Sunday night, sent a messenger to Joe Cannon's hotel asking him to hurry to the White House. "I went at once," Cannon remembered, aware that he was both an old friend of McKinley and also chair of the House Ways and Means Committee. He was ushered upstairs to the oval-shaped library. McKinley met him at the door, and Cannon later wrote that for all the years he had known him, McKinley had never seemed so tense and preoccupied. "It was not his way to show concern," said Cannon. "He had the philosophical temperament that sustained him in times of depression." With neither greeting nor friendly gesture to welcome Cannon into the room, McKinley started talking at the threshold: "Cannon I must have money to get ready for war. I am doing everything possible to prevent war, but it must come, and we are not prepared for war. Who knows where this war will lead us; it may be more than war with Spain. How can I get the money for these extraordinary expenses?"[10]

Cannon remembered the night: "The country was facing a foreign war for the first time in half a century and it was not ready." Cannon referred to the war with Mexico in 1846–48. Indeed, Spain was a European power. "It would mean the transport of troops over sea for the first time in our history. He felt we had reached a crisis and the people were driving the Administration to desperate measures. A sensitive and humane man, McKinley was hurt by press criticism, especially of the sort that held him responsible for sending the battleship *Maine* to Havana on a call of courtesy, only to be destroyed and hundreds of men murdered, and the opposition in Congress hurt him."

Cannon decided that the best approach was for McKinley to send a message to Congress asking for the money he thought he would need. Then Cannon and William Boyd Allison, chair of the Senate Appropriations Committee, would pledge themselves to deliver a bill within a week. The president adamantly opposed this tactic, for it would be taken by Spain as a war message. They discussed other approaches. Finally McKinley asked if Cannon could simply develop in committee a bill making an appropriation for national defense and take it to the floor without unnecessary explanation.

Cannon agreed that he could do that and asked McKinley to write the bill. The president went to the table and took a sheet from a stack of telegraph blanks. With his pen he wrote, "For national defense fifty million dollars."

Cannon later wrote, "It wasn't a bill or a message nor an estimate, but it was the president's memorandum as to what he wanted done, and I put the slip of paper in my pocket." He returned to his hotel and worked most of the rest of the night preparing the bill. The more he considered the challenge before him, the more he liked the idea. "The bill would give notice to the world that we did not have to consult financiers and bankers about raising the money. I thought it would be quite important as it would give the War and Navy Departments [time] in advancing their positions." It was to be his bill, with the support of his committee. "I did not consult any one, for the simple reason that after I had determined on my own action I did not care to argue the question." He considered the many possible effects the bill might ultimately have as an act of Congress. The note McKinley had given Cannon "simply indicated the amount of the appropriation, but it had to be elaborated to enable the President to use the money."

Cannon delivered the goods. Finding enthusiastic support, his bill passed three days later. It changed the course of history, placing the details of war and peace in the hands of the president. The reluctant McKinley, still shrinking at the thought of war, had elevated the presidency to a level of power unknown since the administration of George Washington.

～

John Sherman stepped down from his powerful Senate seat to become McKinley's secretary of state. Mark Hanna was appointed by the governor of Ohio to take Sherman's place in the Senate. Some believed it a design of McKinley's, who, knowing Sherman well, knew his dream for high appointive office and wanted Hanna as a spy and maneuverer in Congress. Although this belief was never really established or dispelled, Sherman took his office with understandable gratification and was sworn in the day after McKinley was inaugurated. Sherman took great pleasure in his new rank, the shower of invitations, and the charming company of diplomats eager to know and please him.

Yet it became a sad transformation. When he took office at seventy-three, he seemed at the peak of health, trim and active. He remained fit, but his mental state deteriorated quickly in the months after he took office. When his wife, Margaret, suffered a serious stroke that left her bedridden and unable to speak, sorrow brewed an undeniable anger in him toward everything. He developed almost a hatred for McKinley, a feeling doubtless rooted in the idea that had Hanna not dropped him, he might have been president instead. He had always previously suppressed any manifestations of jealousy as best he could. Now he made no secret of it. He broadcast his dislike of the president. It became a great embarrassment to McKinley and the rest of the cabinet, all of whom quickly recognized that Sherman was slipping. Staff at the State Department had to compensate for him, sometimes becoming the object of his prolonged rages. Adee naturally had to take the lead. He seemed able to handle Sherman and spent nearly all his time in smoothing out matters of all kinds in the secretary's wake.

Sherman was soon raving anytime, anyplace. Indiscreet and even insulting remarks to diplomats became everyday occurrences, especially on Thursdays, when the diplomats had the privilege of dropping in on the secretary without appointments.

The staff tensed on the sidelines and rushed in to make repairs. Much worse, work could not proceed in the State Department unless it bypassed the secretary. Normally this approval role had been delegated to the second secretary, William R. Day, or to the third assistant secretary, Adee. Sherman demanded to see everything and kept a suspicious eye fixed on all who were around him. Quietly the president began to speak directly to the assistant secretaries when he needed something. An old and close friend of both Sherman and McKinley, Day was uncomfortable with the arrangement, so hid himself from inquiry, deflecting it all to Adee. The result was that the State Department became silent to the outside world. One diplomat complained to a news correspondent, Arthur Dunn, "I am at a loss about conducting business with your government. The head of the department *knows* nothing; the first assistant *says* nothing; the second assistant *hears* nothing."[11]

Secretary Sherman publicly opposed the war. He was a minority in the cabinet for his views on Cuba. McKinley's delay and continual communication with Spain in an effort to keep peace took place in a context of jingoism all over the country. The leaders of the war effort in the Congress, calling themselves *reconcentrados*—the name Spanish soldiers in Cuba called the rebels—forced the subject to the floor whenever possible. Spain's entreaties to keep peace were overwhelmed by war drums. At the Gridiron Club's dinner that year, an impromptu speech by Senator Hanna proved too pacifist for the crowd and someone shouted, "At least we have one man connected with this administration who is not afraid to fight—Theodore Roosevelt, Assistant Secretary of the navy, and tonight a Vice-Admiral by commission of the Gridiron Club."[12] The Roosevelt show had begun.

The assistant secretary of the navy was even more the bane of McKinley's existence than Sherman was. At the end of his thirties, Roosevelt was young and active, indeed bouncy. He called at the White House frequently, verbally pushing the president in tones not always respectful. McKinley listened to exhaustion, too kind to order him thrown out, as Grover Cleveland certainly would have done. Roosevelt, a close friend of Captain Mahan's philosophy about naval power, was eager for the United States to express itself as a world power. In just which war did not much matter, but he looked forward to one. Ten or so days after the *Maine* sank, when the secretary of the navy was at the dentist and out of the office, Assistant Roosevelt wired the United States Asiatic Fleet, harbored in Hong Kong, advising Admiral George Dewey to be in readiness for action. Secretary John Davis Long was astonished when he found out, but not enough to take any particular action, and he let the order sit, remaining in effect through February, March, and April.

In April, McKinley began to yield to cries from all sides and said that he would deliver his war message on the sixth. That day passed, the president wishing for all American citizens to have a chance to depart Cuba first. Congressmen and senators flocked to the White House, crowding the entrance hall and long stairs up to the office, packing into the linoleum-floored waiting room in loud protest. To their indignities McKinley sometimes responded angrily, his fists clenched. He locked his war message in an office safe and said he would take it out when he was ready.

On April 11, with no faith any longer that Spain would stand behind any of the compromises it offered, McKinley asked Congress to authorize him to use force to free Cuba. Debate ensued on the floors of both chambers, and as it did Secretary Sherman paced his office at the State Department, smoldering over McKinley's message. The debate at the Capitol rang in his ears. He had to be there; he should be there in the midst of it; there he belonged. This war must be stopped! He called for his carriage, and it carried him in a blind pursuit to the Capitol. He climbed the stairs to the Senate chamber, where he had spent so many days. He bolted to the floor and went to his old seat, ordering the new occupant, Henry Cabot Lodge, to rise and move away.

Lodge stood up respectfully and stepped aside. The chamber fell to a hush, as Vice President Garrett Hobart, trying to save the situation, graciously welcomed the secretary of state home. The chamber became as still as a church, awaiting Sherman's response. Gradually he seemed to return to reality enough to be embarrassed. He stood up, stiff and straight, and walked out through the silent chamber, looking neither to the right nor to the left. Beyond highlighting the obvious personal misfortune of a once strong and proud John Sherman, the short drama seemed to symbolize the weakening of congressional absolutism that had begun with the Civil War.[13]

The diplomatic world in Washington began firing up its mechanisms to stop the approaching war. Europe became involved. On March 25, the Spanish minister of state, Pío Gullón, sent a circular to Spanish diplomats abroad establishing the point of view they were to take, saying that American inquiry into the sinking of the *Maine* was being submitted to Congress without having been seen by Spanish authorities. He urged the United States to keep the Cuban issues in the hands of the president. "And so convinced is Spain," he wrote, "that reason is with her, and that she is acting with prudence, that if the abovementioned end is not attained she does not hesitate to ask the advice of the great powers [to arbitrate] . . . for settlement of differences now pending and of those which may, in the near future, disturb the peace which the Spanish Nation wishes to preserve as far as compatible with her honor and the integrity of her territory. This is not only for her own sake but also for the consequences which the war, once begun, might have for the other countries of Europe and America."[14]

On April 8, the six ambassadors called on the president once again with a "collective note" appealing to him in the name of humanity to keep peace and hold out against the demands of the angry public. Before they arrived, McKinley, apparently aware of what was coming, summoned Adee and asked him how to dismiss his callers properly. Seated across the cabinet table, Adee took an envelope he found at hand and wrote a response for the president: "The Goverment of the United States appreciates the humanitarianism and disinterested character of the communication now

Sir Julian Pauncefote of Great Britain, first ambassador to the United States, 1893. *Library of Congress, Prints and Photos Division.*

made on behalf of the powers named, and for its part is confident that equal appreciation will be shown for its own earnest and unselfish endeavors to fulfill its duty to humanity by ending a situation the indefinite prolongation of which has become insufferable." The president listened to the ambassadors. When they had made their appeal, he produced the envelope and read Adee's words aloud. This was McKinley's manner of dealing with the six.[15]

Amazed by their reception, the spurned ambassadors gathered with Sir Julian Pauncefote at the British Embassy and tried to decide what they might do next. Their meeting, meant to be kept a secret behind-the-scenes matter, was quickly made public by the German ambassador, Theodor von Holleben, who not only freely told about it afterward without the assent of the other participants but also reported the meeting to the kaiser. Von Holleben's five colleagues were shocked by what he had taken upon himself, as the news spread to the capitals of Europe. His motive seems clear enough: to flatter the territorial designs of Kaiser Wilhelm II. For this the ambassador sacrificed his ethics and his personal prestige, but his first duty was to serve his monarch.

The German ambassador was aware that the kaiser was toying with the idea of allying the other major powers with Spain, against the United States. Wilhelm felt certain that Europe would go along, even if England would take no part. From the resulting conflict, however it might play out—at the diplomatic table or on the battlefield—Germany was to enhance her sea power by gaining control of part of the Philippines and other fueling and deposit stations in the Pacific Ocean. Already the German vice admiral Otto von Diederichs had suggested that the kaiser order German ships in the Pacific to cut through the blockade that Admiral Dewey was holding at Manila.

Ambassador von Holleben's memorandum shaped the story of the meeting at the British Embassy to suit the needs of his emperor: "The English ambassador," he wrote, "to-day adopted in a very remarkable manner the initiative for a new collective step on the part of the representatives of the Great Powers here. We conjecture that the Queen Regent [of Spain] has made representations in this sense to the Queen of England. The six representatives telegraph to their governments by request of the English Ambassador in the following sense. . . . it seems opportune to remove the erroneous impression which prevails that the armed intervention of the United States in Cuba commands . . . the support of the civilized world."[16]

This put Pauncefote in the center of a storm by making it appear that he, the friend of the United States, had schemed behind her back in favor of Europe. The German ambassador added another morsel, claiming that at the meeting Pauncefote had pronounced the Americans "brigands." At this the others who had attended the meeting denounced the German ambassador as a liar. So strong was their response that the brigand story was generally dismissed. It sounded very unlike Sir Julian Pauncefote anyway.

The union of the six ambassadors did continue, with more appeals to the president, more gentle responses, and nearly daily calls at the State Department to try to find some way to stop what seemed inevitable.

Concurrent with the efforts of the six ambassadors, a few days after mid-March 1898, in the midst of the heat of public protest, with war drums pounding, a curious little aside took place at the highest level of government. Stewart L. Woodford, minister to Spain, wired the president that the young Spanish king was a stamp collector and would like a set of U.S. stamps. The note made the rounds at the White House and State Department, and enthusiastic officials dashed back and forth assembling a presentation package. Bruce Cortelyou, the secretary, sat in disbelief and later confided to his diary: "It seems to me that if this matter should become known at this juncture it would cause a vast amount of unpleasant criticism while our sailors are lying at the bottom of Havana harbor . . . hunting up a set of stamps for the King of Spain."[17]

De Lôme's place at the Spanish legation was filled temporarily by Don Juan du Besu, who had been secretary. Du Besu was replaced as minister by an envoy extraordinary, Don Luis Polo de Bernabé, who had presented his credentials to the president on March 12, 1898. By then the *Maine* had been sunk. The new minister began to complain to the State Department that his mail was being opened before delivery, then sealed up again. He called upon Secretary Sherman, who was not available. Assistant Secretary William Day offered little apology but gave the envoy terms the United States would consider from Spain, which amounted to the abandonment of all of Spain's Caribbean possessions in exchange for no indemnity from the United States except where private property was involved. The minister, taken aback, rose and left, saying it was impossible.

On April 24 a proud Spain declared war on the United States. The next day the United States declared war on Spain. John Sherman resigned as secretary of state and was replaced by the former assistant, William Day. On May 1, Dewey steamed into

State, War, and Navy Building, decorated with flags celebrating victory in the Spanish-American War, 1898. *Library of Congress, Prints and Photos Division.*

Manila Bay and destroyed the Spanish fleet harbored there. In Washington, Theodore Roosevelt said, "Didn't Admiral Dewey do wonderfully well? I got him the position out there in Asia last year, and I had to beg hard to do it; and the reason I gave was that we might have to send him to Manila. And we sent him—and he went!"[18]

Recruits collected to ship out from Tampa. They camped among the palms in the gardens of the onion-domed Tampa Bay Hotel, while regular army personnel and thousands of volunteers headed to Fort Sam Houston, in San Antonio. The first transports departed Tampa in mid-June and landed on the twenty-second. Cuba was blockaded, and naval squadrons headed to sea. The war that ensued was bloody and vicious, as horrible as any war during the short time it lasted, notwithstanding the admiration squandered on it at the time. Deadly tropical diseases readily aided bullets in the slaughter. Assistant Roosevelt led his Rough Riders, powdering his legend with glory. Bantam Confederate veteran Joe Wheeler of the Senate led his charges just as well, indeed better, and in the smoke of battle cursed the Yankees, referring to the Spanish. At the close of the summer of 1898 the United States occupied Cuba, Puerto Rico, the Philippines, and the empty Wake Island.

The slim chance that Spain had in the first place was obvious. On April 7, well before the real action, the ambassadors resident in Washington called upon the president once again to plead for Spain. Little attention was paid to this visit in the United

States, but it attracted extensive comment in Britain, where the approaching conflict had been watched with riveting interest. "The scene at the White House yesterday," reported one British paper, "when the Ambassadors of the European Powers waited upon the President as advocates of peace, is one that will be graven deep upon the pages of history . . . as one of the most significant occurrences this generation has witnessed. For what is it in essence? It is the appeal of the greater Powers of Europe, groaning and sweating under the burden of official armaments, to the great Power of the New World on behalf of one of their weaker brethren. Mr. McKinley must have been aware of the dreamlike splendour of the moment. . . . stripped of its formality it resolved itself into an appeal to America for mercy to Spain."[19]

On July 22, 1898, Ambassador Jules-Martin Cambon called at the White House to say that the Spanish ambassador in Paris had asked the French minister of foreign affairs to mediate for peace with the United States. The foreign minister, Theophile Delcasse, assigned the mission to Cambon, who was given power to make a full negotiation.[20] The Spanish minister had departed Washington at the war's beginning.

Cambon was a considerable presence in the diplomatic community. His access to the other embassies and legations and his easy movement among the departments and important individuals in the American government were concealed in a gentle, earnest, even disarming personality. He pursued no public persona other than that of a working diplomat. Photographs recall a dapper man, slim, a little above medium height, with black hair and gold-rim spectacles attached to his vest by a long black ribbon. He was to be the go-between in mediating peace between the United States and Spain. No direct contact was to be made by the belligerents except through him.

Because of uncertainties following a revolt in the Philippines and the mild but threatening stir within the United States against annexing territory without the approval of the U.S. population, McKinley determined that a protocol would first be created in Washington. The resulting protocol or set of terms, when they were as the Americans wanted them, would be turned over to the formal peacemakers. When this was done, the peace conference itself would be held in Paris, the location requested by officials in France and Spain. The objective of the protocol process was to refine the terms as much as possible, so that the protocol taken to the table in Paris would represent both sides and articulate a basic, preliminary agreement that might be honed into the final treaty. For all the apparent smoothness of the sessions, the tranquil-seeming McKinley was no less than a bully, accepting no course but the acquisition of vast foreign territory for his country for the assurance of expanding American trade around the globe.

The protocol was long in coming. Cambon called at the White House whenever summoned and waited in the corridor outside the cabinet room door. Sometimes he sat there for hours on the hard chairs; other times he was ushered to a sofa in the oval library, where the president and Joe Cannon had decided how to fund the war.

Eventually Ambassador Cambon was invited into the cabinet room to answer questions and give comments on the upcoming protocol for a peace treaty. Drafts were read and reread, words weighed and replaced. Adee took the notes, wrote the drafts, and when a new draft was needed, took it across the yard to the State Department typewriters. His fluency in Spanish came to bear in weeding out English words that might be similar to Spanish words but conveyed a nuance or meaning different from what was intended. The meetings in the cabinet room were intense.

The tenseness of the president spilled over into every corner of his house. Once when Hay went to dinner there during this time and the company retired to the south portico, all were struck to silence by an alarming screech from an unseen owl. The superstitious believed owls at night to be harbingers of death. "The President started up in great excitement. 'There he is again!' & a moment afterward an owl flew over our heads and lighted above the window, where he stared down at us with great wisdom and scorn."[21]

On July 30 the president and cabinet made their last changes to the terms. Still, different participants inside brought up points with which they were not quite satisfied. Ambassador Cambon, sent for prematurely in a White House coach, was kept waiting by last-minute details. Two hours passed before the president was ready to receive him. At last Adee brought in a clean, typed copy. When Cambon was called in, the document was placed before him on the cabinet table. As his eyes drank in the text he said, "They are very hard terms."[22] What he read was about the same as Secretary of State William Day, when assistant secretary, had offered back in March to Don Luis Polo de Bernabé. The terms proposed in the protocol kept all the territory the military had acquired and ordered the Spanish out of Cuba.

When Cambon responded, he said that Spain naturally would not agree to every part of the American protocol. He suggested a very general preliminary agreement that allowed for details to be agreed upon later by diplomats at the Paris conference. With this course agreed upon, the protocol was at last signed on August 12, 1898, with some ceremony. A furious thunderstorm blew against the windowpanes. A cluster of electric lights woven into the old gas chandelier overhead provided the only light. McKinley restricted attendance to the actual participants in the work of creating the protocol. This included the cabinet, McKinley's secretaries Addison Porter and Bruce Cortelyou, and the current second secretary of state, Alvey Adee.

At 4:40 P.M., when Ambassador Cambon entered the room, the group seated at the table rose to its feet. These men were not to sit down again. McKinley signed, followed by Cambon. A few words were spoken loudly to be heard above the crashing thunder and rain. The deaf Adee, who had been so central to the work, heard nothing that was spoken but must have felt the thunder. Pens were passed around for souvenirs. No one had thought of taking a group photograph. It was decided that the participants would assemble again in a few days, and Frances Benjamin Johnston, one of the first professional women photographers in the United States, would be invited to take a photograph for history.

In the autumn, when it became clear that Secretary Day's presence was necessary at the peace conference in Paris, the president accepted his resignation and dispatched him to Paris. On Sunday evening, August 13, 1898, Ambassador John Hay and Clara were visiting friends in the English countryside when a telegram brought to him read: "It gives me great exceptional pleasure to tender to you the office of Secretary of State. . . . William McKinley." Henry Adams later recalled that in accepting the job, Hay "took office at a cost of life."[23]

FOUR
World Capital

The close of the "Spanish War" brought to many Americans a new sense of importance in the world, but nowhere more profoundly than in the capital.[1] For Colonel Theodore Bingham, the change gave purpose to his vision of a world-class, more ceremonial Washington. He kept details of his objective as secret as he could, awaiting the right moment to dazzle those who might approve it all at once.

President McKinley, reelected and flourishing, had learned to admire the work of the Army Corps of Engineers while in Congress. Bingham's noted political savvy and his warm reception by the McKinleys at the White House had given him every confidence that he would win anything he went after. He had taken a first step toward his larger vision for the capital by wooing the president with a better, more comfortable White House. At last he set the stage to present his various plans for official authorization. The principal players were invited to a luncheon at the White House, an event clothed merely as a review of upcoming activities attendant to the centennial of the city. Engineers in Bingham's office had labored behind closed doors over drawings and models for extensive urban improvements. The model makers made a miniature of a larger White House incorporating elaborate new wings that sported more columns than any building in Washington.

The lunch took place on December 10, 1900. Guests walked around the Blue Room and East Room, viewing exhibits of amazing architectural drawings and perspective studies, including the mighty *Centennial Avenue*, rendered in ink on linen. When built, the avenue's broad, lamp-bordered expanse would replace a large part of the forests on the Mall and continue to the filled land along the river. Bingham explained a plaster model of the expanded White House, which looked like a giant wedding cake. He had put his program together with the greatest care. But he did not win the day.

Already opponents had appeared among architects. Washington is a web of personal associations. Not only did the overconfidence turn the colonel's head from criticism, but it also loosened his speech to imply his criticism of others who dared question his ideas. Bingham underestimated the quiet political skill of the gifted local

architect Glenn Brown, the most outspoken of his enemies. Brown had been battling him for over a year. Besides being a practicing architect in Washington, Brown
was secretary of the American Institute of Architects, a fledgling Washington-based
"national" organization that lobbied to pass, then enforce, laws that served the architectural profession. The main concern of the AIA at the time was to open government
building projects to private architects, where heretofore they had been almost entirely
in the hands of government-employed architects and engineers. Brown's idea was to
make Washington the showplace for the architectural profession in a resurrection of
the design concepts of the Chicago World's Fair. He and his colleagues espoused a
master plan for the whole, not a piecemeal project like Bingham's. The Army Corps of
Engineers and Bingham stood in the way of something greater for Washington than
anyone might have imagined before.

Brown's political network was strong, and Bingham's luncheon occurred at the
time the AIA was holding its annual meeting in Washington, a coincidence likely
devised by Brown; at least it sounds like him. Participants included the biggest names
in American architecture, not least the makers of the Chicago World's Fair. In their
convention the architects focused on the capital's past and future. Papers were read
and inspiring speeches made. Meanwhile, at the White House, standing up after lunch
before the McKinleys and other political luminaries, Colonel Bingham described his
design for the capital and the major remodeling of the White House. The historic
house had reached the age of one hundred. Through time it linked the names of
McKinley and George Washington, or so went Bingham's pitch.

Senator James McMillan, chair of the District of Columbia Commission, sat back
in disbelief. What was this all about? He had his own plans for Washington, already
agreed upon by his bipartisan Centennial Commission. Not only one but several celebratory centennial building projects were to honor the federal government's century
in Washington. He knew that Bingham was familiar with all these proposals. No individual in the Congress was more devoted to public works than McMillan. The colonel
had met on the friendliest of terms with the District Commission and the Centennial
Commission, in both of which McMillan was very active. Bingham liked to stretch
their sessions by presenting fascinating facts he had learned from studying the historical papers housed in the Public Building office. Bingham was even in part responsible
for the Centennial Commission's adoption of the concept of a Centennial Avenue.
He had seen also that the commission approved an expansion of the White House in
theory. Now Bingham had gone his own way. His presentation at the luncheon came
as unwelcome news to Senator McMillan and the members of the two commissions.
To surprise a public official in public in his own area of authority was a lapse unwor-
thy of Colonel Bingham's reputation.

Senator McMillan returned from the luncheon to the Capitol both puzzled and,
though an even-tempered man, downright annoyed by Bingham's performance. In his

office he found Glenn Brown awaiting him, along with Daniel P. Burnham, of Chicago, father of the world's fair there; Charles F. McKim, of McKim, Mead & White, of New York; and Frank Miles Day, of Philadelphia, also a leader in the field. McKim had brought along Frederick Law Olmsted Jr., son of the distinguished landscape architect, with whom McMillan had worked for years. Rick Olmsted had that morning electrified the AIA convention with an essay he wrote calling for a return of the capital to George Washington's original idea, the plan drawn by the Frenchman Pierre Charles L'Enfant.

The architects urged McMillan to postpone all the individual projects and order a master plan for the city. A month and a half later, in February 1901, McMillan formed the Senate Parks Commission—always to be known as the McMillan Commission—and appointed Burnham and McKim to it. Burnham brought in other prominent participants in the Chicago World's Fair, including Olmsted, the sculptor Augustus Saint-Gaudens, and the painter Frank Millet. Colonel Bingham's plans were set aside.[2]

The McMillan Commission was a self-certain group of men, capable of being overbearing, yet soft-spoken when gentle persuasion was necessary. Each member played his role carefully, no one of them a stranger to collaborating on great works. Skilled in their own fields, convinced of the validity their ideas, their professional characters had been honed in practical terms by long years of experience negotiating for opportunities to show what they could do. In building, between the creative spark and the finished object, lie money, the coordination of diverse efforts, and many compromises. At the AIA convention in the previous spring, the younger architects had been inspired by Olmsted's address calling for a revival of the original plans L'Enfant made for George Washington. In the idea was the beginning of a near-perfect historical basis for the renaissance of the American capital in a grand plan. The idea included the promise of work for many architects.

The sensitive political nose of Senator McMillan's chief aide, Charles Moore, a newspaperman who came to Washington with the senator from Detroit, had caught a whiff of Bingham's program long before it was unveiled, and he feared the program's results. Through his friendship with Glenn Brown, Moore stirred opposition to Colonel Bingham. Brown could not have secured a more valuable ally than the aesthetically sophisticated and politically wise Moore, who was stimulated by the neoclassical architecture of the Chicago World's Fair to wish ardently for a return to similar historical inspiration in the design of public buildings. No question that gaining the support of Senator McMillan was fortuitous for Brown, but the involvement of Charles Moore buttoned it all down. He conducted all the follow-up, urging Senator McMillan to take the capital's future design away from the Army Corps of Engineers immediately and put it with leading American architects in private practice.

Even with so powerful a champion as McMillan, achieving such a turnover was no easy objective. The corps was powerful with both the House and the Senate. The belief that successful public works depended entirely upon the engineers had been well-established since the Civil War. Architects, on the other hand, appeared to many lawmakers as impractical men who drew ambitious pictures. Congress absolutely supported the corps's unseating of the architects on the Library of Congress, praising the engineers for being realists who finished what they started. Congress was proud of its library.

Yet McMillan was universally respected in such matters. His interest in parks and civic improvements was well known by his colleagues. In his adopted hometown of Detroit, the native of Canada had fathered one public building project after another, with a particular triumph in the landscape of the celebrated Belle Isle Park. It was a site oddly situated geographically so as to be north of Canada's southernmost border, yet attached to the city of Detroit. The elder Frederick Law Olmsted turned the open land into a place of beauty and popular public resort. The presence of Olmsted's son among the architects can only have pleased the senator. McMillan praised the Chicago World's Fair for showing how clean and inspirational a city could be. While as chair of the Centennial Commission he had been the one who led his commissioners toward big projects, he now willingly stepped aside in favor of what seemed the better idea of having the architects create a master plan.

Philosophically Colonel Bingham had more or less the same ambitions as the architects, only he lived professionally in the relative confines of a particular government milieu. He was a commendable researcher but no artist.[3] His was not the battleground of creativity achieved through business competition. Charles Moore would one day write the biographies of both Burnham and McKim, men of about the same age, who stood tall in American formal architecture of the late nineteenth and early twentieth centuries. Burnham learned architecture in Chicago architectural offices, rising to partnership with John W. Root, a Georgia man who had practiced in Chicago but was by now deceased. Developing more through business than art, they built ever taller buildings, pioneering in the use of steel construction. The firm Burnham & Root played a major part in the genesis of the skyscraper. Burnham began as an architect of commercial buildings. His interest in neoclassicism and planning came later and culminated in his master plan and supervision of the 1893 World's Fair. McKim, reared in Philadelphia, was born among intellectuals, his father a lawyer, both parents active abolitionists. He was self-taught about architecture for the most part, thanks to an early passion for the subject. Following a smattering of college at Harvard, he took the big step of studying at the École des Beaux Arts in Paris. After extensive travel, he returned to pursue a career in New York, first as an employee of H. H. Richardson's architectural firm. He later formed McKim, Mead & White with two associates and close friends at Richardson's office: Stanford White, a designer like himself, and William Rutherford Mead, an architect with strong business skills. By 1890 their firm was one of the leading architectural practices on the East Coast, and in 1892 and 1893 they worked with Burnham in building the Chicago World's Fair.

Olmsted, heir to his late father's Brookline, Massachusetts, landscape architecture practice, had known the other commission members all his life and had gained their professional respect. The fourth member was the sculptor Augustus Saint-Gaudens. In Washington, Saint-Gaudens was best known as the creator of the mysterious mourning figure that Henry Adams placed over his wife's grave in Rock Creek Cemetery in 1891.

Burnham, the most openly vocal of all, admonished his colleagues to think big. He had started the planning of the fair with this challenge, and he extended his enthusiastic approach to Washington. By the spring of 1901 Burnham had decided that for the enrichment and credibility of the commission's report, its members must have their thoughts fueled by a tour of the capitals of Europe. He believed Washington should have as great a capital as any in the world, an objective with which McMillan agreed. In June 1901 the architects set sail and spent seven weeks talking among themselves and looking at the monuments and civic improvements of the capitals of Europe. While it was not unusual at all for the government to send agents and official parties out to study different things in foreign places, McMillan made a special effort to bury the cost of this trip. He put the party in first-class travel accommodations; on the books it was called an open-ended expense of the commission.

Little of what the party saw can have been new territory to them, but they discussed it in terms of the capital. Their diaries make clear that their study—of Paris, Vienna, Venice, Rome, and London—though leisurely was nonetheless diligent. McMillan's aide, Charles Moore, who accompanied them, would remember the trip years later as one of the most stimulating times of his life.

⁓

President McKinley was assassinated on September 5, 1901. It was six months after his inauguration to a second term. The fatal shots were fired while he received the public at the Pan- American Exposition in Buffalo, New York. The suddenness of the death's effects, as with all assassinations, created confusion, which turned to fear, followed by a frantic reach for reassurance that everything would remain the same under a new leader. It was discomforting to some who walked the halls of power to consider that the man now in the White House was the bombastic, sometimes unruly, and very young Theodore Roosevelt.

The Senate Parks Commission Report—a document containing both text and a master plan—was presented in January 1902, four months after McKinley's death. The report as shaped by Burnham was not at all the concept that had been authorized but a comprehensive city plan. It projected urban improvements and modern facilities for running the city, such as those espoused in the 1893 fair. On the surface, however, and what people remembered of the plan, was what they saw most clearly: the magnificent architecture. This would transform the old American capital into a proper seat of government for a new world power.

Members of Congress uncomfortably took note of Burnham's presumption to enlarge the original scope of the centennial plan. Some spoke of stopping the project in its tracks. The architects, anticipating a struggle to achieve their vision, set about to court favor wherever they could find it. Unable to depend upon Congress, they sought to attract the support of the new president, Theodore Roosevelt.

They knew that one model was worth a hundred drawings. The Senate Parks Commission plan was therefore presented to the president and Congress in model form. With care the architects selected for their stage the only Washington building they could all agree was appropriate to their idea, the new Corcoran Gallery of Art, an Italian palazzo in pinkish marble, completed about five years earlier.

The best architectural model makers that Burnham and McKim could engage worked in the Corcoran for weeks, filling the marble galleries and the Corcoran's Statuary Hall with an exhibition that brought three-dimensional life to the plan, a display of beauty sure to bring delight. One could stand beside it, bend the knees, and get a bead on one of the avenues lined with trim model trees, running from monuments to imposing buildings. Mirrors made pools and lagoons. Expanses of lawn opened up the plan and gave the great white buildings room. Large drawings were mounted on the walls, but it was the model that most captivated those who saw the exhibit, for in it they could understand the new city grown large and beautiful among the familiar places in the Washington they already knew.[4]

Colonel Bingham disliked the Senate plan and never stopped calling his own plan the official one. To his mind the architects destroyed everything that was Washington and replaced it with something too imitatively European. But in truth, Bingham's plan was dead to everyone but him. The architects soon learned, however, that Bingham's politics had been absolutely correct on one point: the way the president's support for the plan stemmed from his wish to preserve the White House, which he dearly loved for its historical associations. "His very first remark," wrote McKim after he had explained the plan to Roosevelt, "was that he was glad that the Commission agreed with him, as he did with it, that the White House should not be disturbed. He regards it as a historic monument and a landmark, and will not listen to any proposition looking to its alteration."[5]

The plan was presented to Congress in the morning of January 15, 1902. That afternoon Congress and President Roosevelt visited the exhibition. While the lawmakers were surprised by the extent of the plan, the visitors who saw it were delighted. It was clear enough without saying that what Burnham, McKim, and the other architects had proposed was, in spirit at least, partly a revival of the shimmering glory of the Chicago World's Fair and Washington's adaptation to it. Colonel Bingham insisted that it was nothing more than an impractical rehash of L'Enfant's plan for Washington. The architects, who knew less about L'Enfant's plan than the scholarly Bingham, were pleased to agree with the L'Enfant part of his observations, for the analogy proved useful in selling their product.

Olmsted's had been a good idea: a resurrection of the old plan, at least in theory. The salesman in Burnham, reaching for analogies and symbols, saw power in the forgotten Frenchman's roots in late eighteenth-century France as a connection between his world's-fair-inspired Washington on the one hand and the neoclassicism of Versailles and the cities and palaces of Europe on the other. Tying the plan to this actual history brought local significance to the Mall, circles, avenues, and other devices L'Enfant had called for in his plan of 1791. Associating the new plan with L'Enfant worked very well. This world capital was to be as modern as the fair, incorporating the best up-to-date technical principles in housing for the government, sewage, lighting, and transportation, but the ceremonial heart of this modern city, like the main part of the fair, was to wear a cloak of neoclassicism, its public buildings boasting colonnades and pediments, domes and entablatures, all rendered in white marble, light granite, or sand-colored limestone, gleaming pale and white through orderly avenues of trees. Inspiration in the architecture was the modern classicism of Europe that followed Renaissance ideals. In other words, the buildings would mirror not ancient Greece and Rome but ancient classicism as adapted in later times.

Legal regulations, some already in place, were to guarantee continuity, such as in the heights of cornices, which would keep the levels low and provide the horizontality one saw in the streetscapes of Paris. A certain conformity of secondary buildings would frame and enhance the major monuments and buildings that terminated the vistas formed by the avenues that passed arrowlike through the urban grid, as L'Enfant had intended. The Mall was to be stripped of its groves of trees, the ground graded more or less level and planted with grass, bordered and crossed judiciously at right angles by graveled drives and paths. Opposite the Capitol, westward two and a half miles at the banks of the Potomac, was to be a memorial to Lincoln, a building of yet undetermined style but large and impressive. Across the Mall and perpendicular to it, the axis from the White House southward was to be terminated at the Tidal Basin, by a memorial to the American Revolution, about where the Jefferson Memorial stands today.

The most detail was given to the greatest change, which involved the ceremonial core, a giant, elongated diamond- or kite- or coffin-shaped area cut in half east to west by the Mall and north to south by the axis from the White House. Lesser streets of the composition created secondary cross-axes, such as that from Eighth Street, which formed an axis between the old Greek Revival Patent Office on the north and the site where today the National Archives has been built on the south. Existing features were corrected to serve a better symmetry. For example, the Washington Monument, which was not centered on the Mall, was brought in line by shifting the boundary of the Mall twenty-five feet to the south.

A massive program of demolition was anticipated. All the red-brick and dark-colored buildings on the Mall were to go, including the relatively new Department of Agriculture Building and the Smithsonian Castle. Removing the encroaching

Baltimore & Potomac depot was a leviathan challenge. These were to be replaced either with open land or with white neoclassical buildings. The same was to take place on Lafayette Park, where the surrounding mansions of the square, including the double house of Hay and Adams, were to be demolished and replaced with official buildings in the prescribed style, facing the White House.[6] Senator McMillan's health worsened, and he died in August 1902 at his summer cottage near Manchester-by-the-Sea, Massachusetts. It was Charles Moore who changed the name of the Senate's Washington plan to the McMillan Plan in the senator's name and memory. The name brought honor to the plan and, at least for those years, a measure of protection to it.

~

Theodore Roosevelt remained seated quietly, for the moment, in the presidency of the United States. He was restrained out of respect for McKinley but also because he was looking around. Then he emerged as no president before him. His political career had been varied, from police commissioner in New York City, to governor of that state, to Republican political appointee as assistant secretary of the navy, and after a relatively short time as vice president, he became president at the age of forty-two. In the second month of his presidency he turned forty-three. Theodore Roosevelt was the first president too young to have served in the Civil War. McKinley's pitiful, deluded assassin, long gone by midautumn as the fiftieth casualty of Auburn Penitentiary's electric chair, had opened the office of president to a man who at that time could probably never have been elected on a general ballot. The new president would prove to be a new sort of a man for a new century. He was different from his predecessors. But so was the world different from what had gone before. For the nation it would take awhile for the idea of a changed America to sink in, but Americans took quickly to President Roosevelt.

Most people thought of Roosevelt less as a politician than as a flashy hero of the Spanish War. However, there was much more to know about the man. Ornithologists were likely to know his book on birds; historians knew his book *The Naval War of 1812*. His subsequent book, *The Winning of the West*, followed a theme of racial superiority that would repel today's sensibilities but received wide acclaim in its time. As a verile Rough Rider and activist, he projected a new American ideal that captivated the nation and eventually much of the Western world.

Washington became *his* Washington, and along with it came the McMillan Plan. At first Roosevelt moved unobtrusively through the fall of 1901, almost constantly in company with Bruce Cortelyou, upon whose knowledge of the presidency he wisely relied. Adee, too, who had known Roosevelt for years, entered this early orbit, giving advice and writing speeches. Colonel Bingham was an old friend. As a place, the White House offered an elegance of its own but had only limited modern comforts. This situation was not immediately recognized by the president and his wife, Edith, for they loved old houses, old furniture, and old gardens. The high-back Victorian beds,

Theodore Roosevelt in his office in the new west wing of the White House. *Library of Congress, Prints and Photos Division.*

tall four-posters, and marble-top tables were their delight. Their children rode bikes on floral carpets and incorporated velvet portieres in their games of hide and seek. The Roosevelts, however, at last realized they must make some changes that would ease daily living at the White House without lessening its historical charm.

McKim, mindful that the White House was the key to winning Roosevelt's support of bigger plans for the capital, accepted at once Mrs. Roosevelt's request to drop by for advice about making the house more comfortable. She spread before him some domestic issues that concerned her and became a mouse in McKim's trap. Skilled in obtaining business with a certain class of people, McKim spoke convincingly. The needs of the White House increased to such an extent that in the spring Congress set aside half a million dollars for its improvement. It was to be "restored," a word gentler and even more elastic than *reconstructed* or *replaced*. With Glenn Brown, McKim studied the house from attic to cellar. They sat in the moonlight on the lawn and imagined the Georgian facades without the Victorian additions. At their drafting tables in New York the supporting architects of McKim, Mead & White transferred sketches to working drawings.

In June, Mrs. Roosevelt and the children went to Oyster Bay to remain until fall, when the restoration would be complete. The president remained in the house,

Edith Roosevelt in her White House garden, 1903. *Library of Congress, Prints and Photos Division.*

declaring that he could put up with anything for a mere three months. Plaster dust soon sent him packing to Senator Scott's row house on the west side of Lafayette Square. McKim then cut into the house seriously. Away from the Roosevelts' watchful eyes, not a historical brick or an inch of plaster was allowed to block the progress of his alterations, and at the climax of the demolition, one could stand in the basement beneath the Blue Room and look up through the timbers framing two stories all the way to the attic ceiling.

When Roosevelt returned in the fall a miraculous renovation had taken place. The White House was at once the same and different. Victorian additions, notably a great, rambling conservatory with attached greenhouses, were gone. The old west wing service area beneath the greenhouses had been restored to how it had looked in Jefferson's time. At its western end a new office building had been added, the "Temporary Executive Office," which would one day be called the West Wing. This moved the presidential offices for the first time out of the White House proper. On the east side, where Jefferson's matching wing had been demolished long before, a new east wing rose on the old foundations, to be used as a new entrance to the house. One passed through this wing into the arched "ground floor" as the basement was restyled, then up a flight of stairs to the formal rooms on the state floor. This was a real innovation: guests no longer had to wander upstairs in search of a toilet.

Once inside, the plan of the rooms seemed about the same, but the décor had become European. The former warmth of a wooden interior now yielded to cold marble and stone. Corners and edges were sharply defined, as they would appear in an architectural drawing. Bare parquet floors of bleached oak replaced the wall-to-wall carpeting. Glass chandeliers and bronze wall lamps from the finest suppliers in New York replaced what had been there before. Wallpaper was gone; stretched silk took its place. The East Room, no longer like a hotel ballroom, was paneled in white-enameled Louis XIV–style boiserie, copied from the Château de Compiègne, north of Paris.

Dark, waxed oak paneling in the enlarged State Dining Room gave the impression of a Georgian country house in England. Stuffed animal heads mounted high on the walls symbolized Roosevelt the outdoorsman.

Electric power served the house to its farthest corners, from the bedside lamps, to the toasters in the kitchen, to the three great chandeliers in the East Room. It turned fans that conveyed warm air from the coal furnace through ducts to the rooms. Technological convenience was everywhere. The house functioned better for all the gadgets. By removing the president's office and cabinet to a new wing on the west, the upstairs was freed for more family living space. What had happened was a transfiguration. From a long past of being fashioned as merely a bigger version of Everyman's house, the White House was glossed by McKim to serve in every sense the needs of the chief of state of a new world power. And it was about as grand a house of state as the American public, who provided this roof over the presidential head, would readily allow. McKim and Brown's ninety-day wonder actually took longer but was ready for the first state dinner in December, still smelling of paint and wax and suffering from an unreliable elevator. The Roosevelts set up their Christmas tree in Edith Roosevelt's sitting room, next to the room with Lincoln's high-back, carved bed, in which she and the president, whom she called "Ted," slept. Five stockings hung from the mantel. There was a new exuberance in the White House.

The transformation at the White House reflected more about change in Washington than a mere restoration of architecture. Roosevelt's role in dramatizing the world power and the "new" presidency bequeathed to him by McKinley was never better expressed visibly than in the transformed White House. Social forms and domestic management were soon modernized to present a White House more vivid in its elegant representation of the presidency than anything known in Washington before. Some of the social forms were borrowed from diplomatic usage. Others continued or adapted White House traditions. No notes seem to have been kept from the sessions that established these changes. Edith Roosevelt, Bruce Cortelyou, Alvey Adee, and Colonel Theodore Bingham seem to have met as an ad hoc advisory.

Because President Roosevelt had great and justifiable faith in his wife's judgment in such matters, he likely left the final decisions to her. The object of the new social program was not to change arbitrarily the way the White House had always worked but to make it function more efficiently. Many of the patterns of operation had been developed successfully over the years and were, if unique, useful to the particular demands of the place. What the reformers wished to do was to simplify where possible, not only for greater convenience, but in ways that would allow for the accommodation of ever larger numbers of guests. They also wished to feature the president as he had never been before. Nothing was more naturally compatible to Roosevelt than the spotlight. Those supporting his performance knew better than to make mistakes. Set rules were thus essential.

Judging the relative contributions of the four who set things in order and institutionalized White House living is not easy. Each was a strong, opinionated individual. Surely the most deference was shown to the first lady, yet neither Bingham nor Cortelyou was a bench-warmer. Bingham liked to talk. Adee sat by silently with his pen and note slips. Cortelyou's way was to wait quietly and listen, then often provide the definitive solution as a summing up of what others had said. The four approaches are certain: Cortelyou and Bingham were concerned with logistics; Adee, with standards of ceremonial conduct and interaction with diplomats; Mrs. Roosevelt, with proper social and especially moral conduct in the house of state.

Written instructions had been issued heretofore only on presidential train trips. Eighty or so years before, President James Monroe had created a social rule book for the White House, but it garnered more amusement behind his back than an ordering of behavior. Social activities surrounding the presidency were fairly predictable, footed in forms that had worked over time. Institutional memory was with the individuals, nearly all men, who had worked there through at least several administrations; a few, such as Tom Pendel, a doorman, and Colonel William H. Crook, an accounting official in the office, went back as far as Lincoln. Questions more complicated than the staff could answer were reviewed by the State Department, which meant for the past twenty years they had been taken to Adee.

To end reliance upon memory, "Blue Books" were now printed with the rules stated simply. No justifications were given for any rule, only the mandate that it be obeyed to the letter. Outside the White House the rules would have appeared finicky, even a little silly, but the Blue Books were not to be shown elsewhere. The little books were specifically for those who worked at the White House, and every person who had one was accountable for it and had to produce it on demand. Most rules had deep roots in a century of trial and error. What was new was seeing them in print. Each category of work had its own particular book.[7]

For example, there was the book titled "Social Aides." Well before McKinley's death, Colonel Bingham had introduced the use of social aides to mingle with guests and generally keep public events moving. The aides were young officers stationed in Washington, enlisted by invitation to serve at the White House in addition to their military duties. Most of them were in their twenties. Good looks and a distinguished family name were recommendations for the job, but more important were tact and social sophistication. The Blue Book for the aides defined their responsibilities carefully: they should wear their dress uniforms, dance well, and engage in charming but never controversial small talk; they were to be courteously aggressive in breaking up noisy arguments, gentle but firm in removing drunks, and perform many other thorny jobs while always appearing cool and friendly. Bingham had observed this arrangement in royal courts during his years as a military attaché to American legations in Europe and found it a very useful application to the White House.

The president's office staff had Blue Books, telling them what to wear and that they must leave their desktops vacant at the end of each day. Members of the press had a Blue Book to keep them in line. Ushers who managed the domestic establishment had a Blue Book, as did every chambermaid. A Blue Book was sent to guests who were invited to ride horseback with the president. It explained that when they rode abreast of him it was to be one at a time; they were to keep their stirrup even with his, and when he nodded they were to fall back and allow another guest to move to the president's side.

For all the rules and Blue Books, the White House is ultimately the personal domain of the person in office. Tradition must bend to the current administration's wishes. Edith Roosevelt considered that as first lady she was automatically the head of society in the capital. It was a presumed status never so boldly articulated before her. No glimpse, no matter how fleeting, of official Washington society at the time is complete without an awareness of Mrs. Roosevelt's looming, often unsmiling, judgments. In contrast to the shy, little-town Ida McKinley, to whom such presumption would never have occurred, or even to her predecessors, such as the intense Carrie Harrison, who would have found it objectionably snobbish, or the gay, youthful Frances Cleveland, who would not have troubled herself, Edith Roosevelt was a first lady who took her role very seriously. Perhaps the changes since the Spanish-American War called for a tighter leash on the federal city. She seems to have thought so. But she was also a practical woman who realized that to avoid the chaos that could easily result from so many changes, her hand must be kept tightly on the wheel.

As soon as the Roosevelts were back in the remodeled White House, Mrs. Roosevelt summoned weekly late-morning meetings with the cabinet wives, when she was in town. Traditionally the cabinet wives had met at the White House to fill out invitation cards for the president's wife. However, under Edith Roosevelt, the White House meetings resembled a Star Chamber. The ladies were seated facing each other in a double row of chairs, with Mrs. Roosevelt seated at the head; there was no table. A name might be brought up, some individual or group that was in conflict with what was acceptable at the White House, and a solution discussed. What the cabinet wives thought of this stint at being ladies-in-waiting is not known. Good-hearted Clara Hay sat through it all. It is not likely she would have been comfortable with some of it.

Nor was Edith Roosevelt opposed to judging moral issues in the official community, even venturing into areas not really her business. She and Roosevelt were prudish. A couple having an affair or even suspected of having an affair was warned in person by a military aide sent by Mrs. Roosevelt that if they did not cease their indiscretions, they would be dropped from the White House list. For a diplomat, being culled from the social list of the head of state was a professional death sentence. Most of Mrs. Roosevelt's problems in the moral area came from foreigners at the embassies and legations. Diplomats accustomed to the loose codes of worldly courts elsewhere, particularly the younger ones, could draw a sharp contrast to American ideas of propriety. Treatment of diplomats stationed in America had indeed changed over the years since the 1820s, when a Mediterranean emissary requested a concubine and was duly provided one at the expense of the American government.

Mrs. Roosevelt's ideas verged on a snobbishness that the president did not always share. On one occasion the president sent her a message asking that she join him with visitors in one of the parlors. When she went there, he was with two women of whom she disapproved, one being Mrs. Edward Harriman, wife of the Union Pacific Railroad magnate. She entered the room, remained standing, offered neither tea nor other refreshment, said very little, and turned and left. When the embarrassed president later asked how she could be so curt with her guests, she told him that she had no time to give to "painted women." Roosevelt found the response hilarious and confided it to John Hay, who repeated it in a letter to Clara in a tone that suggested he and his wife had discussed the first lady's attitudes before.[8]

Guest lists were thus seriously scrutinized, and individuals evaluated and categorized as to whether they merited being included in the restricted numbers the White House could accommodate, even at large receptions. Adee always reviewed the guest lists and seating charts. He knew better than anyone whom it was wise to seat next to whom and how the menu might have to be adjusted to suit the tastes or allergies of some important guest. "Mrs. Roosevelt entertains not occasionally but constantly," reported Collier's Weekly.[9] New ideas for events made it possible to invite ever greater numbers of guests without disturbing the formal context traditional at the White House. The musicale was one of the cleverest devices, not a new idea, but never institutionalized at the White House before the Roosevelts completed the renovation. After coffee in the Red Room, dinner guests walked to the East Room, where they took front-row seats, joining 150 to 350 other invited guests. Cortelyou, himself a pianist and vocalist utterly dedicated to music, used his connections with the Steinway Company in New York to book accomplished musicians, who agreed to perform gratis.[10]

Singers, harpists, and pianists usually appeared only as professional performers, rarely, if ever, considered as dinner guests. After a short music program, light refreshment was served from a table in the hall outside the Blue Room, and then the guests went home. Those who lingered too long saw rows of social aides walking toward them and so, like sheep before collies, headed for the door. A state dinner now provided an evening for three hundred guests, including dinner and musicale guests, each of whom received an engraved invitation, and the idea made political hay in a big way. The Roosevelt method had been established, and it was followed to the letter for the duration of the administration.

As the public got used to new customs at the White House, shifts of personalities from one position to another came quickly. Of those who had helped remold the White House, only Adee and Mrs. Roosevelt would remain attached to the social

concerns of the administration. Roosevelt would appoint Cortelyou secretary of commerce when the department was founded in 1903 and thus bring his former assistant
into the cabinet. Colonel Bingham soon became a burden the president wearied of
bearing. But they were old friends. When Roosevelt's former job as police commissioner of New York City came vacant, Bingham, dispatched with the president's blessings, moved to New York. He took on the commissioner position with customary
vengeance and became legendary as the purifier of the wicked "tenderloin district,"
the present-day Times Square. Commissioner Bingham became the scourge of every
gambler, thug, and whore in town. He was a familiar feature in the crime sheets. Alas,
his personal opinions, expressed freely in so public a job, would eventually send him
into a new city job in Manhattan, then retirement. Manhattan politicos were less tol-
erant of a martinet than those in Washington.

Where the city's improvements were concerned, progress was slow. Presidential
support was not aggressive, although Roosevelt favored the architects' plan and was
willing to make a pitch for it when he could. In the revamped White House he had
the stage he wanted. Improvement of Washington seemed a good idea and certainly
visionary—and expensive. But with McMillan dead, the planners had no powerful
champion on the Hill. The politicians were suspicious of anything by architects that
was so ambitious and came from outside the government, outside Washington. The
negative feelings of many members of Congress toward the architectural profession
were intensified by the brazen way in which Burnham and his fellows reached far
beyond what the Senate Parks Commission had been established to accomplish.

Moreover, if Senator McMillan's concealment of the cost overrun had been
exposed, it could have meant the death of the City Beautiful movement in the capital.
Beyond the grace of the model, the program had a tone of downright un-American,
Old World, princely extravagance to some—Uncle Joe Cannon, for one. European
monarchs had sponsored costly civic improvements in their capitals throughout the
nineteenth century. Other than for adorning its own halls, Congress has never been
generous with public art. Though adherents might point out that the McMillan Plan
was more than decorative, having attributes for residential areas, including sanitation,
street lighting, and parks, Congress was still seldom a patron of city planning. Even
the original capital had been designed and laid out under the strong hand of President
Washington, not Congress. Most grand plans of any kind looked like pork barrel to
the beleaguered lawmakers. It was clear that the McMillan Plan would have to seek
its patrons outside Congress. Yet, external meddling with federal work in the early
twentieth century invited political trouble, because the Congress, a jealous master,
considered the construction of public government buildings its own domain.

As it happened, luck intervened in this paradox. The architects' first project came
not directly from Congress, or according to any specifics in the McMillan Plan, but as
a result of a design competition that the Department of Agriculture had held in 1901

for a structure to be built directly on the Mall in a grove of old trees. The existing Agriculture Building, with its gardens, sat along the edge of the Mall, as we have seen. The project for the new building was beyond the design stage when the McMillan Plan was made public, and it had not followed the McMillan Plan's specifications. Through the ensuing chain of events, the architects came to understand that timing was often the source of the difficulty in their work in Washington.

After some hesitation the architects decided to try to intervene. They turned to the president, who was reluctant to take sides about the new Department of Agriculture Building. Finally, because his heart was with the architects, he expressed his support for a reconsideration of the new building's location and how it might be designed. With some persuasion, Congress, eager to settle the matter and be done with it, agreed to lean toward the idea of accommodating the McMillan Plan in the placement and design of the new Agriculture Building.

It should have been a smooth win for the architects. But it brought controversy and a protracted land suit by them, which to Congress made the architects look greedy. Construction on the building was delayed for three years. No one was happy about it. McKim jockeyed himself into position for forming a committee with Burnham to select the architect of the new agricultural building. Their choice was disputed, further disparaging the project in congressional opinion. Fees seemed too high. New inquiries to architects were made, until finally the Philadelphia firm Rankin, Kellogg & Crane got the job and construction began.

The new Agriculture Building was a long structure built of highly veined white marble with L-shaped wings that flanked a central colonnaded block. First the government built the wings, without the middle part. In their design the architects had translated very loosely the pair of late seventeenth-century neoclassical government buildings by J. H. Mansart facing the Place de la Concorde, in Paris. When it was completed five years later in 1905, the new Department of Agriculture Building, which stands on Independence Avenue between Twelfth and Fourteenth Streets NW, was not the great architecture the McMillan Plan had anticipated for Washington. Its stubby colonnades and boxy form did little to recommend it as a child of the 1893 World's Fair, nor did the vicissitudes involved lessen the congressional view that architects were a lot of trouble. But its significance was that it overlooked the Mall rather than standing upon it, and it established for public architecture in Washington the neoclassical motif that would later come into full flower.

The second project that threatened invasion of the McMillan Plan was the United States National Museum. The idea of building an annex to the Smithsonian Institution had been current for a long time. A rather obvious approach was suggested, to build a red-brick building on the north side of the Mall to balance compatibly a new Smithsonian building that had been erected next to the 1840s Castle, which had been the first building on the Mall. This is what the Smithsonian board wanted, but they did not consult the McMillan Plan, which called for the demolition of the fifty-year-old Castle along with the relatively new annex structure that stood next door to it. However, no competition was launched, and McKim and Burnham pressed the board to agree to another idea.

Washington architects Joseph C. Hornblower and James Rush Marshall, who had produced the red-brick proposal the board already had in hand, made a new design in 1901 for a white building that would have been perfectly at home at the Chicago World's Fair. Despite this, the board found it too French, its neoclassicism too foreign and high-flown, and had McKim not intervened, penciling some key modifications to Hornblower and Marshall's new plans, their previous red-brick design would prob-ably have been dusted off and used. Victory in this case resulted from the addition of a dome based upon the Pantheon in Rome; one can almost feel Burnham and McKim's relish in revealing to the board members this noble source. The board liked the dome the most of all, and construction began in 1904, bringing to the Mall another rather accidental, though more successful, ghost of Chicago's great fair.

The McMillan Plan came to be a goal mutually agreed upon by a few people, who retained power enough to gain approval for parts of it or for unplanned elements that were in the spirit of it, such as the Department of Agriculture Building and the Smithsonian Institution Building. It was a frail arrangement, for some members of Congress hated everything about the plan. As Washington grew and obviously had to change, the McMillan Plan was conveniently at hand, with no rivals in view, the clos-est charted path and not difficult to defend as the desirable way to go. The snow-white neoclassicism was fresh and unquestionably beautiful, and to that all could agree. So the architects spread the plan out on the table whenever improvements were consid-ered by the federal government, if only for justification. They were not always wel-comed in the offices of the government officials, but largely thanks to Charles Moore, they had enough connections to get them in.

~

The most dramatic building to appear was Union Station. Plans for it were pre-sented after the completion of the White House in the fall of 1902, although maneu-vering for the new station had begun earlier, while McMillan himself was still alive. This building's story reveals another instance of the unexpected. Daniel P. Burnham's trademark was railroad stations, which he had built for many municipalities. He called them his "city gates," reflecting a time when most people came to a city by rail. Burnham was a man who usually had his way. He was a handsome, heavy-set man, less scruffy than most fat men; he dressed expensively, allowing himself the vanity of a walrus mustache and parting his thick reddish hair high in the middle of his head. His was a jolly, disarming manner that covered powerful determination with seeming unhurried patience. Burnham was one of the most brilliant architects of his genera-tion, a man with an artist's eye but, unlike McKim, with a business head as well. Since the 1893 World's Fair he had yielded his pursuit of largely commercial projects to one of civic design. His interest in urban planning stemmed from important public building projects such as the railroad stations.[11]

While the McMillan Plan was being made, the Pennsylvania Railroad Company had decided to tear down the thirty-year-old Baltimore & Potomac depot, the massive red-towered structure that, to the architects' eyes, was an old-fashioned obstruction to the east end of the Mall, in its prominent situation near the Capitol. The Pennsylvania Railroad, owners of the Baltimore & Potomac, or B&P, planned a new, much larger station nearby and of the same castlelike design. Burnham took the opportunity to intervene and redirect this plan toward clearing the Mall of a number of elements that blocked the path of the McMillan Plan, including a whole network of tracks, bridges, open sewers, and yards, in addition to this station and another very large one. These obstructions to the the Mall were even more objectionable to him than the ruddy old Smithsonian Castle. The plan was to remove them all eventually along with the depot, but when Burnham saw the Pennsylvania Railroad's decision, which shortcut his goal, he first made an inquiry, then launched an attack.

Early on, Burhham had gone to Senator McMillan with the idea, and the senator had warned him that to relocate the railroad would be impossible. But Burnham began to push the idea, using his personal prestige as a designer of railroad stations and a master of the immortal Chicago fair to open doors to key people. At last he seated himself with the Pennsylvania's president, Alexander Cassatt, the greatest business figure of his time in American railroading and thus a member of America's commercial peerage. Having doubled the company's revenues since taking over a few years earlier, Cassatt naturally felt very comfortable and good in his position, with the approbation of his board, and was not inclined to welcome disagreement. Perhaps he was more receptive to the famous Burnham than he might have been otherwise, for it was Burnham's Chicago fair that had spirited Cassatt's sister Mary to fame through the mural she had painted in the Woman's Building.

Discussions between the two men, who met in offices, hotel lobbies, and a private train car, warmed them to a pleasant friendship. A deal was struck. In exchange for removing certain crossings on city streets, the railroad would receive government land north of the Capitol for the new station. When he was told of a merger planned between the Pennsylvania Railroad and the B&P line, Burnham returned to the agreement: What if the proposed station were to house not only the two railroads but all the railroads that served Washington? Cassatt was amenable, provided that the railroads would all contribute to the building of the station itself. Burnham was to persuade Congress to cover the costs of necessary tunneling beneath the Capitol grounds to make the new station function.

He took this challenge to Senator McMillan. Encouraged by the practicality of the idea, McMillan in the summer of 1902 began the process of gaining congressional funding. By the time of his death in August, the railroad effort had already gained enough power to carry on without him. After about a year the idea was confirmed, and the design and building of Union Station began. Burnham had been sketching, developing his idea for many months, even when it was still uncertain whether there would or would not be such a station.

The plan for the station, which would involve a combination of railroads and tunnels, was approved by the Senate Appropriations Committee. That was but one step; the road through Congress promised to be rocky, assuming that Speaker Cannon would let it pass through at all. Ardent proponents of the station in Congress hesitated. Burnham took up the problem of the station on his own, for in his opinion it would ensure a future for the McMillan Plan, even though at the time it was clear that Congress was not yet ready to adopt a master plan. Creating consensuses was an important aspect of Burnham's skill as a negotiator. Burnham gathered politicians and people of influence at his Cosmos Club dinner table in the evenings, regaling them for hours, and it was not long before Union Station seemed a good idea to most people.

Burnham was able to take the design of the new station under his control. His numerous railroad clients yielded fairly well to the main client, Cassatt, with whom Burnham worked very compatibly. Congress built the complex of tunnels that took railroad tracks off the streets of Washington. Union Station would be the main place of entry into the capital for most people traveling cross-country by train. Burnham's station design, with its large central section, arcades, and grand forecourt, was both a screen to cover the train yard and a gate of welcome.

There was of course no functional precedent in classical architecture for a train station. To create his "city gates" as simple statements in architecture, yet ample enough inside to house lobbies, offices, train sheds, and other functions, he took classical architectural design themes from arches of triumph and other Roman structures with facades broad and open enough to swallow mundane function, yet carry an expensive, inspiring sense of entrance and exit.

The long horizontal elevation drawings for Union Station were hung up in the construction office for all to see. Drawn in Burnham's office in Chicago, they projected a structure of great beauty, the central part adapted from the Arch of Constantine, the last of the great processional arches built in ancient Rome. This academic virtuosity was integral to the philosophy of the Beaux-Arts school. The creator (the architect) was to be so steeped in factual knowledge of the buildings of the past that he could design freely, and the perfection of history (the lessons of time) would come through in new work. Burnham was not building "historical" buildings at all; he was building "modern" buildings that spoke to his own age, the latest technology clothed in designs evoking the past. McKim had used an actual historical building when he modernized the White House in quite the same sense, only with less freedom, because the past he was using was actually there and not imported from academic studies.

His approach, however, was no less modern than Burnham's, only not built upon an abstraction of history.

At Union Station all the shortcuts of modern innovation were present. For the arcades and domed ceilings, there was no longer any need for complex, heavy stone arching such as the Romans had built. Now the stupendous vaulting that adorned the station was load-bearing, like that of Rome, but, by the genius of Rafael Guastavino, of Massachusetts, consisted of layers of light tiles held together with plaster of Paris, glue, and mortar. The vaulting looked classical; who could tell the difference? Column screens had steel cores. Marble veneer was applied to a superstructure of concrete blocks. Steam heat, ventilation fans, miles of electrical wires—all would be brought to completion in five years. The station was ever more beautiful as it took form. Like some angel of purity, it was barely touched by the political battling that took place regarding it, just up the street at the Capitol.

FIVE
Diplomats

The hastened pace of activity in the Washington diplomatic corps reflected the vibrations of world power, as well as a new press of responsibilities. Diplomats now moved faster in their efforts for their countries, rented larger houses, traveled more to make speeches. Paperwork increased. But at the ever-crucial workaday point of contact between American officials, notably over Adee's desk each week, it was business as usual. Change among the diplomats in Washington was more an adjustment—like tailoring a suit of clothes—than a turnover.

One refinement of the diplomatic routine appeared in the White House. On the ground floor, McKim created the Diplomatic Reception Room for Roosevelt by converting a dingy, low-ceilinged room immediately beneath the Blue Room into a private entrance hall for diplomats, who passed through it to events at the White House. The long, oval room that was now the reception room had begun life in 1800 as a servants' hall, but for as long as anyone could remember it had housed the furnace. Accessible to the outside beneath the columned south portico, the space was central, and McKim had taken advantage of its limited architectural qualities. Both Adee and Bingham must have been glad. For years they had heard the complaints of diplomats, who resented collecting beneath the dubious shelter of the very lofty north portico, where rain might soak or snow might frost their golden epaulettes while they waited for the front door to open.

Those who came either to call or to attend state functions now directed their carriages along the south driveway to the door of the Diplomatic Reception Room. In status the space was a cut above the new, more general social entrance in the east wing, although it shared with other callers the men's and women's lavatories nearby. Few ever sat in the straight-back chairs that lined the stark plaster walls of the Diplomatic Reception Room. Here at state functions the diplomats shed their coats, tweaked their moustaches, and otherwise prepared to enter.

If a diplomat was not pleased with something or felt affronted, especially at the White House, the State Department was sure to hear about it. With or without the

Diplomatic Reception Room, Adee found that conflicts continued in the renewed White House, despite all the effort that had been made to make it conflict proof. The erratic elevator sometimes did not function or was otherwise occupied, and arriving diplomats were diverted to the "back stairs," a service stair used by the domestic staff. Use of this secondary stair, though good enough for Lincoln during the Civil War, was not so for the diplomats in the early 1900s.

The Russian ambassador Count Cassini wrote in high annoyance to Secretary Hay about this stair, and Hay passed it on to Adee with a smirk at the count's pettiness. "The Diplomatic Corps," wrote the count, "was admitted to the main floor through a very narrow service stairway, on which servants carrying platters of eatables were to be met; again in order to reach the Blue Room that was reserved for the corps, it had to work its own way through a close throng, owing to the absence of officials charged with maintenance of order. In view of the readiness which has always been character-istic of the Diplomatic corps in Washington when the expressed wishes of the Execu-tive Power were to be met, it becomes my duty to draw your Excellency's most earnest attention to these particulars."[1] Adee's response was pleasingly apologetic.

The expansive character of diplomatic Washington in this period can be under-stood best in the general context of diplomacy in the nineteenth century, which influ-enced it. Historically, ambassadors formed a network linking the Western world as a result of the Congress of Vienna in 1815. That grand convocation of kingdoms, exhausted from a comprehensive war, indeed a world war, aimed to set the kingdoms right again after the general upset by Napoleon.[2] Fallen crowns were brushed off and restored to royal heads, if not always replaced there as absolutely as previously. The great majority of the crowns remained for most of the nineteenth century, no matter the character of government that functioned beneath them.

America was otherwise occupied at the time. Emerging victorious over Britain in the War of 1812 and emotionally charged up, the young nation turned its inter-ests inward to begin taming the rest of its continent that had barely been touched. If the Congress of Vienna was noticed at all in distant America, it was not observed with much interest. Although American commerce covered the seas, the business of the great kingdoms of Europe otherwise concerned the United States very little. The actions at Vienna, however, would eventually have an influence on the manner of America's conduct of foreign affairs, but not for the better part of a century. When a second congress, the Congress of Berlin, was held in 1878, the Americans were not invited. Fifteen years later European ambassadors began to appear in Washington.[3]

Diplomats became a key safety mechanism in the restorative efforts of the Con-gress of Vienna. Representing their kingdoms, the diplomats existed to prevent all-out wars. Their heads of state also wanted no repeats of the revolutionary waves that had so suddenly and destructively swept Europe and the colonies over the past quarter cen-tury. The way to halt rebellions and the wars that inevitably followed them was to keep a tight lid on Europe, so the congress resulted in a cooperative arrangement in which each kingdom pledged to help the others in avoiding any more bloody chaos. Through the nineteenth century, the system was gradually fragmented into smaller alliances involving fewer nations, arrangements considered more useful at the moment. There were wars. But the Congress of Vienna did achieve what it set out to do, and what followed was nearly a century without major wars in Europe, so peaceful a stretch of time that people forgot how terrible major international turmoil could be. Indeed the war greatest in scale fought in the nineteenth century was the American Civil War.

Communication was essential to implementing the world designs of the Congress of Vienna, so the conduct of diplomacy was institutionalized, with universal rules codifying a system of its own in place of the more arbitrary system that had gone before. The structure, although tediously elaborate, was effectual. Ambassadors were defined as the personal representatives of their sovereigns. Ministers plenipotentiary, although representing their country, represented not the sovereign but the foreign office and thus, on foreign soil, had to go through that country's foreign office to reach the head of state. Ministers resident addressed only the foreign office.

Venice is believed to have sent out the first resident ambassadors, many years before the Congress of Vienna. The word *ambassador* itself came from Italian. Major kingdoms, such as England and France, received resident ambassadors through the seventeenth and eighteenth centuries; an Austrian ambassador, for example, always lived at Versailles, and a French ambassador resided at court in Vienna. *Ambassador* was a word sometimes used to denote a special and important mission. For example, the seminal Japanese visit to the United States just before the Civil War was called an "embassy," and its top officials "ambassadors." It was not an embassy in the usual nineteenth-century sense, and in the 1890s temporary legates would more properly have been called envoys extraordinary. By the early twentieth century the network of diplomats had vastly increased in number over the world, far beyond what could ever have been projected in 1815 at the Congress of Vienna. The results of their work were usually of merit, and at that work's core the art of diplomacy remained very strong.

Even an institution so carefully crafted as diplomacy, however, still sees some change. Intimacy between ambassadors and sovereigns meant less as the nineteenth century grew older. The meaning of sovereignty—popular power—was no longer exclusively expressed by the king in some countries. In America, sovereignty was held entirely by the people and exercised through their votes. The idea of absolute monarchy vanished in most places, and kings fell under constitutions, as had Britain's already in the later seventeenth century. With telegraph and telephone, now and again the question was asked, as it was by Theodore Roosevelt: did nations really need ambassadors? But the diplomats and the rules by which they worked proved their usefulness repeatedly, and so they prevailed, crisscrossing the world with their safety nets. Theirs was the most stable system of communication that existed among nations.

Alliances were the age-old means by which European nations obligated themselves to help other countries in case of trouble from outside. The alliances that followed through the century after the Congress of Vienna, for all the comprehensiveness of their paperwork, required constant maintenance and called for ever more functionaries and supporting staff in the foreign office, which Americans called the Department of State. Each country organized a corps of professional diplomats, elite specialists trained to monitor the activities of foreign countries. Over the years, experience in the field generated rules and customs that became part of the language of diplomacy, and the diplomats felt safe in these rules, trivial as they sometimes seemed to outsiders. Procedure and conduct among the diplomats were one and the same.

At the turn of the nineteenth to the twentieth century, the major powers of Europe built military strength using all the muscle of modern technology. To those who sensed danger coming, diplomacy began to seem more important than ever. Kaiser Wilhelm II in his long orations seemed ever more threatening than simply a royal braggart. Captain Mahan was his gospel. He was passionately determined that through sea power he would raise Germany above Britain. In Austria-Hungary, the aging emperor Franz Josef fell increasingly under the influence of military generals and industrialists. France and Italy, stifled by internal turmoil, pursued active colonialism, along with Britain and Germany and, after 1898, the United States. The ascent of power carried a thrill with it in the early years of the century. Diplomacy and pure good fortune kept energies under some control that otherwise might have exploded on contact. For all his warlike chest beating, Roosevelt privately feared what would soon enough be called a "world war." The concept cannot have escaped many others either.

American diplomats had always been reticent about taking on the showy aspects of international diplomatic formalities, lest they appear monarchical before the suspicious eyes of democracy. Rather, most diplomats had gone out of their way to avoid showy formalities. Flamboyant Henry Clay had weighted himself down with feathers, gilt, and embroidery at Ghent in 1814, but few American diplomats had been so bold. All of them complained of the complications of not having official uniforms like diplomats from other countries. Clay's "uniform" was not official but of his own design and purchase. "Royal" garb did not belong on a red-blooded American. Congress stood pat in denying court attire.

For a century American diplomats delicately navigated the international rules and forms to compensate for the refusal of Congress to allow them to function as other diplomats did. Andrew Jackson's foreign ministers squeezed permission from a begrudging State Department to sew a few gilt stars on their stiff, high collars. Conversely, later on James Buchanan, American minister to Britain in the 1850s, was turned away from a court function in London for wearing mere dinner attire. Whenever the subject of uniforms came up in Congress, orations of protest followed, calling up a cherished image of Poor Richard while totally misunderstanding Franklin's motive for drawing attention to himself by appearing in a homespun suit before the court of Versailles.[4]

The United States appointed six ambassadors to foreign countries in the spring of 1893, pursuant to the act of March 1 of that year, which authorized the nation to send ambassadors to countries that sent ambassadors to Washington.[5] Six ambassadors reported for duty in the United States that year, and six U.S. ambassadors went to those same reporting countries. Ambassadors from seven nations greeted Theodore Roosevelt on his accession to the presidency in 1901: Britain, France, Germany, Russia, Austro-Hungary, and Mexico. Spain, whose representative had been absent briefly after Enrique de Lôme departed, sent an interim minister, the Duke d'Arcos, then elevated him to ambassador immediately after the peace treaty was signed in Paris.[6] Since all of these envoys represented monarchies, except for those from France and Mexico, diplomacy in the capital was spangled as never before with court practices from Europe. Even in the French Embassy titles abounded, for no matter the legal status, Frenchmen rarely dropped their evidences of family rank.

The second level below the highest rank, the ministers and ministers plenipotentiary, were numerous in Washington. China, Japan, Siam, Korea, the countries of Central and South America, Haiti, the Netherlands, Denmark, and Turkey all sent ministers. Sweden and Norway shared one minister in Washington. The Dominican Republic had no minister in Washington in 1900 but did maintain a diplomatic representative with a legation in New York.

Foreign embassies and legations in Washington were considered rather romantically as standing on the soil of the nation they represented. Diplomats enjoyed immunity from criminal and civil laws in the country of mission. Cases challenging this proliferate in State Department records, almost from the beginning of the nation. Immunity was not honored every time, but usually it was, so that Americans would be honored similarly in foreign countries. Sometimes the public was aroused by inflammatory incidents, such as rape—the earliest being in 1818—and other high crimes.[7] The State Department's reaction was to remove the problem quickly in any way it could. Usually further trouble was avoided by the secret flight of the erring diplomat. On the other hand, sometimes the offense was that of the Americans and too big for the diplomat from the offended country to avoid. When a group of immigrant Italian truck farmers were lynched in Tallulah, Louisiana, in 1899, Baron de Fava, declaring the outrage of the Italian crown, called for his passport at the State Department and left the country until some agreeable settlement could be made.

Consuls in the major ports and economic centers addressed personal and business problems at the level of everyday transactions, dealing with commerce and passports, arranging business contacts, negotiating with customs, seeing to shipments of goods and personal possessions, attending to burials or forwarding back to America remains of deceased fellow citizens, starting investigations, negotiating over civil and criminal issues, and responding to requests of every other sort. Consuls had no diplomatic rank. They were expected to be the eyes of their country in foreign places, and reports of their observations are plentiful in the State Department archives.

In Washington the embassies and legations worked at the highest levels of international politics. Little of this was glamorous, not even enough to generate books about it in most cases. Apart from dealing with treaties and relations between nations, the embassy's work was not so different from that of the consulates and charges d'affaires. Given the sensitive nature of diplomacy, a diplomat was expected to be at his post. In his absence his chief aide, nearly always identified as the secretary, became charge d'affaires until the diplomat returned; this secretary was never "acting ambassador" or minister, as Adee was, for example, at one point "acting secretary of state." The diplomatic secretary had authority to do only basic management and keep the lid on things, as it were, until the top official returned. Ambassadors and ministers left their posts only on formal leave, with permission both from the home office and the U.S. State Department, where their passports were held while they were in Washington. They were usually permitted one month free, during which they went home to attend to personal business or relax. In the event of major need, the chief diplomat, if out of town, was expected to hurry back to his post. Many an ambassador took the train from Newport to Washington and arrived worn-out, only to be transported to the state reception room in the State Department for a conference of many long hours.

"To Americans in general, diplomat means less than dentist," wrote Lionel Strachey in the *New York Times* in 1903. He continued to observe correctly, however, that in Washington a diplomat was an important man, "the pink of polish, the sovereign of social suavity, the artistic aristocrat, the complete conversationalist, decorous and dignified in deportment, possessing unusual intelligence and universal information, pre-eminent in his acquirements of history, languages, international law and usages, familiar with all politics and ways of thinking of all nations and possibly esteemed by his own Government for services previously rendered elsewhere."[8]

Diplomats were social by necessity. They made themselves celebrities in Washington as well as in the major cities and watering places of the rich, notably Newport, New York, Boston, Chicago, and New Orleans, although out west they barely made a ripple. Diplomats welcomed being soft news; scandal, of course, was fatal, more so perhaps in America than in Europe.

The world of the diplomats was at once big and small. Like the upper military, the corps involved many people and was crisscrossed with friendships made during missions and remade during later assignments. In Europe the diplomatic service was highly organized. A young man at entrance level went through a strictly supervised educational process that included an apprenticeship before a slow, step-by-step climb up the ladder. For Europeans, diplomacy was a lifetime career. No matter who one might be, a single faulty move could terminate a promising future. In America there was no formal training for the diplomatic service. For clerks at the State Department, experience on the job constituted training. Most of the employees below the level of "assistant" were usually clerks; they had trained to be teachers or lawyers or for some other pursuit. Few had a background specific to foreign service. Adee was an example of one who did. He obtained his job with educational qualifications in composition and translation. He moved into a very responsible position abroad. His early career was hurried along by his ability but also by his personal contacts. Top-level employees were rarely as well qualified as he when they started. Still, the State Department always boasted a distinguished roster.

Europeans devoted their lives to it. Ministers and ambassadors sent from Europe were usually men of family prominence. Young men of respectable social background, many with titles, with or without private fortunes, gravitated to the foreign offices. The government provided generous allowances for the costs of maintaining high state at foreign embassies and legations. American ministers and ambassadors on the other hand were typically rich men who could privately pay the costs attendant to the job. For all his other gifts, Hay could never have functioned at St. James's without his wife's fortune. Ambassadors from the United States made a little under twenty thousand dollars a year, about a third of what the president made, but with very few of their expenses provided. An ambassadorship was a coveted job for a man who could afford it, and for the president a good place to satisfy a political obligation. Even so, the late nineteenth and early twentieth centuries produced some remarkable American diplomats.

Society was part of a diplomat's job. Roosevelt called this side of diplomacy the "plush business."[9] To the outside world looking in, diplomats had a festive time. However, society was more hard work than pleasant. In company a diplomat could not drink too much, smoke too much, or talk carelessly. He had to use great restraint, as did his wife, with even the most casual interactions with other diplomats and their wives. All but the most studied informality was hazardous. Impressions counted as much as words, so even in personal friendships a wise diplomat never lowered his guard. They presented themselves with the attention an actor might give to a performance.

Like everything else in diplomatic life, social conduct was tightly bound up in rules. This helped avoid unpleasant incidents and embarrassing faux pas. The tone naturally was very reserved, and all the more so in Washington with the appearance of ambassadors. Most rules followed the usual codes of formal social conduct, but there were also diplomatic rules. These were never relaxed for any reason, and there were more rules than even the most fastidious private host might feel obliged to follow. Recognition of rank was the most significant part and was an element in all official entertaining in Washington.

In the American capital as in any capital in the world, deference among diplomats was based first on one's official position and second on the longevity of service in

Washington. For example, all things equal otherwise between, say, two ambassadors, the one who had been in the post longer took precedence.

The president by tradition did not attend diplomatic dinners at legations or embassies, the building itself considered to be standing on foreign soil. When he did attend, perhaps at a hotel or other venue, he was at the head of the table, just as he would have been in his house. All other guests descended by rank from him. Next came the vice president, who did attend embassy parties as often as he wished, the Speaker of the House, the chief justice, and the secretary of state, after which the ambassadors, then the other diplomats, who were received and seated by their status in the corps, determined by chronological order, established by the date and time when they made their original Blue Room presentation of credentials.[10] It was not unusual in Washington, or considered especially odd, if the diplomat wrote to his host prior to a dinner to make sure in advance that he would be seated properly at table.[11]

The shape of official rank was followed in every embassy and legation and by all who entertained high officials in diplomacy or individuals elected or appointed to government service. Wives were considered as having the same rank as their husbands. Sons and daughters, friends and sisters, had no rank, unless the wife was deceased or out of town and the family member was the attending diplomat's temporary hostess. Even then there was likely to be some question that had to be taken to Alvey Adee to answer. It was a touchy area, this matter of rank, and everyone involved with it took it very seriously.

To those diplomats who had served in European courts, Washington at its most formal seemed almost informal. The difference was one of setting and the degree of ceremony, which in European courts was at its most elaborate when it framed and enhanced the presence of the monarch. Except in France, where there was no king, European courts were given an intrinsic sort of power by the attendance of the king. The French made up for their absence of state ceremony in magnificent décor and food and a flavoring of noble French titles. When foreign diplomats commented on the American way as being lax, most of them blamed it upon ignorance and isolation and the typical American cynicism about ceremony. In fact it was the absence of a visible sovereign in the American system that made some of the more princely ceremonies seem meaningless. Even so, foreign emissaries seemed to have appreciated the stark ceremonies of the Americans as appropriate, and the carefully tailored ceremonials of the Roosevelt administration rather threw the idea up a notch and redefined democratic restraint.

By contrast to American ceremonies, regulations in European courts seemed foreign indeed to U.S. emissaries. Strangers exposed to it were wise to take instruction in advance, and every foreign capital offered practitioners—consultants—teaching court form and costume. To engage these experts was not a thing to hide; indeed, rank was found even among them.

Rules extended beyond the palaces. Under the reign of Kaiser Wilhelm II in Prussia, for example, the rule that nobles not be invited to dinners given by persons beneath their rank did not necessarily mean that nobles stayed away. Far from it. When a noble heard of a dinner or learned of it in the court register or by some other means, and he wished to go, he simply informed the host that he and his party would be there or, for that matter, might even appear at the door unannounced. The theory behind this practice was that nobles of Prussia were welcome wherever they might wish to go. Curiously enough, it was generally true.[12]

Carrying the idea further, a noble who wished to honor a host or hostess with his presence but was otherwise occupied might send a photograph, autographed and framed, for the host to display prominently in the entrance hall. This counted the same as if the guest had attended in person. After World War I in almost any junk shop in Germany, or in Austria, Romania, and other countries of eastern Europe, among the gilt chairs and dusty mirrors, the porcelain vases and baled tapestries, one was likely to find these portrait photographs for sale for a few cents, relics of a time that had disappeared.

Full explanation of court etiquette was found in the numerous volumes published by the lords chamberlain and other high court officials. Copies were readily available in bookstores or through the chamberlains' offices. Compared with Roosevelt's little Blue Books, they were ponderous indeed. Conduct in every situation was given a form. Costume, equipage, manner of bowing, walking, nodding, maneuvering the hands, wearing swords, and eating and drinking at table were the subjects addressed. In the diplomatic context they were important, all part of the system set down in the Congress of Vienna. Continually adapted and improved, they helped bind ever more tightly and strongly the diplomatic system spread over the capitals of the world for the preservation of peace.

In the American capital the British ambassador entertained the most frequently. His was almost certainly a budget that outstripped all the others and indeed that of the White House itself, where a mere twenty thousand dollars for extra costs was allotted the president for four years.[13] Lord Pauncefote's embassy allowance, apart from his salary, was almost four times the salary of the American ambassador to St. James's. On both sides of the Atlantic, a very great point was made of the kinship between the United States and Great Britain. Like all British ambassadors, Pauncefote was presented with table silver in banquet quantity and porcelain and fine table linens as well, but the wealth he had achieved originally as a barrister, practicing in Hong Kong, and cultivated through the years of his public service was also called upon, if not to the extent it would have been for an American ambassador abroad.[14]

Of the diplomatic houses in Washington, the palatial Second Empire–style mansion occupied by the British on Connecticut Avenue was the largest. Not only was it the finest in Washington; it was also one of only two embassies there, along with

Germany's, that were actually owned by foreign countries and the first built entirely for diplomatic life. If one spoke of "the embassy" in Washington, the term referred to that of Great Britain. Occupied in December 1874 just days before the opening of the social season, what was then the British legation, and in 1893 became the British Embassy, had among its features a ballroom so spacious that an ample house could have been slid into it comfortably, like a dresser drawer. When the building was originally designed, the director of works in London protested to Her Majesty's minister in Washington that the proposed house was larger than Britain's embassies in Paris, Vienna, and Constantinople. "In the capitals in Europe," explained the minister defending so large a house, "the distinction of classes is so plainly marked and so strictly observed that Her Majesty's representative may select his society and ensure its not being too numerous. But in this Republic, where all classes claim equal right and the lowest aspire to and may attain the highest positions it is impossible to restrict invitations, and everyone who is accustomed to Washington Society well knows how desirable it is to have plenty of room for the guests whom Her Majesty's Minister is called upon to invite."[15]

British Embassy, Washington, D.C., 1895, the largest diplomatic headquarters in Washington. *Library of Congress, Prints and Photos Division.*

It was built of brick and limestone. The Foreign Office even allowed a porte cochere, in recognition of Washington's fickle weather. Upon entering the finished building, one could hardly doubt where he was. From within a heavy gold frame, at the landing of a colossal free-standing staircase, stood Queen Victoria in robe and crown, painted on canvas as big as life. To her left, following her death, a portrait of Edward VII was added. Sir Julian and Lady Selina and their daughters occupied eighteen rooms upstairs, while on the lower floor formal apartments of state, including the ballroom, interconnected through broad openings. Other rooms apart from the formal saloons served the chancery, offices, and other functions of the embassy. Other legations and embassies had the same functions stuffed uncomfortably into smaller accommodations. Only the staff of the Chinese was larger than that of Britain.[16]

While the other embassies may have continued to pale beside that of the British, the coming of ambassadors, creating such change throughout the diplomatic community, sent all the diplomats hurrying to improve their quarters. This flush of ostentation gave a new breath to society. The capital was fascinated with the noble titles—dukes, counts, princes, marquises—appearing in greater number than ever before. Ambassadors were addressed within the corps as "your excellency," which was strange to the American ear and, while much enjoyed in society, was used very little elsewhere in Washington. Some politicians, looking on, still feared that the presence of titles and the ornaments attached to diplomatic life would spoil American youth and make them ambitious for similar social distinction. In general their fear was unfounded regarding youth, but mothers with daughters of matrimonial age were quite another matter.

A glamorous marriage was a fairy-tale dream sparked in girls' imaginations from the day they first read Cinderella. Another side of the story was that many an impecunious though noble title came to America in the employ of the diplomatic service, looking for a rich American wife, so that he could patch up the family premises back home and live the life his title suggested. And many a marriage of this sort was made, the young lady's money restoring what had been lost and the man's name nourishing a sickly family tree. Some of the foreign services had regulations forbidding their employees to marry U.S. women, but these were rules to which no one paid much attention.[17] Nothing was new about crusades for advantageous alliances, but Washington, with a few exceptions, had never been an especially fertile field for it. By the early 1900s, romance in the capital's winters rivaled that in Saratoga and Newport summers.

By general agreement the "season" in Washington was in full force from the middle of December until Lent in February but continued at a slighter pace until mid-May. The first state dinner at the White House opened it, and the last White House garden party closed it. Large events with dances were usually winter affairs in December, January, and February. Each hostess, each embassy, each legation wished to hold at least one of these. Small dinners and public receptions continued through all the months. The organization of so much of the diplomats' activity relied to a certain extent upon the oversight of Lord Pauncefote, who was dean of the diplomatic corps by virtue of rank and longevity in Washington. More particular questions, even small ones, found their way to the office of Alvey Adee.

In this office Adee kept a registry book. It lay open and available for all to see. Notations were by day and month, rendered in ink. The first entries were the White House events, of which there were four regular state dinners, under Roosevelt normally five, and the state reception on New Year's Day. Cabinet receptions were also noted. These events were considered givens. No other official entertainments, or entertainments that aspired to official guests, diplomats, or otherwise, were to be held at those reserved times. Otherwise the five winter and spring months were open, and it was first come first served. The book began filling the minute it was opened in October. No social event had notable importance unless it was listed in Adee's book. People called in person or sent secretaries or butlers to mark spaces.

Adee's register helped avoid collisions. If two embassies were to have dinners on the same night, an uncomfortable situation might result and, depending upon the circumstances, would require complicated peacemaking. To hold a ball at the French Embassy on the night the German ambassador celebrated the kaiser's birth could be interpreted as an insult to Germany, for the French ambassador was naturally expected to be at so notable an occasion held by another major power. Cancellations of any registered event could be ordered directly by Adee in the instance of a national tragedy or the death of an important figure. This was more a favor to the host than the intrusion it might appear to be. Likewise, if diplomats anticipated personality problems between their guests, they requested Adee's assistance, and he obliged. If asked, he reviewed seating charts and menus. Private hosts came to him as well, to untangle the confusion that sometimes accompanied the mixing of diplomats at even the most innocent social functions.[18]

A diplomatic dinner was an event of significance in Washington. Engraved invitations embellished with the arms of the host country announced the hour. Everyone in the diplomatic community, invited society, political and military realms, and many others as well, soon knew the guest list. Who was not invited was often as important as who was invited. In the 1890s, diplomatic affairs usually had outshone those of the president, but Roosevelt's imperial shine brought the spotlight back to the White House.

Men wore full dress, white tie and tails, but gloves for them were optional. Ladies were expected to wear elbow-length gloves, to be removed at the dinner table. Their court trains by definition extended three yards from shoulders to tip end; some gymnastics were required in moving the train about, as it was a no-hands process. Soon after arrival, the train was looped over the lady's arm, out of the way. Now and then a cluster of three white plumes, set straight up from the back of a woman's high coiffure, bobbed over the heads of the assembled group, attesting the bearer's presentation at court. The plumes were more in evidence in the early 1900s than they had ever been before in Washington.[19]

For a brief fifteen minutes after the stated time on the invitation, the event began with a reception. This period allowed leeway for unanticipated delays in arriving. Guests removed their coats before they entered the reception room, where they were greeted by their hosts. Everyone stood. Sitting down during this short reception was condoned only in the aged or infirm. Sometimes flutes of champagne or cups of soup were passed. Serving cocktails was not usual before about 1905. Even then, a woman usually drank wine or a light punch, leaving the prevailing scotch whiskey to the men.

Seasoned guests, which included all diplomats, set their watches with precision for formal events. When dinner was announced, exactly fifteen minutes from the time stated on the invitation, any arrival past that time was late. Tardiness, whatever the reason, was a rude affront, suggesting that one had more important things to do than to honor the invitation. A sin committed in this particular was likely to be a topic of discussion all through the diplomatic community the next day. Proper form was serious business. During the reception, a seating chart or a butler informed the arriving male guest of his place at table and the name of the woman to be seated on his right. He was to "hand," or escort, her to dinner. Alternatively a small envelope was provided to him upon his arrival with the dinner partner's name on a card inside. Seating arrangements were very carefully made, all sensitivities and preferences taken into account.

The march to the dining room called for a "figure" of sorts, with dinner partners departing the reception room two by two. In the earlier nineteenth century these figures could be very fancy, almost like a slow square dance, but by the early twentieth such old-fashioned ideas were deemed silly, and the trip was likely to be a chatty walk, women taking their dinner partner's arm on the right, with their train thrown over their left arm. In large houses built for such activities, as the British Embassy was, the prescribed processes of dinners and receptions were naturally easier than in most other diplomatic headquarters, where several domestic-scaled rooms and a stair hall were the formal areas. Complaints were universal that the houses were too small for the formalities. Still the social custom was followed, no matter the size of the house. Because nearly all of the legations and embassies were relatively small, most diplomatic dinners of any large scale were held at hotels. Of these the Arlington was at the top for its ballroom with adjacent smaller rooms and the residential quality that diplomatic formalities preferred, although the Willard, which was much larger and less intimate, also was engaged for major dinners. No matter whether at the legation or a hotel, procedures were followed to the letter.

Host and hostess sat facing one another across the center of the table. A battalion of waiters hired from a list maintained by approved Washington caterers served the dinner. The table was always elaborately outfitted, with cloth of linen, lace, or even silk, flowers, and usually three to five wine glasses and a water glass at each plate. Nothing was passed in the French style; all was served separately and in sequence *à la russe*, by waiters.[20] Until all guests were seated, no one lifted a fork or took a sip or a bite. Spending three hours at table, now and then more, was not uncommon. Conversation generally went to the sides rather than across the table. When the host or guest of honor looked up and spoke, the table was expected to fall silent and listen. It was considered rude to leave the table then return, and savvy dinner guests exercised their bodily functions in advance. "Make water when you can," the admonition of the Iron Duke to the youthful Prince of Wales, was backed by the wisdom of experience. Yet in an emergency, etiquette took precedence over upholstery.

With rare exceptions, the dining table was covered with white damask, starched stiff, the sharp creases rising razorlike, revealing where the cloth had been folded and pressed. Great napkins of the same material, a yard square and a little less painfully starched, lay folded in some decorative way on the dinner plate when the guest sat down. Flower arrangements were made low, so as not to obscure cross-table visibility. The flattering light of candles nearly always illuminated the table, although it was likely supplemented by shaded electric lights around the walls. The general rule was to allow a width of twenty-seven inches for each guest's plates and tableware. Wine glasses could be as many as eight to a place, depending upon the hosts' generosity. A single table was always preferred. When the party was for thirty or so guests, a number of tables usually became necessary, with a head table for the honored guests and others of high rank, backed by flags of the host nation. Normally each woman guest found a favor at her plate—a fan, a silk reticule for jewelry, a small vial of perfume, a book of poems. Men received a boutonniere or cigarettes.

The custom of toasting, if fairly well abandoned for the time in other official circles, always prevailed in diplomatic usage. President Roosevelt had revived toasting at the White House at the dinner he held in the East Room for Prince Henry of Prussia in 1902. At a diplomatic dinner the principal toast was likely to be offered by the ambassador at the conclusion of the main course. If others followed, and they did not necessarily, they were started by the male guest of honor. Toasting did not go on and on, as at a wedding supper. Nor did jokes and ribald humor shade the little speeches; they were serious, often very literate and elegantly turned, in Washington nearly always in English. Jules Cambon's were legendary in the diplomatic circle, showcasing his great charm and experience at speaking on his feet. Toasting was terminated by the ambassador, if necessary, by standing up and thanking the toast makers with a gracious nod. At this point the ambassador was likely to depart from the table, leaving his guests some time to relax a bit over champagne and dessert.

Women guests rose after dessert and assembled elsewhere for about half an hour. Port was passed around for the men, who remained in the dining room and came and

Alice Roosevelt and Prince Henry of Prussia, brother of Kaiser Wilhelm II, at the launching of the emperor's American-made yacht, the *Meteor III*, February 25, 1902. *Library of Congress, Prints and Photos Division.*

went from the table. After about half an hour an announcer informed the men that the ladies awaited them in the drawing room, where coffee and liqueurs were poured. Cigarettes, formerly offered only to men after the women had left the dining room, were proffered to all among diplomats by the late 1890s, a European touch not always well received by Americans. The ambassador might join the final episode, but not necessarily, for if he bid his good-bye at the table, his wife or a member of his household likely remained with the guests. Politeness decreed that the guests stay over coffee only briefly before going for their coats. If the dinner began at eight, it was almost certainly over by eleven-thirty. With so much alcohol offered, it was wise to drink coffee, lest loosened tongues and perhaps also emotions turn the occasion into a madhouse to be regretted the next morning. A diplomatic community never seemed to forget unwelcome explosions. If the offense was serious enough, both the incident and the names of the participants traveled the network that crossed the oceans.

Smaller, less starchy dinners also marked the diplomats' Washington season. These were the occasions for ten or twelve at table, rarely more than eighteen. Typically an embassy had formal dinners only half a dozen times during the winter but probably three "suppers" a week. During the Washington season a diplomat rarely ate at home, unless he was entertaining. A gathering of sophisticated, world-wise people well accustomed to conversation with strangers and subtlety of language, well-read, much-traveled, possessors of some leisure, was bound to be charming. These were the diplomats who came to Washington, veterans of life in capitals great and small throughout the world.[21]

Receptions for large crowds were a less enjoyable fact of diplomatic life. Washington had receptions of all kinds during the season, and in the diplomatic community most were exercises of duty, not pleasure. The traditional reception at the White House on New Year's Day was of long standing, whereas the other White House reception, on the Fourth of July, died out in the 1870s when President Grant finally rebelled against the Washington heat and started the custom of taking a summer vacation at the beach for the last half of the summer, returning in mid-September.

Every embassy and legation had at least one large reception a year. Like those at the White House, these were attached to symbolic events, as a historical commemoration or a king's state birthday. The French celebrated Bastille Day on July 14; Mexico held open house for Mexican Independence on September 21. Some receptions were by invitation, while others admitted the general public, subject to a dress code, the choice usually determined by available space. The White House received an estimated average of six thousand on New Year's. A legation could expect at least a thousand at a public reception, particularly at the British Embassy.

Most legations rented their houses, so the quarters were simply not built for crowds. One solution was to send, say, five hundred invitations, with staggered reception times assigned in them. These receptions might be likened to flowing streams, for the guests rarely stopped moving in a line that began well outside the front door and poured out a side door. Formal admission of the diplomats and high-ranking officers was managed somewhat the same all over town, including at the White House, with the doors opened an hour earlier for this select group, who lingered rather on display for the general guest list, arriving later.

Because of the difficulties of accommodating large crowds, most diplomatic receptions were not public, although they had carefully crafted invitation lists that penetrated usefully into the government service for goodwill and extended also into society, to assure reciprocity. Held in the winter, they were gala events, orchestra playing, tables of food and drink, and garnished most of all by the sheer delight of place. One observer commented, not without validity, that a main duty of a diplomat was "to be generally agreeable. So doing, he can better exercise the functions of a legitimate spy upon our operations as a government and a people."[22]

~

While it was commonly remarked that one went to an embassy dinner for celebrity, not food, the food was, from all accounts, excellent. The diplomats sometimes served a dish or two native to their countries, but the favored fare was French, the special recipes and techniques, the mingling of ingredients and subtle sauces, that had emerged in Paris in the hard times of the late eighteenth and nineteenth centuries, when penury in market supplies stimulated creativity in French cooking. Menus boasted soufflés, casseroles, all manner of baked meats swimming in succulent sauces, green and jellied salads, breads, all prepared in the French way, and served with multiple French wines and rivers of champagne, the signature wine of diplomatic entertaining. By 1910 people were still grumbling about Lord Pauncefote's insistence upon "digestive port" in place of all other wines. His successor, Sir Michael Herbert, was blessed for restoring the banished champagne.

Clever chefs augmented the more orthodox French menus with wild game from the woods of Maryland and Virginia. The important Washington dinner that did not include one or another of wild turkey, venison, rabbit, goose, or duck was rare, it seems. Baltimore's enticing favorites were pillaged and adapted to diplomatic tables: from the Chesapeake Bay fried soft-shell crab and from the rivers broiled shad row. A kind of regional oyster then eaten but no longer seen today was unusually large, as big as a salad plate. Local turtle, flavored with sherry and a concoction of herbs and cream, made a superb soup with which to begin a meal. So popular was "terrapin" soup that wet bins appeared in many cellars, where captured turtles lived until visited by the cook with his cleaver.

Washington's city markets were supplied by farmers with produce-laden wagons early in the day, and apron-clad cooks were there before most citizens, walking stall to stall, followed by assistants with large baskets to fill with fish, lobster, oysters, venison, chicken, beef, pork, and greens and other vegetables. Farm families made cheese and bread and rolled them to town on push-carts. The capital city was surrounded by a breadbasket in the cultivated hills of Maryland and Virginia, and with the railroad, produce also came from farms in Pennsylvania and West Virginia. Some of the more resourceful cooks had regular arrangements with particular farmers, just as they did with their ice men. Farm wagons called at those legations at daybreak. The figures seen earliest in the morning on Washington streets were the purveyors of farm produce.

~

Lord Pauncefote of Preston had accompanied the United States in its international dawning, the first ambassador on her shores. Personally he was ready to lay down his epaulets and go home. By 1901 he was tired, nearing his midseventies. The British Foreign Office repeatedly declined his requests to retire, and when he renewed his appeals, he at last resorted to complaints of ill health. The Foreign Office countered coldly, alluding to pension complications that might be remedied if he were to remain in Washington a little longer.

After each episode with the home office, he agreed to serve one more year. But his heart was no longer in his work. The ambassador was a familiar sight in Washington, riding out to Arlington National Cemetery in his carriage or taking the streetcar alone, apparently for his own pleasure, and riding up and down Pennsylvania Avenue. Many an evening he spent sunk in a chair in John Hay's library, talking with his host. They had become closer friends after Hay was appointed secretary of state, and they conducted much of the business of their respective countries in Hay's comfortable library, which looked out on Lafayette Park. Such personal contact, after all, represented diplomacy at its most effective.[23]

Pauncefote was considered by his foreign office the most effective of all ambassadors in the British system. His expertise fit the diplomatic modus operandi of the time. In diplomacy, the key word *alliance* had been replaced by *arbitration*, the diplomatic art of negotiating treaties that established a ready framework for discussion between countries. This was judged the most effective way to keep peace. Arbitration was better suited to lawyers than most diplomats, whose training was usually more general. Pauncefote was a successful lawyer, and the pairing of him with the Boston lawyer Richard Olney, successor to Gresham as secretary of state under Cleveland, produced the Olney-Pauncefote Treaty, a collaboration between two brilliant men who added to the mix the valuable attribute of becoming close personal friends. Rejection of this treaty by the Senate was devastating to Pauncefote. Better luck came with the Hay-Pauncefote Treaty of 1901, the treaty with Britain that cleared the way for the United States to pursue construction of the Panama Canal. Henry Adams believed that Hay's inexperience was compensated by Pauncefote, who "pulled him through."[24]

The Hague Conference in 1899 was called by Czar Nicholas II, of Russia. Recoiling from the grim prospects of technology applied to war machinery, the czar made an effort to encourage an international system based upon arbitration for preserving world peace. It was his idea, and it parted from various motives of his advisers. The impulse in the young ruler was stirred ostensibly by the ominous threat of world disaster that seemed the obvious conclusion of a clash between the great powers. Britain selected Lord Pauncefote as the senior of two representatives. Twenty-six countries attended in May and June of 1899. The character the arbitration might take was the opening issue. "Pauncefote," wrote his biographer, "was completely in his element." With the Germans in firm opposition to arbitration, he pressed on, gathering support and writing what ultimately became the statement of the conference, which was signed by the participants on July 29, 1899. Pauncefote received high praise all over the diplomatic world.

On May 23, 1902, at the peak of his diplomatic fame, Lord Pauncefote died unexpectedly in his sleep at the British Embassy. A deep shock ran through Washington's diplomatic community. Several thousand people passed through the embassy ballroom, where the ambassador lay in state, to pay their respects. Atop the pall, in a spray of flowers, was his silver dress-sword. The embassy naturally followed British diplomatic procedures to the letter.

President Roosevelt took upon himself the American response and ordered a state funeral at St. John's Church on Lafayette Square. The service somewhat resembled the memorial Pauncefote himself had designed to mourn Queen Victoria at the same church one year to the month previously. He had given the public something "foreign" to look at with fascination, scheduling the service to correspond with the hour in England that the train carried the royal remains from London to the tomb at Windsor. Lord Pauncefote's own funeral had no such compelling parallel, but St. John's high-domed sanctuary was draped mournfully in the purple velvet accorded by his peerage and massed lavishly with spring flowers. Attendance was strictly by invitation. The State Department, through Adee, worked closely with the British Embassy on details, giving consideration for Lady Selina's wishes, but the show was Roosevelt's. The diplomats wore full court uniforms. Seating was by rank. Pauncefote's empty pew was filled with lilies. Spectators in thousands lined the streets and followed the hearse on foot to the receiving vault at Rock Creek Cemetery.

Lord Pauncefote's remains were sent home with full honors aboard the USS *Brooklyn*. At Southampton two other American navy ships met the Brooklyn and escorted her to the dock. While Roosevelt told the press that the ceremony was not for an ambassador but for a "damned good fellow," the *London Times* called the American mourning "excessive." Still the British government turned out in full dress to continue the American honors, transporting Pauncefote to London aboard a special train to lie in state in Westminster Abbey. The state funeral was attended by King Edward VII.[25]

～

Embassy life in Washington was, unavoidably, a world distinctly apart from the general flow of life in the capital. Daily private interactions of the diplomats are difficult to trace. Their communications to the foreign offices are discreet and usually brief. *Private*, however, is not an entirely relevant word to apply to them, for everything they did was subject to scrutiny from others. The younger employees of the legations and embassies especially seem to have had good times outside office doors, most of them single men, many living in boardinghouses elsewhere in town. By the early 1900s the ambassadors and ministers found that greater visibility of their own activities benefited their countries. Particular diplomats had always stood out from the rest, giving a certain tone to the diplomatic community as a whole.[26]

One of these, in the first years of the twentieth century, was the Chinese minister Wu Ting-Fang, a rich Hong Kong businessman and lawyer educated in England and France. Master of five languages, he spoke each one without a trace of a foreign accent. He was a friend of Pauncefote from their Hong Kong days and a man of cultivated tastes, with admiration for Western culture. Invitations to his dinners were rarely declined. The sheer luxury of his domestic staff kept even the most jaded guests wide-eyed. He brought with him a retinue of fifty Chinese servants, in addition to a large number of aides. Thus served, the Chinese legation, both office and home, seemed something mystical from the foam of the sea. An attendant in crisp silk attire received calling cards in the dimly lighted hall, where palace urns and bronze statuary stood before embroidered tapestries. The air in the house had a wonderful scent. Flowers from the conservatory were arranged throughout the public rooms.

At work in the Chinese legation on Dupont Circle, ca. 1895, by Frances Benjamin Johnston. *Library of Congress, Prints and Photos Division.*

The Chinese minister's wife, a tiny woman with ivory skin, her feet bound in the traditional way, accompanied Wu to Washington. While the minister's predecessor had also brought his wife, she had been much more secluded, since it was not the usual practice for Asian legations to have women in residence. Madame Wu, as she was known, spoke good English, however, and so became well acquainted in the diplomatic community. She was well spoken, and her informed conversation decried the silence required of upper-class Chinese women outside the confines of their homes. When she was in public shopping though, carried along the sidewalks downtown in an enclosed palanquin and accompanied by a flock of attendants, she honored the tradition of silence. Her steward went into the shops and brought merchandise outside to her chair for her inspection, for surely no Chinese woman of her rank would compromise her dignity to enter a commercial establishment.

Wu's successor, Sir Chentung Liang-Cheng, was equally popular. He had been educated in the United States, spoke American English with amusing informality, and loved odd American dialects. He joked that he was "the complete Occidental." At his celebrated entertainments he always used American waiters, because he suspected that Americans preferred not to have Chinese people serve them. Julia Foraker, wife of Senator Joseph B. Foraker, of Ohio, recalled an incident in Minister Chentung's drawing room after dinner. When a female guest went to retrieve her fan from the dining room, she returned quickly, saying in amazement, "Do you know there are thirty Chinks in that room? Every white has vanished."[27] The economical minister had sent the part-time help away and assigned his actual staff to clean up.

"How Chinese he remained at heart," Mrs. Foraker said of Minister Chentung. Yet his sons played sandlot baseball outside on the lawn with the local boys, and his wife moved about fairly much as she wished. Only Chentung's teenage daughter, who "fluttered forward on tiny, bound feet," was kept behind closed blinds abiding by old Chinese ways. The Chinese minister loved almost everything about the West. One of the main dishes at his dinners was Maryland terrapin. "I know it's expensive," he told Mrs. Foraker, "and that I am very extravagant. But I adore it, so I always order a large quantity for dinner, thus there will be always some left for me next day." Then he winked, "Luckily, one must give dinners."[28]

The typically slow turnover of diplomats in Washington served some of the ambassadors well. Ten years was a usual period of service. Pauncefote's tenure, for example, was very long, nearly twenty years. It is hard to imagine what the British Embassy might have been like without him. His successor, Sir Michael Herbert, with his sharp wit and bouncy manner, brought about what seemed from outside a slight relaxation of what had been the stiff tone of life at Pauncefote's embassy. If Herbert's appointment did not elicit full support at the British Foreign Office, he still seemed to the secretary of state a good choice to fill Pauncefote's big shoes. A public sort of man with strong American connections, Herbert was the type to win friends. He was forty-five, the younger son of Lord Herbert of Lea, the Sidney Herbert who was secretary of war under the Palmerston ministry, during the Crimean War, and the cherished colleague of Florence Nightingale. Sir Michael had successfully served in Washington under Pauncefote on two previous occasions and had been a close friend of Theodore Roosevelt well before his presidency. He was wholly unlike the dour Sir Julian. The American-born Belle Wilson was his wife, whom he had met in Newport during the first of his American assignments.

He had written dreamily of Newport summers back in the 1880s and of the beauty and wealth assembled there promising perhaps a marriage into American prosperity. One of his colleagues from the legation, visiting Newport along with him, wrote that Herbert was smitten with "a pretty and graceful Miss Wilson. . . . Her sister married a rich man [Cornelius Vanderbilt] and has yachts and diamonds."[29] As Herbert's wife, Belle Wilson, both wise and charming, proved to be an asset to his career, joining him on missions to the courts of Russia and Prussia, where she made a memorable impression as her husband ascended the diplomatic ladder.

By the time he returned again to Washington, in the top place, more than a decade had passed by. Belle and "Sir Mungo" were greeted joyously at the White House. For a while Herbert seemed to take over the diplomatic community, the most talked-about ambassador yet to come. The Herberts lighted the season of 1903 with both their hospitality at the embassy and the good cheer they brought elsewhere as guests. Their entertainments always included music. Crowds were mixed, as in London society, including artists and writers, even news people, with fellow diplomats. Sir Michael reigned socially over the other ambassadors until he called down the wrath of his foreign office by supporting Roosevelt's move to settle the Klondike boundary question, when British officials had no idea of surrendering an inch of their authority in the matter. In 1904, during the course of this unhappy difference of opinion, Sir Michael, who had already been diagnosed with tuberculosis, died suddenly before any solution was reached. Roosevelt ordered another state funeral at St. John's. Sir Michael loomed in the diplomatic history of the time, a brilliant young ambassador struck down in his prime.

Then from London came a man unlike either Sir Julian or Sir Michael. Like Sir Julian, Sir Mortimer Durand was not a trained diplomat, but he was a less obvious choice for the job. He had served for many years in the Indian civil service, before the Foreign Office transferred him to a more typical diplomatic mission: "I do not regard the life as a fine wholesome one," wrote Sir Mortimer of diplomacy. "There is practically no work or responsibility until a man becomes a Minister, which he may never do. At all events until a man is forty, he may expect to spend his life in copying dispatches, writing up registers, deciphering telegrams, and generally performing the duties which a subordinate clerk could perform in India."[30]

An outdoorsman and sportsman, Sir Mortimer had been ambitious to become ambassador to the United States. Forces were at work against that in America though, for as soon as Sir Michael died, President Roosevelt revived his efforts to have his friend Sir Cecil Spring-Rice appointed British ambassador in Washington. The Foreign Office in London, annoyed by what it considered presumptuous conduct on the part of the president, ignored Roosevelt and appointed Durand.

Roosevelt never liked Sir Mortimer. In spite of their similar interests, both literary and athletic, the president never could relate to the ambassador. He wrote to an American diplomat in London, "Now I wonder if you could arrange to have the Foreign Office send Spring-Rice over here to see me for a week? I understand he is to be in London for a little while. There is no one in the British Embassy here to whom I can talk freely, and I would like to have the people at the Foreign Office understand just my position in the Far East, and I would like to know what there is [to know]. . . . I do not know whether it is my fault or Sir Mortimer's, but our minds do not meet; and in any event I should be unwilling to speak with such freedom as I desire to anyone in whom I had not such absolute trust as I have in Spring-Rice."[31] He was not to have his way, nor was Spring-Rice to become ambassador to the United States until after Roosevelt had left office.

In contrast to the other diplomats, the German ambassador Dr. Theodor von Holleben was a bachelor, a scholarly, learned man who kept a sparse, austere household that very few were ever invited inside. Now and then he assembled a small company for what he called "family suppers," which by name warned in advance that nothing more than simple, substantial food and beer would be served. The plain-spoken doctor usually rather receded into the corps but could present surprises, such as when he released a diplomatic snakebite in 1902 by sharing with news reporters the confidential secret memoranda and telegrams that shed unfavorable light on Sir Julian's and the other ambassadors' motives when they made an appeal to McKinley at the time of the Spanish-American War, as described in chapter 3.

A further sampling of prominent diplomats in Washington would include Jules Cambon, of France, who had performed such useful service to the peace process in 1898. He lived simply in the relatively modest French Embassy. Although good company, he was not notably "social." He kept no chef and only a small number of servants. Most of his clerks lived under his roof, the rest in a French boardinghouse on Capitol Hill. Cambon's wife refused to move to America, so he was single while in Washington and entertained little on his own but was not likely to decline a dinner invitation elsewhere. The only large celebration he held, besides a few official dinners at hotels, was on Bastille Day at the embassy. Cambon celebrated the French Revolution with a reception and liked to annoy aristocrats on his staff by praising the Reign of Terror.

Ladislaus Hengelmüller von Hengervár was notable for giving small dinners at the Austro-Hungarian Embassy and appearing in public only when diplomatic duties required it. He declined the theater and other amusements and was considered socially dull. In summer he nearly always went home to Vienna, where he remained at his vacation house until fall. His thundering wife, Marie, however, who was not so quiet and private, added to his distinctiveness in other ways. Substantially younger than he, she had been reared in diplomatic life and had her own ideas about how things should be done. The baroness, a large, handsome woman with penciled eyebrows and rouge-crimsoned cheeks, was determined to correct whatever she saw wrong in Washington. Her overbearing manner made people avoid her when they could. Nothing aroused her temper more than a breach of protocol at some official event. It sent her storming to Adee's office, where she pushed her way in, to rage at one who, happily for him, could not hear a word she said.

Perhaps the grandest diplomat, in a theatrical sense, was Count Arthur Cassini, a seasoned Russian professional who had served with distinction in China. He rented from Alexander Graham Bell a Queen Anne house on Rhode Island Avenue, near its junction with Massachusetts Avenue, with pointed tower, steep roofs, and a scattering of stained-glass windows over its red brick, and there held court. It was a house of a type that could have been found in most any American city, but under Cassini's occupancy it became a choice place of fine dinners and intimate, small gatherings around his samovar.

The family situation with Cassini was one of those curious entanglements accepted in diplomatic circles but, ten steps away from an embassy doorway, in

Salon, Austria-Hungary Embassy, 1905, by Frances Benjamin Johnston. *Library of Congress, Prints and Photos Division.*

Washington or anywhere else in the United States, never would have been understood. Ambassador Cassini's sixteen-year-old daughter, Marguerite, was his hostess. Her mother posed as her nurse. Being a woman not of Cassini's class, the mother had no status with the czar, who had refused to approve the marriage. The morganatic marriage of the count was known in the foreign office in St. Petersburg and was no secret in the diplomatic community in Washington. A little make-believe was not alien to diplomatic life, so Marguerite was given the rank of an ambassador's wife at all official functions; her "widower uncle," being dean of the corps, pushed her status higher. Astonishment at the sight of the petite, bright-eyed girl taking the place of honor at her first dinner, above the other diplomatic women—to the utter rage of Baroness Hengelmüller—led to an avalanche of letters to the State Department the next day. But Marguerite's presence as hostess was all perfectly proper, no matter what the baroness might otherwise demand.[32]

The work of the diplomats covered the world. They existed a bit above the earth, moving in a sense in their own strata. Even Secretary Hay was philosophically apart from the lawmakers; he was the first secretary of state with a worldview and thus light-years distant from the opinion in Congress and surely more mature in his intellectual awareness than the president. By its customs and structures, the U.S. Foreign Service was different from those of other countries. While some diplomats believed that an American diplomatic profession would raise the bar in the diplomatic interaction between the United States and foreign governments, the American ambassador George von Lengerke Meyer strongly disagreed: "If we had men in the service permanently, many of them would become un-American, due to the modes and habits of life [abroad] being so absolutely different from ours. Our diplomats would also get out of touch with American ideas and sentiment, as we progress so much more rapidly at home [than they do in Europe], and our objects and aims in life are so very different."[33]

President Roosevelt, fresh from a diplomatic triumph of his own in the Russo-Japanese peace agreement, wrote in 1905, "I do not believe that as things are now in the world, any nation can rely upon inoffensiveness for safety. Neither do I believe that it can rely upon alliances with any other nation for safety. My object is to keep America in trim, so that fighting her shall be too expensive and dangerous a task to likely be undertaken by anybody; and I shall try at the same time to make her act in a spirit of such justice and good-will toward others as will prevent anyone taking such a risk lightly, and will, if possible, help a little toward a general attitude of peacefulness and righteousness in the world at large."[34] Notwithstanding the president's rather personal view, the diplomats continued to carry the greater burden of maintaining world peace.

SIX
Progress in Marble

The international capital of builders' dreams was eventually to take material form in monumental public architecture, but by 1903 the evidence was slight. Most of the buildings planned were either not started or not completed. Those underway were not a part of the McMillan Plan but were certainly inspired by it. Union Station, the proudest example, was the result not of the master plan but of the outgrowth of brilliant ideas by Burnham, fitted into a puzzle of particular circumstances that only a capital can present.

Nevertheless, Burnham's and McKim's satisfaction with the results in Washington could hardly be exaggerated. The panic of 1893, which had ravaged that decade, seemed a distant history in the prosperous third year of the twentieth century. The white marble Department of Agriculture Building, a milestone inspired by the 1893 World's Fair, was to be far outstripped in its style by the new Smithsonian Institution Building, the exquisite national museum, awaiting groundbreaking in the spring of 1904. Its drawings projected a low, elegant dome, smooth granite walls, and a lofty basilican rotunda exploding beyond a stately colonnaded facade, all of which not only epitomized the buildings projected by the McMillan Plan but also were the classical antithesis of the ruddy Gothic Castle that faced it across the Mall.

Well ahead of the Smithsonian museum, Daniel Burnham was under way building Union Station already by the close of the summer of 1903. It still seemed impossible to those who knew the slow-moving cranks and gears of political Washington that any project so politically complex could actually have happened as quickly, Burnham's noted genius notwithstanding. Mule-drawn wagons hauled loads of fill dirt for lifting the grade, a scene like the one observed for many years on the western end of the Mall. The station's location seemed off and away from things, down the hill north of the Capitol and the Library of Congress. Laborers with shovels and mule-drawn wagons, then small trolleys on tracks, dug tunnels that would admit trains coming into the international city from all directions, from New York, Chicago, New Orleans, Nashville, and Los Angeles.

New neoclassical Smithsonian Institution Building on the Mall, completed 1911. *Smithsonian Institution Library.*

Burnham remained close to his basic design while continuing his sketching with soft lead pencil, devising refinements. He kept his political contacts close, to assure that his project did not get into the wrong hands, which meant to him the Army Corps of Engineers. He knew they considered him and McKim and the rest usurpers. And they were not, as Burnham knew well, entirely off the mark.

As the steel frame established Union Station's outline, the architect was confirmed in his wish that the station be white, like the buildings of the Chicago World's Fair, except sheathed in stone, not plaster. Georgia marble was the material that came first to mind, but Burnham hesitated. It was a highly sculptural marble, pure in color, indeed somewhat translucent in its creamy whiteness, but for this building the faintly yellow warmth of Georgia marble was not right. He wanted something harder, with the colder cast of blue. At last, when the perfect stone was found, obtaining it presented problems. A family quarry in Vermont yielded just the right white granite, with just the right hint of blue, but the owner, in mournful tribute to a son tragically lost, permitted only tombstones to be made from his quarry. Characteristically, Burnham went in person to meet the quarrier. No amount of coaxing, no words of patriotism or compassion, could move the disconsolate father to open up for Union Station. Burnham stood firm in what he wanted. Only after the quarryman later died was the way cleared with his heirs for Union Station to be faced with the granite Burnham desired.[1]

Burnham's splendid Union Station, 1908, with its Columbian Circle forecourt, as completed 1912.
U.S. Commission of Fine Arts, Washington, D.C.

The meddling of individuals within the Congress nearly cost Burnham the site
at one point. With Senator McMillan gone, the architect was left struggling in quick-
sand without a powerful congressional advocate for the Union Station legislation.
Although McMillan's former secretary, Charles Moore, who had gone into banking,
had lost his secure political base when the senator died, he had cultivated his past
connections and not for a moment turned from his support of the City Beautiful
movement. Burnham relied on him as protector and guide at the Capitol. A shrewd
Moore was far from faint-hearted; he took on battles neither Burnham, nor McKim,
nor Olmsted, nor any of the other designers of the City Beautiful had the brass ever to
attempt. The razor edge of Moore's rhetoric sometimes angered seasoned politicians.
Yet in the last count Moore had a way of bringing them to his side, for they respected
him for past associations and trusted his integrity.

Speaker Joseph Cannon was one who believed that Union Station was a bad deal for
the government, declaring that the citizens spent too much and the railroads spent too
little. Burnham heard his and all the other complaints. Even those who favored Union
Station were sometimes a threat with their myriad ideas for how they might improve the
plan. For example, an idea that gained currency in the political community was that statuary of some sort representing American heroes would be obtained for the new station.
Fearing what he had seen of government taste, Burnham struck quickly in settling the
sculpture program by awarding artists' contracts to people he trusted. This quick move
and others of the sort bypassed the dangers posed by those who would violate his plan.[2]

Burnham's railroad station, when completed in 1908, seemed to scorn old, red-
brick Washington, which was still all too visible from it. The white blocks that made

the station walls were luminescent any time of the day; sunlight made them brilliant, as did the electric lights at night. Even moonlight gave them an unearthly magic. The central five-part "city gate" was modeled after the ancient Arch of Constantine, in Rome, but Burnham had stretched the facade horizontally and surmounted it with statues representing the "Progress of Railroading," in allegories of mechanics, electricity, fire, freedom, and imagination, all served by inscriptions cut into the marble from text by Harvard's venerable president Charles W. Eliot. On the interior the soaring aches and vaults, the statuary, and the watery greenish glass in the clerestories were a modern interpretation of ancient Baths of Caracalla, in Rome, and rendered in blocks of white marble and Rafael Guastavino's white tiles. Light played as dramatically in the grand inside spaces as it did on the exterior. Beauty in architecture as interpreted in the Beaux-Arts manner was rarely closer to perfection than in Burnham's Union Station.

A formal forecourt was designed by Burnham after the completion of the station itself. It was envisioned as a generous ceremonial place of arrival and departure that would enhance the station's grand marble facade while minimizing the raw effect that might have resulted otherwise from the sprawl of pavements approaching it. Congress funded the forecourt willingly, and Burnham chose the Chicago sculptor Lorado Taft in commissioning a full-size white marble statue of Christopher Columbus clutching his charts of the Ocean Sea, windblown on the bow of the Santa Maria. It symbolized the first spirit of the westward movement of European civilization, taken up centuries later by the American people.

~

Another great, unexpected public building project seemed to fall from the sky into the hands of the architects. Whether by accident or pure luck, McKim was invited to appear before a committee of army officials in 1902 while he was in town looking over the White House remodeling. The generals showed him campus plans they had developed for the Army War College; they were not comfortable with what they had produced on their own. Emerged from the experiences of the Civil War and during the forty years since, the army had developed an educational system for officers, which was now respected the world over. With enthusiastic support from Congress and President Roosevelt, the army wanted to build a permanent campus that was functional but also proclaimed the greatness of its schooling.

McKim studied the plan and redefined its zones to suggest ceremonial areas while taking advantage of a beautiful river view. The generals knew they had their man and gave him the project. McKim spooned the campus carefully into the McMillan Plan, which had provided no war college. He walked the site, making notes and sketches to take back to the drafting rooms of McKim, Mead & White, in New York. At the cornerstone ceremony in 1903 probably half of Washington stood in attendance as President Roosevelt delivered the dedicatory address. The site was a sprawling plain along the

Potomac River, where the federal prison had stood. McKim had designed a city within the city, reflecting the army's requirements for barracks, office structures, classrooms, a parade, and a row of substantial red-brick houses for the officers. Orderly, tree-lined streets organized the site, which was climaxed by the monumental main building, which McKim placed on an inspiring rise of earth where the Anacostia River poured into the Potomac. His scheme for the main building was neoclassical, of course, and massive in scale, boldly proclaiming its purpose as a school of war.[3]

Executed in red brick and trimmed in limestone, the main building was massive without being heavy, light in the manner of some eighteenth-century English buildings built of brick. It faced the parade ground, with the rivers to its back. A dramatic central block was crowned with a shallow imitation of the ancient dome on the Pantheon, in Rome, thus a link to the new Smithsonian on the Mall. From the central section with its lofty ceremonial spaces, long wings to the sides, designed wholly for function, housed stacks of lecture halls and classrooms opening off long corridors. McKim made an effort to give the building the lanternlike lightness of the 1798 Boston Statehouse, only not so vertical. This he did by reducing the dimensions front and back and receding the uppermost story from the plane of the walls below. This centerpiece of the U.S. Army War College was then and still remains one of Washington's most successful public buildings.

As the new capital experienced physical changes, Roosevelt, a most unusual president, proved less successful with Congress than he was with the diplomats. The biggest changes in politics during this time were in reaction to the president. Roosevelt's was a difficult journey. He lacked the patience of a Burnham and at times wavered in his focus, which Burnham never did. Some of his most effective enemies were in Congress, because he never really understood how to cultivate support within the carefully joined framework, yet was often boisterously chopping at it with flamboyant language that annoyed the lawmakers. The president's attacks upon great wealth were delivered with emotion, but a significant number in Congress believed that his arguments lacked basis and that his performance was merely another feature of the ongoing vaudeville with which he captured public favor.

Congress remained uncertain about the international United States that Roosevelt spoke about so frequently. Neither he nor McKinley had been able to assure a large part of Congress that America was on the right track in her world outreach. For all their doubts, however, the two chambers of the legislature gave fairly constant support to the arrangements and treaties that buoyed the United States as a world power. Congress, like most of the citizens it represented, retained its age-old suspicion of the intentions of foreigners, especially diplomats.

By the basic tenets of the Constitution, the president was in charge of foreign relations but could make treaties only with the "advice and consent" of the Senate. Although the Congress took the most interest in the economic implications of foreign treaties, it seriously minded its power of advice and consent in all aspects of them, fully understanding that the first word was vague and the second implied final authority. Whether the head of state liked it or not, the nation's awakened presidency, in all the glory of power, always had Congress to contend with.

President McKinley had first addressed the forces of change that involved the United States with other countries. But with the nation's new position in the world, beginning with the Spanish-American War, international relations had become more complex than the United States had ever known. Roosevelt was sensitive to this and believed that closer communication with other countries was not only possible but also necessary. Senator Chauncey Depew was one who felt strongly that Americans needed a schooled, trained, professional foreign service, such as one found in Europe. But in the Congress he "found there was a very strong belief that the whole foreign service was an unnecessary expense." When Roosevelt became president, Depew brought the issue to him, and Roosevelt said, "This foreign business of the government, now that the [Atlantic] cable is perfected, can be carried on between our State Department and the chancellery of any government in the world. Nevertheless I am in favor of keeping up the diplomatic service. All the old nations have various methods of rewarding distinguished public servants. The only one we have is the diplomatic service. So when I appoint a man ambassador or minister, I believe that I am giving him a decoration, and the reason I change ambassadors and ministers is that I want as many as possible to possess it."[4] Roosevelt, then, stood somewhere between the congressional view and that of Senator Depew. It was feeble support indeed for what Depew believed was necessary.[5]

Roosevelt ran for president on his own in 1904, his first presidential campaign, and he counted upon the votes of the reformers or "progressives." Harry White wrote to the president from the American embassy in London, saying that Senator Henry Cabot Lodge, in England on a visit, told him that the election was in the bag for their friend. Roosevelt wrote back, "Do not take Cabot's over-sanguine view of matters. Nobody can tell how this fight will come out. I have been astonishingly successful in getting through the policies in which I believe, and am achieving results; but often the mere fact of having a good deal of a record is more against a man than for him, when the question is as to how people will vote; for my experience is that usually people are more apt to let their dislikes than their likings cause them to break away from their party ties in matters of voting."

"Politicians," he continued, "proverbially like a colorless candidate, and the very success of what I have done, the number of things I have accomplished, and the extent of my record, may prove to be against me. However, be that as it may, we have a big sum of achievement to our credit." In May he was ready for battle and wrote again to White: "I think there will be a lull before the actual campaign begins; then there will be no lull as far as I am concerned until it is over one way or another."[6]

After Roosevelt's overwhelming election and the festive beginning of his first full term as president on inauguration day March 4, 1905, he faced a hostile Congress. This was to remain the case until he left office in early March 1909. His worst troubles lay in his own fellow Republicans, who had believed since the Civil War forty years earlier that the party, not the president, should dictate policy. They wished to return to the relationship between Congress and the executive as it had been before the Spanish-American War. Roosevelt's presumptuous style—imperial and overbearing—did not fit the idea of the president as head of a corporation, the chief executive, answerable to Congress, the board of directors.

Republicans in Congress believed Congress was rightly the dominant branch of the three because it sprang directly from the grassroots ballot boxes. Yes, the president was elected by popular ballot, but not entirely, for the electoral college intervened. It had been the populist Joe Cannon, after all, who had helped McKinley create the new presidency through war powers assumed in 1898. This, Cannon said at the time, he was allowing as an emergency measure, but events carried it on, and he lived to see a permanent result in greatly increased presidential power. Having been reelected to the House in 1903, at the age of sixty-seven, Cannon represented the return to power of the old guard, who, in spite of Theodore Roosevelt, now dominated Congress again.

Heady with his power, the congressman was always on guard to have his way. Beneath the iron dome of the Capitol, Cannon had earned his crown with energy and perspicacity. Reigning as Speaker of the House, he was the most powerful man in the capital, next to the president, and sometimes even that distinction was subject to question. Cannon commuted by streetcar between the Capitol and the hotel where he lived with his wife of forty years, Mary Reed Cannon. He mingled in good spirits with people on the street but otherwise was not especially social. Sponsors feared he might not appear at the testimonial dinner given in his honor at the Arlington Hotel in 1906. A thousand paying guests had accepted the invitation; two hours passed and no Cannon. Drinks and sandwiches were passed around. And finally he was there, shaking hands and making jokes for the evening as though he was right on time.

After he became Speaker, Cannon perused the White House social schedule for the season. There was a reception for the Congress, a dinner for the Supreme Court, and one for the ambassadors. What about the Speaker of the House? The question was put to Roosevelt, who in 1905, obligingly, introduced the custom of a White House dinner honoring the Speaker. A young Douglas MacArthur, who was a social aide, recalled the Speaker's dinner. During the reception before it, Roosevelt, receiving in the Blue Room, asked that Cannon be brought to him. MacArthur went to the Speaker, who was telling one of his tales to a group gathered in the Red Room, and said with a flourish, "Mr. Speaker, the president will receive you now." Cannon snorted, "The hell he will," and, after due pause to savor the laughter, resumed his story.[7]

Both Cannon and Roosevelt carefully tailored their public characters, and no other two people seemed more opposite or had more opposite views of how an American government should be. Roosevelt was, for example, committed to building an ever more professional civil service, with life tenures for federal employees. He might point to a model bureaucrat like Alvey Adee, who had devoted his extraordinary mind and judgment to the well-being of his fellow citizens through public service; he might point to Bruce Cortelyou, who had graduated from presidential secretary to cabinet member. Cannon believed Roosevelt's civil service concept impractical, and he warned that it paved the way for an aristocracy of bureaucrats, like in Russia and France. In such a case Washington, he believed, would become a cave in which men could hibernate and do nothing yet thrive under the protection of the law.

He believed in the spoils system of old. It served as a routine cleansing of the government, indeed a purgative, as well as an affirmation of party loyalty. "The harvest of victory," he said, "is to be garnered in the Federal offices." Cannon believed in low taxes and a thrifty government; his contempt for the architects and their City Beautiful plan was perfectly in character. Roosevelt's big, participating government cost too much for him, taking money out of the citizens' pockets that they might better spend doing business of their own. Cannon's secretary wrote of him, "He was always a politician, always a partisan, and he felt no shame in being either, or deemed it required an apology."[8]

In recalling his tug-of-war with the White House during his speakership from 1905 to 1907, Cannon observed that Roosevelt had emerged from the convention and election of 1904 as the "dictator" of the Republican Party. Everyone had pushed behind him to make the Republican victory a landslide; every Republican knew that without Roosevelt the presidency might have been lost to the party. However, neither Democrats nor Republicans had much confidence in Roosevelt's knowledge or experience. His first administration seemed to confirm their doubts about his ability in key aspects of the job of president. "Economics, figures, statistics, schedules, a glance-sheet, all those things meant nothing to him," wrote Cannon. "They made no appeal to him—they seemed to him dull and sordid things. A curious thing considering that Roosevelt was a man of powerful imagination, and to a man of vivid fancy one would think the romance of business, which has been the inspiration behind all our marvelous achievements, would stir his pulses."

Cannon continued, describing what did move Roosevelt: "When he recalled the pioneer battling the elements and the Indian, he glowed with pride at the recollections of the heroes of civilization over mountain and plain and who could rely only on their own courage and resources to ward off death and suffering. . . . To Mr. Roosevelt, I think, the pioneer, the hunter, the trapper, the soldier were heroic figures almost heroes of mythology, while the business man he pictured safe and secure from attack who thought only of his profits and was indifferent to the onward sweep of civilization. I think, if the truth be known, Mr. Roosevelt rather despised trade and failed to understand that without commerce there could have been no civilization."[9]

In a sense, Cannon understood Roosevelt better than one might think, but what he said about Roosevelt points also to what he did not perceive about his own era, which Roosevelt represented well. Idealism was in the air. Call the people of the time the children of an age of innocence, or naive, or victims of American isolation, whatever may fit, but romantic idealism permeated the American psyche. It was romanticism that inspired the Chicago World's Fair, the murals of such painters as Violet Oakley crowding the walls of new public buildings, showing adventurers and pathfinders in bluish hazes and setting suns; romanticism met with popular acclaim in literature, music, art, and, to Cannon's distain, political philosophy, where it fueled such movements as socialism, expressed in a formidable political party. As for Theodore Roosevelt, he too whiffed the age but was practical at his core and a solver of problems, well able to step aside from ideals. Cannon was reluctant to acknowledge that characteristic.

Thus, while the nation looked to the broader world, at the core of politics, new ideals moved forward with difficulty alongside conservative economics and historical concepts of practical government and democracy. The past was not easy to give up. Yet as white stone appeared among the old red brick and trees fell to open space, the new progressive ideas of a younger generation began to burrow more and more effectively into the system so long dominated by the generation that had won the Civil War. That victory for the Union was separated from Roosevelt's 1904 reelection by only thirty-nine years and was still cherished in memory by Americans.

To the great surprise of adherents of the City Beautiful, Congress all of a sudden joined the movement. While Joe Cannon would never have granted that Congress had approved the McMillan Plan, or even part of it, in 1905 the legislators authorized major improvements on Capitol Hill, in the construction of office annex structures. Even Speaker Cannon was enthusiastic. Both chambers of Congress suffered from overcrowded offices in the Capitol, a situation that became intolerable with the increasing number of members and the ever-larger volume of work. On the recommendation of McKim, Mead & White, Congress commissioned the New York architectural firm Carrere & Hastings to design the new offices. Having previously done residential work in Washington, John Mervin Carrere and Thomas Hastings became the first of a younger generation of architects not associated significantly with the 1893 World's Fair to design public buildings in the capital.

While Carrere & Hastings worked in various historically based idioms—notably, the romantically Spanish Ponce de Leon Hotel in St. Augustine, Florida—their great affection, and especially that of Carrere, was for the neoclassicism of seventeenth- and eighteenth-century France. They had borrowed handsomely from this treatment of neoclassicism in 1897 in their winning design for the New York Public Library, which bested that of their mentors, McKim, Mead & White, among other competitors. The building committees of House and Senate requested that they use the same French style for the office buildings.

Although the congressional buildings needed to signify a powerful presence, it was important that they remain secondary in scale to the Capitol. The architects selected an actual model for the offices: the Garde Mueble, the great pair of furniture warehouses built in the time of Louis XV on the Place de la Concorde, in Paris. These eighteenth-century structures had inspired the Department of Agriculture Building. For the new housing of Congress, the adaptation of the French model was subtler and closer to the proportions of the original French buildings. When the office plans were laid before Congress, the two buildings, quite similar to each other but each magnificent in its own right, did not intrude upon the great domed symbol that stood on its sprawl of lawn in between them.

Constructed with exterior walls of Vermont marble, the office buildings stood across the avenues flanking the Capitol. Toward the Capitol, they presented long colonnades mounted on arcades and rising to roofs ringed by balustrades. The singleness of material, sharpness of detail, and restraint of ornament were so successful in the buildings as to capture worldly monumentality appropriate to the nation, yet a practicality of purpose as well.

In the space inside the House and Senate office buildings, more liberty was taken with design. To study the architectural richness of the interiors even today is to marvel that the thrifty Congress approved them. The long corridors extended from grand marble rotundas, the Senate's main one patterned on the royal chapel at Versailles. Marble staircases rose to important meeting or caucus rooms, each heroically dressed in marble columns and rococo decorations in cast plaster. Landscaped courtyards pierced the volume of the structures, allowing light into the rooms that faced inward. The architectural impression of the buildings was distinctly urban. In their essentials, the buildings were practical in that the restrained neoclassical French architecture simply provided a vessel of external importance to hundreds of rooms separated by relatively simple corridors. The House building on the south would one day carry Joe Cannon's name, the Cannon House Office Building, and thirty years later the other would be named the Richard Brevard Russell Jr. Senate Office Building.

This architectural project of the Congress took less construction time than any other project of the era except the War College, for over its own works, Congress does not tarry. Three years elapsed between groundbreaking and the occupation of the buildings. The dazzling white offices flanking the Capitol made an interesting juxtaposition to the Library of Congress, still one of the most admired buildings in the nation. To the practiced eye the library, with its florid detailing, seemed a gray phantom from another time, even though its completion was separated from that of the new House and Senate office buildings by only eleven years.

~

The embellishment of the international capital was not entirely in the hands of architects and engineers, or congressmen and senators, or even men in general. In Washington there was a determined woman of means who took a piece of the challenge for herself. Mary Foote Henderson was experienced in politics—the daughter of a U.S. senator and the wife of another—and she was good at getting what she wanted.

Her husband, former senator John B. Henderson, was close at hand. His place in history was established early, in his authorship of the Thirteenth Amendment to the Constitution, which abolished slavery, and his vote, one of seven in the Senate, that saved President Andrew Johnson from an impeachment conviction. One month before the latter episode, which ended his political career, he had married Mary Foote. The couple lived in St. Louis for twenty years, where he made a fortune in several smart endeavors, then decided to return to Washington. On a steep hill outside the settled part of town they built a massive stone house, an improbable castle with towers, battlements, and a front porch. They called it Boundary Castle, after its location on the northeast boundary of the District of Columbia. The byway of rutted dirt that ran beside it was an extension of Sixteenth Street, linking Boundary Castle to the White House, a bit more than a mile to the south. Most people knew the rambling pile as Henderson Castle, for the Hendersons easily became fixtures in Washington social life, particularly among the diplomats, who loved to gather around their abundant, albeit dry, dining table.

An early and devoted worker for women's right to vote and the prohibition of alcohol, Mary Henderson had from youth used her social and political connections to further those causes. Senator Henderson, who by 1900 was seventy-four and in weakened health, had withdrawn from most public activities, but his wife remained out there in full force. Just about the time of the Spanish-American War (although the date is not certain), Mary Henderson became enthralled with the idea of a new, international United States then taking shape. The dream of a world-class Washington thrilled her. About the time that Colonel Bingham and Glenn Brown began rolling up their sleeves for battle, she cast upon the scene her own independent idea of how America's world status might be reflected in some key additions to its capital.

She quite agreed with Bingham that the White House, if historic, was outdated and inadequate for McKinley's elevated presidency. To make it a museum seemed wise. Working with the architect Paul J. Pelz, whose plan for the Library of Congress had been usurped by the Army Corps of Engineers, Mary Henderson conceived a plan for developing the large farm acreage around Boundary Castle, linking it to the city by way of a much improved Sixteenth Street. This street would be named the Avenue of the Presidents. At the northern terminus was the elevation known as Meridian

Hill; at the southern end the avenue was to terminate at Lafayette Park and the White House. But at the north end there was to be a new residence for the president, a palace with colonnades, terraces, and gardens, built at the top of Meridian Hill, straddling the Avenue of the Presidents. From this monumental palace the avenue would extend south, and embassies would be built alongside, beyond the rows of clipped trees. She had seen this sort of ceremonial planning in the capitals of Europe. It was how she thought a world capital should be.[10]

Invigorated by the nation's new international position, she made her appeal to the diplomats, congressmen, and senators at her dinner table. Who was to say no? Although she may have been feminist beyond a doubt, it was men she gathered 'round her, encouraging them to relax and have fun, all the while drawing on their power to help sell her plan. She bound printed plates of Paul Pelz's schematic drawings into folio books for selected distribution. A few of these survive, preserving her idea, which fit into the orderly McMillan Plan. Most of what her efforts obtained was polite encouragement. It is true that to please her, Congress renamed Sixteenth Street the "Avenue of the Presidents" as she wished, but the name was returned to the original after a year, because it was awkward to say, and its residents protested having to change their calling cards and stationery.

Mary Henderson had plenty of money, thanks to her personal inheritance and the questionable fortune Senator Henderson had made in St. Louis, notably from collecting devalued wartime county and city bonds and obtaining a court judgment requiring the state to fund the bonds at face value. At sixty Mrs. Henderson still had the pep of a younger woman, an attribute she credited to abstinence from not only alcohol but also coffee and tea and to adherence to a strict vegetarian diet. Putting her energy to work for her plan, she began building big houses along Sixteenth Street for the purpose of renting them to embassies. The ambassadors and ministers, most of whom were still crowded into houses too small, were delighted to move from the dour brick houses into something that reminded them of official living in Europe. Before Mrs. Henderson was finished, she had handsomely housed the representatives of Cuba, Spain, Poland, France, Italy, and Mexico. Together, her "palaces" on Sixteenth Street, following the historical European architectural styles, contributed to an "embassy row," an element of a world-class capital not articulated in the McMillan Plan.

~

In the larger picture of the new capital, the proposed cityscape was still very slow in being finalized, even in design, notwithstanding the flurry of building in the first decade of the twentieth century. The development of the McMillan Plan remained in a sense a dream, resting in the Senate Parks Commission, an outgrowth of Senator McMillan's original committee. At the Parks Commission's behest, proposals were continually entertained to move the grand plan forward. Charles Moore was behind most of these. Giant public buildings were rendered in watercolor, an amusement center with playgrounds, a public bath and gymnasium, office blocks for thousands of federal employees, all screened in neoclassical sheathing, columned and pedimented, balustraded and terraced. The gifted brush of Jules Guerin translated into sublime paintings the architects' concepts for formal avenues of trees, fountains, and lawns; drawings of stone pavements and reflection pools suggested enhancement for the starkly simple Washington Monument.[11]

Studies were made, and committees met to plan memorials, the main one being that to Lincoln, which would terminate the west end of the Mall and complete the symbolic trio, joining the Capitol and the Washington Monument. John Hay had headed a committee planning a memorial to Thomas Jefferson. Drawings were made—sketches really—but Hay's death cooled the interest to carry the project through. Jefferson's monument was laid aside, not to be revived for thirty years.

Yet for all its promise of a spectacular open sweep, the Mall, central to the grand plan, remained a grove of trees, the winding drives in place and maintained as though they would always be. Only at certain points on the Mall could one discern the Capitol dome through the trees, although at a greater distance it was visible from nearly everywhere. The Mall was more a forest than an open stretch one might call a mall. The public did not like seeing trees cut, especially the old trees, and if challenged could make warm public protests. This attitude made planners cautious in their advance, but a greater fear was of spending too much money—or of having the appearance of spending too much—and angering Congress. Burnham had doubtless hoped the plan would be well along to completion in his lifetime. McKim had wished the same, but their clocks were running faster than that of the City Beautiful movement.

Except for the few new buildings, ceremonial Washington looked just about the same as it had before the City Beautiful movement began. The engineers carefully fenced construction sites while keeping the grounds elsewhere in perfect order. Even the existing railroad stations looked as they always had. Tourists wandered in the Baltimore & Potomac Railroad depot to see the spot where Garfield had been shot, where he fell onto the tile floor. As the new city started to take some form, the times seemed to outpace it. For example, the McMillan Plan had made no provision for automobiles, although by 1905 automobiles were everywhere, rolling uncomfortably over old carriage drives but tempted to speed on the smooth pavement of Constitution Avenue. Sporting citizens took their machines to a roadway around the Tidal Basin, then nicknamed the Speedway, to see what they could do.

In contrast to the gentle movement of public change was the busy hustle of private building. Those individuals changing the capital the most visibly during Theodore Roosevelt's administration were private businessmen. Given an increasing and affluent population, Washington had become a prime field for development, resulting in a building boom. Improvements unmistakably American in character began to fill vacant lots along the streets and avenues. The jump in private investment brought new office structures, theaters, hotels, and most of all apartment buildings. The apartments eventually would replace most of the boardinghouses. As more people needed to be near the government for their own purposes, and the government payroll grew, the apartments became a feature of capital life. Some were simple, while others featured full-service dining rooms, ballrooms, and comfortable living space rented in many different sizes. Servants' quarters were not uncommon in the more ambitious apartments.

Connecticut Avenue and K Street were the most notable of the early fine apartment districts. But apartment buildings of every quality were likely to be built nearly anywhere in the city.[12] Residents of the capital were generally suspicious of the apartment structures, seeing them, first, as intrusions and, second, as perhaps appealing to a sleazy class of profiteers. Washington had always had those types, but they had stayed in hotels and left after Congress adjourned. When the developers took an interest in building flats on Mary Henderson's Sixteenth Street, she issued a protest that brought action and kept them out. No apartment house was going to pollute her Avenue of the Presidents.

Another boom in buildings was in large private houses, indeed some of them palatial. The diplomats' gloss and the shine of official society had combined already in the 1890s to attract winter residents from all over the country, to set themselves up well, put out their silver trays, and wait for the calling cards to appear. By the turn of the century, during the Washington season, the city's social life, as it pertained to society, took on the ceremonial sham of court life in a European capital. The presence of the winter residents each year was felt all at once in early December with the appearance of fine horses and carriages, visions of busy servants dusting and polishing behind tall windows, and new crops of fine houses, seemingly built overnight.

Principal among these residential streets was Massachusetts Avenue, a long, diagonal artery that extended northwest from the Capitol, passing beyond the White House neighborhood into new territory. The avenue climaxed about two miles away at Dupont Circle, which in 1900 was considered quite a distance away from the center of town. Farms with dairies and vegetable gardens were within easy walking distance, and forests touched the edges of the avenue.

Although the avenue was a remote place, it was soon to be lined with grand houses. It had been notable early on for two such houses, the largest being Stewart's Castle, rented to the Chinese legation at the time of the Spanish-American War but a vacant lot by 1901, the structure demolished mostly because it was too costly to heat. The other house was two long blocks away, a big red edifice associated with its most famous occupant, James G. Blaine, former presidential candidate and secretary of state under two administrations. This Victorian pile, frosted over with intricate wooden embellishments, was of a type that had delighted house builders in the times of General Grant and Rutherford B. Hayes. Although it was out of style and not especially remarkable to begin with, in Washington it had cachet. George Westinghouse purchased it in 1891 for an alternative to his residences in Lennox, Massachusetts, and his permanent home in Pittsburgh. From this auspicious, if gloomy, seat overlooking Dupont Circle, the inventor and electricity magnate who built the great generators that lit the Chicago World's Fair kept an eye on Congress, in which he wielded power.

Dupont Circle had secured its name in the late 1880s when Congress permitted the erection of a statue of Rear Admiral Samuel Francis Du Pont, whose stellar Civil War career had been clouded by a failed attack on Charleston. Before Admiral Du Pont was stood up on his tall pedestal, the surrounding had been called Pacific Circle; the name Dupont Circle was adopted almost immediately. The admiral, cast in heavy bronze, surveyed many vacant lots. Back toward the center of town, Massachusetts Avenue passed between a dozen or so large houses on it or adjacent streets, all versions of Washington's red-brick residential vernacular blown up big, their brick walls composed of various shades of red-rose to red-orange, the largest of the houses being at least four stories. They were so tall as to seem ready to topple over into the street. For the most part they had been built in the 1880s, several as Washington residences for rich senators, and until 1905 the Spanish Embassy also numbered among them.

Those occupied part-time were originally only a few, but that would change with the floodtide of "winter people." Among the permanent residences, for example, was the hulking brick house that had been built in the 1880s, a block west of the circle, and willed by the Irish-born widow Anastasia Patten to her five daughters, Mary, Augusta, Josephine, Edythe, and Helen. With sweat and grit, their father had reaped a fortune in the gold fields of California and Nevada, which he and Mrs. Patten had managed well, leaving the girls rich. Augusta left the nest when she married a man her sisters despised. The second and last adventurer, Edythe, went out into the world to marry but soon returned a widow. The Patten sisters staked a claim on the emerging Washington society as few other permanent residents were able to do, considering themselves several rungs above nearly everybody else. The new winter residents, who knew the world elsewhere, found the Patten sisters charmingly provincial and learned that they had to be contended with. From their rugged house, the sisters judged all they saw, never keeping secret their disapproval of unacceptable performances in those who passed before their doorstep.

Interspersed with these houses and many more vacant lots were a few churches and some old-fashioned cottages tucked away beneath shade trees. In the other direction from Admiral Du Pont's statue, heading northwest and around what was to be called Sheridan Circle, were woods all the way to the Naval Observatory and beyond. Even a walk out that way took effort, not a foot of it paved. For Edith Roosevelt it was a favorite path of escape. With a few friends, baskets on their arms to collect plants and flowers, she was driven from the White House out beyond Dupont Circle and rambled on foot over the wooded paths in fall and spring, dreaming that she was light years away from the burden of public responsibility.[13]

SEVEN
Business and Friendship

The working heart of American diplomacy remained in a line of rooms in the State, War, and Navy Building. No matter the anathema it was to the architects of the new Washington, the powerful granite structure was held in affectionate regard by those who pursued their careers in it. To pass inside beyond the heavy doors was to be captured in a majestic unity of design and materials. Over the marble checkerboards of its floors, beneath the richly frescoed ceilings, the eighty-seven officials of the State Department worked every day, fully occupying three floors of the south wing, five days a week, seven if called upon.

On Tuesdays and special occasions the foreign diplomats stationed in Washington came, when necessary, to interact with the U.S. State Department staff. Hay's office, number 208, ringed by tall, carved bookcases and crowned by painted clouds, was only a door away from Alvey Adee's and a few doors from the great State Reception Room, numbers 212–214, where Hay received the diplomats. In its time, the huge saloon was called the finest room in Washington, rivaled only by the Cash Room in the Treasury Building, at the other end of the block, and by the ballroom at the British Embassy. The secretary of state met here with the representatives of kings, a splendor not overlooked by Americans privileged to tour the room when it was not in use.

Unlike ordinary federal offices, the Department of State did not slow down between administrations. State's work never stopped; involved as it was in the business of treaties and negotiations of every kind, it could never simply stand still and await the political appointee who would appear as its secretary. In an interim of any kind, when the office of secretary was empty or the secretary was away, an assistant secretary moved up. Secretaries of state never left the country on diplomatic business as they later would, but they did leave for vacations and speaking tours. The surrogate might be the second secretary, also a political appointee, but the role was more likely to be filled by the third secretary, a career man who knew the ropes. This was Alvey Adee, and it was nearly always Adee who pinch-hit in the absence of the secretary. He was the continuity of that whole department of the executive branch of government.

John Hay photographed in his State Department office by Henry Adams, 1902. *Massachusetts Historical Society, Boston.*

Beginning in 1903 he was "acting secretary of state" in the ever more frequent absence of Secretary Hay.

Adee was at his best as a second in command. Although he made many important decisions that often seem to have been accepted, in fact he only suggested the choices he made, and he did not hold responsibility for them outside the office. His assistance to John Hay seems to have been an exception to this part of the time. Hay, who was more often absent than not from 1901 to 1905, trusted Adee as a nearly life-long friend, so did not object to Adee's making decisions without him. During Hay's illness, Adee had more control and more of a presence in the State Department than he had ever known before. His physical stamina was seemingly boundless. But he demanded his summer trip to Europe, which must have helped him recover at times from near exhaustion.

Adee was a sound decision maker but always working with details, some of which could have been handled by others. His manner of doing business was naturally unusual, given his severe hearing difficulty. Those who worked closely with him had to learn how to communicate with him his way. Some claimed if they talked very plainly, separating their words, keeping the tone down, he could hear perfectly well. This was only imagined. His collapsible ear trumpet might have suggested a slight ability to hear, but he used it more as a baton when giving orders or for effect when he slammed it shut loudly to terminate a conversation or presentation. He himself was not able to hear the high, shrill voice he had taught himself as a child, so he spoke as little as possible. The vast paper archives of the Department of State are flaked with scraps upon which he wrote his orders in long-forgotten moments. In his world of silence he had developed a remarkable ability to read the lip movements and physical stances of others, and in that sense he was not encumbered at all by deafness. At times his being silent transcended necessity and gave him a certain useful distance from others, when it was advantageous.

John Hay's general health weakened when he was in his midfifties, and he would no longer experience the familiar rally from his illnesses that he had known over the years. Unlike some men who suffer repeated sickness, Hay never seemed less than healthy, but from time to time he lay bedridden, under Clara's ministrations while recovering from some malady or another. By his second year as secretary of state, Hay's heartbeat became irregular. Through the first few years of the twentieth century he held his own, but in 1902 there was no mistaking that he was a sick man. He drew ever closer to Adee. "I am rather good for nothing," he wrote to Adee that summer, "and should be altogether wretched if it were not for the comfort I take in your being on deck."[1] Already four years before, he had written to Clara Hay: "Dear old Adee comes fluttering around twenty times a day at the Department to see that I don't overwork or to tell me a new joke he thought of, but with that exception I know nothing of human companionship."[2] Nothing else had much changed, but he was weaker and worse off than ever before.

Hay's physical state offered no protection from the severe depression that tormented him following the death of his twenty-three-year-old son. Delbert Hay had grown from an unpromising boyhood to stellar postgraduate achievement in the diplomatic service. Following an early, distinguished career in British South Africa and London, Del returned to America in the summer of 1901 to work under Bruce Cortelyou on McKinley's staff. While attending commencement at Yale, he climbed out on a dorm windowsill for a smoke late at night and slipped to his death on the pavement below. "I do not know yet whether I shall get through it or not," an emotional John Hay wrote to Henry Adams. "I am not making any progress. I am waiting to see if my nerves will stand the strain."[3]

Hay was never able to absorb Del's death. "I have hideous forebodings," he wrote. "I have been extraordinarily happy all my life. Good luck has pursued me like my shadow. Now it is gone—it seems forever."[4] Clara Hay, always the stronger of the two emotionally, guided his thoughts to a measure of peace—Hay's loss being hers, too—but Hay's physical health declined rapidly. All of a sudden, at sixty-four, John Hay was an old man.

At the office Adee assumed more and more of Hay's duties. Although the telephone increased expediency in the office, it was of no use to Adee. Letters and notes track his frequent contact with Hay, most of them handwritten, even though Adee was a proponent of the typewriter. When summer came, the letters between Washington and Hay's New Hampshire farm were frequent. "The president kindly excused me from meeting him at the station," Adee wrote, happy to avoid the ceremony of Roosevelt's return from Sagamore Hill. "To tell the truth, I dreaded to be put in the forefront of the reception as if I were Acting John Hay. People do not seem to comprehend that I am not representing you personally. . . . I am merely a designee to perform certain official acts you would do if present."[5] In response to Adee's apology for sending a note over Hay's signature, the secretary of state responded, "If it were not that I believe your judgment is better than mine in these things I should not be here."[6]

Hay attempted to resign. He had tried with McKinley; now he tried with Roosevelt, who, like McKinley, declined the request. Hay had no choice but to remain. He had periods of good health and bad. Traveling to Europe was regenerative, more of spirit than of body, for the scenes he loved to travel diverted his thoughts. Adee, ever the adviser on health, urged him over the years to go to the healthful springs that Europe provided: "The baths act like external champagne—the carbonic acid bites and tickles the skin as it does the tongue. The circulation is stimulated, the tired nerves wake up and the whole ganglionic system is put in the way of regaining strength but . . . *nature won't be hurried*. Do take more time. When you are through with the Nauheim course, go to Evian or Como or Vichy and take the needed month rest-cure."[7]

It was well known in the department that Adee was taking up the slack in business left by the secretary's long absences. Friendship between the two men simplified the process. In keeping each other informed, their letters were chatty, often joking even when conveying weighty business. Adee did not hesitate mixing diplomatic discussion with medicinal advice and encouragement to exercise, sometimes sounding urgent, as though he could not imagine another man's illness in the light of his own good health. In letters he tried to amuse Hay, to cheer him up and make him laugh. When Adee informed Hay he had bought a canoe, the implication was that the Hay might consider joining him for a ride. Both knew better. In September 1904, Adee wrote to Hay, who was in New Hampshire: "This has been a more irksome day than usual. It took me just one hour and 29 minutes to sign the mail, and I have been signing driblets ever since. A wave of careless imbecility seems to have passed through all the bureaux, and I think I must have made at least forty corrections."[8]

Adee had been called upon by Webb Hayes, the former president's son, a spirited man whom both Hay and Adee had known in earlier times as his father's secretary. After working in the White House, Webb Hayes made aggressive use of his Washington connections to build a fortune. "I had a pleasant interruption of twenty-five minutes from Webb C. Hayes," Adee wrote to Hay, "who has just gotten back from Korea and Manchuria. That young man should conduct his conversations with a phonograph. I tried to say something several times, but he cut me short at the third word, and went on like a rusty corn-sheller. It was like Mme de Stael's conversation with that remarkably intelligent and well informed deaf-mute. I did manage to get in one phrase. When he told me he had got through the lines disguised as a miner, I said, in a weary tone, 'But you have been a major.' 'Oh yes,' he replied, 'but my grade was lieutenant colonel.' Then I collapsed."[9]

Among the diplomats in the summer of 1904, tension was widespread as a result of Japan's building anger over Russia's arbitrary takeover of Manchuria two years earlier and the resulting control that Russia assumed over Port Arthur (Lushun), the Manchurian port on the Yellow Sea. These acts ignored the Open Door policy of 1899–1900, devised by Hay and drafted by Adee, in which the United States demanded that trade with China be open to all nations. The apparent appeal to fairness masked a primary interest in keeping American trade routes open. The British admiral Charles Beresford reviewed the policy and conveyed his government's unqualified approval. Britain had been calling for an "open door" policy between the powers and Japan for some time. Most of the other nations did not respond, thus registering no actual objection.[10]

When the United States took the Philippines in 1898, the nation's sudden presence in Asia gave it a voice of authority that had not existed before in that part of the world. British proponents of an open door treatment of China believed that America's advocacy would have the strongest impact because it had no history of exploitation in China, whereas the other powers, for the most part, did or, if not, at least looked upon China as a resource for the taking. But the Open Door policy attracted little notice from the other major powers until Russia, which had big ambitions for taking territory in Asia, began to challenge it.[11]

The stage was set for conflict. Russia's quest southward for an ice-free port that could connect to European Russia by the Trans-Siberian Railway was compelling. In 1903 Russia had been poised to cross the Yellow Sea to Korea to take control of that country. Japan's reaction thus had already begun in a significant military buildup. Diplomatic relations began to crumble. The State Department recoiled at Russia's defiance of the Open Door policy. Hay had already anticipated trouble in a personal letter written to Ambassador Harry White three years earlier: "The Chinese, as well as the Russians, seem to know that the strength of our position is entirely moral, and if the Russians are convinced that we will not fight for Manchuria—as I suppose we will not—and the Chinese are convinced that they have nothing but good to expect from us and nothing but a beating from Russia, the open hand will not be so convincing to the poor devils of chinks as the raised club. Still, we must do the best with the means at our disposition."[12]

The State Department's task was to use American influence to keep China neutral. Russia made this difficult by ignoring the "neutral ports" the Americans recognized as part of the Open Door. Ambassadors and ministers called at the State Department. Adee, having at last been moved up to second assistant secretary by Hay, met with them.[13] Count Cassini expressed Russia's position, which received no assurances in the American capital.

The Japanese ambassador Kogoro Takahira attempted to reassure Americans, through sessions with Adee, that matters were better than they seemed. Takahira— whom Adee called "tug-a-hair-out" in some of his letters to Hay—described mass evacuations from coastal areas of Manchuria to avoid the oncoming Russians. Wrote Adee, "Takahira whispered to me that so far as the open door policy was concerned the part to be evacuated [in October] appeared to cover about all the territory to which it was at present applicable."[14] As the meetings transpired, the Japanese government built a military machine greater and more modern than seemed possible in so short a time. In St. Petersburg, negotiations between the Japanese and the Russians failed ten times, and by February 5, 1904, when the Japanese diplomats prepared to return home, the Russians were clearly in conflict over what to do. By then Japan had decided to use force against the Russian invasion. On May 5, on the Yalu River, the border between China and Korea, Japan successfully fought the first battle in its history against a white nation. When the telegram arrived informing the U.S. State

Diplomats calling on John and Clara Hay, New Year's Day, 1899. *Newspaper clipping, Hay scrapbook, Library of Congress, Manuscripts Division.*

Department of the battle, the location on the Yalu River could not be found on the department's maps.

~

Hay was back in Washington in the fall of 1903 and brought resolution to an issue of long standing in American diplomacy. On November 3 that year, Panama revolted against its Colombian overlord. This was neither objectionable nor less than a happy surprise to Americans, who had determined in the Hay and Pauncefote Treaty that the canal to cut across Central America would be in Panama. Philippe Bunau-Varilla, mastermind of the revolution, came to Washington two weeks later and sat with Hay and Adee in the reception room at the State Department. Hay hurried the negotiations between the caudillo and administration officials over lunch, turning the preparation of the documents entirely over to Adee. The second assistant secretary had been working on drafts already for several years.[15] At 7:00 P.M. on November 18, 1903, Adee carried the treaty across Lafayette Park to Hay's house, where the secretary of state brought out a treasured memento, Abraham Lincoln's pen, and scratched his signature.

Crises at the State Department were always plentiful in the early years of the 1900s. Most of them were likely to be small aspects of large issues. The Russians presented repeated problems beyond their incursions into other areas of Asia. Anti-Semitism, long smoldering in eastern Europe, found bloody expression in mob attacks on the homes and businesses of Jews in the old town of Kishenev (then the capital of the Bessarabian province of the Russian Empire), where hundreds were wantonly wounded or even killed, dragged from their homes and slaughtered while the Russian police looked on, refusing to intervene. Press stories of the massacre incensed the American public somewhat, as had reports from Cuba some years before. Cries for intervention were accompanied by American Jews' proposals for sanctuaries to which the persecuted Russians might flee, among them Israel, the Holy Land, where an already large and growing population of Jewish exiles had moved in among the Arabs. There they envisioned a Jewish nation safe from persecution.

Further atrocities and discrimination against Jews in eastern Europe, notably Romania's

State Reception Room, Department of State, Washington, D.C., ca. 1900. *Author's collection.*

prohibition of Jews from citizenship, and the resulting American protests led to what Adee called the "Roumanian Jew instruction" in 1902. That summer while Hay was away, Adee wrote a document with that title. Extensively edited, it represented an effort to convince the powers that had signed the Berlin Treaty of 1878, which recognized Romanian independence, that they must honor Article 44, which made religious freedom a guarantee of citizenship. "When I drafted it," wrote Adee of the instruction, "I had in mind the next logical step, namely, an appeal to the Berlin signatories to see that the provisions of Article 44 are carried out in Rumania in purpose and spent as the framers intended it."[16]

"Now," he concluded, "the seven signatories of the Berlin treaty are: Great Britain, Germany, Austria-Hungary, France, Italy, Russia and Turkey. Of these Russia, Austria and France are openly anti-Semitic, Germany is virtually so. Turkey can hardly approve the Roumanian continuation of the Ottoman treatment of the indigenous non-mussulmans of her conquered province, for the only rationale of the Roumanian policy is the old Mohammedan doctrine that all infidels are aliens. . . . As for Italy, we need not look for support in that quarter. England alone remains in her normal splendid isolation as our sentimental ally."[17]

Hay's inclination was to issue a note—a request, comment, or opinion—to the foreign offices of other countries. As unobtrusive as the term implies, a note was an exchange between diplomats, a professional communication, a step intended toward mutual understanding. Through the 1890s notes had increasingly been sent out by the United States, most dramatically in the second administration of Cleveland. For the reasons Adee gave in the correspondence above, he wrote individual notes to the players instead of sending a "circular note" to each.

When it was made public, by nearly universal agreement the document was so striking in its humanity that the American secretary of state was hailed as something of a hero, not only by the Jewish community in the United States, but also by many other Americans who wished action to be taken to assure the well-being of the oppressed in eastern Europe. A petition of protest containing thousands of names was taken to the Russian Embassy and placed before Count Cassini. He rejected it on the spot. The sponsors carried the original, bound in a volume, a few blocks away to the State Department, where Hay received it graciously in the State Reception Room and ordered that it be preserved there as a "precious document of history."

By the late summer of 1904, Hay was very ill and with his family at the New Hampshire farm. Adee spent August 25, a hot and difficult day, at the office. That night he wrote to Hay: "The incredible is coming to pass. After defying all Chinese efforts to enforce neutrality . . . Russia now announces that she will no longer consider the Chinese government neutral." Adee added what seemed to him implicit in this: "Russia may be planning to seize a Chinese winter port and hold it with the Baltic fleet." Russia, which had been taking a terrible beating from Japan, declared in a note its intention to "regard the Chinese Empire, or at least part thereof, as being within the sphere of active hostilities" and, added Adee, to "treat the agreement to respect Chinese neutrality as a 'dead letter.'" What Russia's plans were was not clear. "Perhaps," wrote Adee, "she is counting on what she may be able to do next year or the year after, and contemplating the enlargement of Manchuria by the additions of a goodly slice of the Chinese coast, with harbors available in winter—Russia has the men and money to raise gigantic armies and carry on a land-war for years."[18]

The Japanese ambassador Takahira had called on Adee that day to say that unless a disarmament was agreed upon, Japan would take the Chinese situation into its own hands and drive the Russians out, occupying the ports for itself. Late in summer a Russian warship, *Lena*, cruised into San Francisco's harbor for repairs. Japanese ire over this was considerable, because the presence of the *Lena* brought into question American neutrality in the Russo-Japanese War. The combination of events, as reported to President Roosevelt by Adee, concerned the president. Now in the throes of campaigning for his first full term, Roosevelt nevertheless turned his attention to Asian issues. He wondered if diplomacy on his part might end the war between Japan and Russia. Adee knew Ambassador Takahira well, but Ambassador Cassini, heavily pressured from home about Russia's position, had issued public statements in Washington that made him persona non grata there. Disgraced at his St. Petersburg foreign office as well, he was known to be packing to leave Washington, the auction house wagons seen daily loading the furnishings of the embassy. The situation rose to a crisis in the summer of 1904.

Meanwhile, a new ambassador from France had arrived in 1901. Jules Jusserand was an elegant-looking man with a highly refined presence. He was every inch the diplomat. Intellectual and learned, Jusserand, at forty-eight years of age, was a well-established professional. Like Roosevelt and like Hay, he was also widely published in essays and monographs. His subjects were usually literary; he knew Roosevelt's books and those of Hay; Adee's critical works on Shakespeare were also familiar to him; and Adee, being himself a Shakespearean scholar of note, was aware of Juserrand's publications in French. In a sense Juserrand might be compared to both Hay and Adee. He was too soft spoken to become very close to Roosevelt, although they had a warm friendship nonetheless.

Jusserand would grow to love the United States in his twenty-two years as ambassador. In the first years of the century-old nation's emergence in the international scene, he knew he stood on that threshold and was every day more aware of it. He had come to the scene fresh and saw it all anew, without the historical context shared by Americans. He was fascinated and amused by Theodore Roosevelt, whom he had first heard speak at the dedication of the War College in 1903. "I noticed the vigour, the insistence on the important words, the premptory gestures of the president," wrote Jusserand, "his bitter condemnation of limp individuals, of 'weaklings' adverse to

J. J. Jusserand, ambassador of France to the United States, 1902–25. *Library of Congress, Prints and Photos Division.*

effort, his praise of energetic minds and his picture of that world power of the United States which they are not free not to fulfill but which they [will] fulfill well nor not. The attitude they should observe is that of the armed just man."[19]

The French ambassador's fascination with the boldness and color of the president's address led him to draw closer to Roosevelt than a prudent ambassador ordinarily might. Access proved surprisingly easy. When the accreditation ceremony took place, the two began to talk, standing in the middle of the Blue Room, laughing, skipping from one subject to another, as the assembled guests looked on restlessly, wondering what to do next. Ambassador Jusserand, if a little taken aback by the lapse in ceremony, never underestimated the value this bonding had for his country.

Diplomacy, however, was only one aspect of Jusserand's instant admiration of the very American character of Roosevelt. They were often together during Roosevelt's seven-year presidency. Jusserand was encouraged by the president's openness with him and was intrigued by and hoped to understand the American gregariousness in the man; the president in turn marveled at the luminescence and erudition of the ambassador. They were both intellectuals, but of different sorts: Roosevelt, with his appetite for history and science, his books and articles, his seeming passion for all knowledge; Jusserand, a few years his senior, with a sound reputation among academics and with some of his books attracting a popular following in France.

Jusserand's witty exchanges with the president were legendary. The president liked to challenge the ambassador's physical ability. On one of his macho "point to point" hikes in Rock Creek Park, the line of males came to a creek bank, and the president stripped naked before crossing the deep stream, dressing again on the other side to proceed with the walk. The rest of the party followed suit obligingly, hoisting their clothes over their heads as they waded into the water. Only Jusserand retained his gloves. When Roosevelt asked why, the ambassador responded, what if ladies should appear?[20]

It was their easy association that tempted Roosevelt to a personal journey into diplomacy, about which he knew very little, apart from what he had observed with Hay and the State Department. He was, however, very interested in the subject and wished to try his hand in the dispute between Russia and Japan. He turned to Jusserand as his instructor.

The French ambassador was preparing to spend the summer of 1905 at his farm in France. Just before his departure, his trunks stacked in the hall, he received a summons from the White House. "I have not Mr. Hay by me," Roosevelt said to Jules Jusserand. "You must give me your opinion." The ambassador could hardly believe he was being asked to advise the head of a foreign nation.[21]

Roosevelt not only liked him but also admired him as a diplomat. Jusserand had moved to Washington after several years of duty in the embassy at Copenhagen and nine years earlier in London. He was considered by his foreign office in Paris one of the most valuable diplomats in the French corps. In cultivating his friendship with Roosevelt, Jusserand was ambassador in the historical sense of having personal access to the head of state. At their meeting, Roosevelt put before Jusserand the draft of a cable response to George von Lengerke Meyer, the rich Bostonian who was the much esteemed American ambassador to Russia. Meyer had responded to a previous cable that Alvey Adee had sent to him over the president's signature, instructing Meyer to approach the czar on the subject of possible American arbitration in the war with Japan.

Meyer wrote, "I had hoped I should see the emperor alone, as the English ambassador had told me that the young Empress was influencing her husband to continue the war and gain a victory. I delivered your instructions as cabled by Adee on March 27, and she drew nearer and never took her eyes off the Tsar. When I pronounced the words, 'At proper season, when the two warring nations are willing, the President would gladly use his impartial good offices towards the realization of an honorable and lasting peace, alike advantageous to the parties and beneficial to the world.' His Majesty looked embarrassed . . . but instantly turned the conversation on to another subject." Ambassador Meyer added in a postscript, "It is already said by a certain Grand Duchess that the Tsarina was present on purpose to prevent the Tsar committing himself in any way or my having an extended conversation."[22] It was an issue now of seeing the czar alone.

Jusserand concealed his surprise at being consulted by the president on so sensitive a matter. But directness was Roosevelt's way. In the absence of the secretary of state, who had been closely involved in the issue until recent weeks, the president took up the challenge himself. Jusserand took the draft back to the embassy and worked on it. He and the president agreed at last upon instructions to Meyer. With these in hand, threading the ins and outs of imperial court form, Meyer set a day when the empress was otherwise occupied with celebrating her birthday to arrange an interview with the czar. In the *presence*, the diplomatic term for being before the crowned head, Meyer read Roosevelt's instructions aloud, "laying stress on certain points." Czar Nicholas agreed to the plan.[23]

Meanwhile, Jusserand entered as adviser to the president. Just how one might class his efforts is difficult. He was not truly acting as ambassador of France, and to call him a confidant would be inappropriate, considering his official position. "Friend" is close but is no piece in the mosaic of diplomacy. In any case, the advising was carried out very much behind the scenes. The ambassador postponed his trip to France. He was at Roosevelt's side when Ambassador Takahira, a close friend of Jusserand, answered Roosevelt's invitation to call at the White House. Already Takahira had attempted to reach the Russians through Count Cassini, who, having been kept out of the loop himself by his own foreign office in Russia, felt it best not to forward the request to Russia. Takahira's various other efforts had also been futile. Both Japan and Russia were possessed by passions of pride and greed. Roosevelt now stepped forward as the mediator between two battling empires. Earlier, Americans had been mediators and arbitrators over many years but never on so high a level. Nor were these preliminaries carried out ceremoniously in gilded hallways, as heirs of the Congress of Vienna might prescribe, but rather beneath buzzing electric fans in the president's private study upstairs in the White House, in the hot, sweaty atmosphere of a long Washington summer, about which everybody complained.

Once Roosevelt's lines of contact were confirmed with the envoys, he went to work with them in close association with Jusserand, welcoming his advisement. "Dealing with senators," Roosevelt wrote, "is a time-excellent training for the temper, but upon my word, dealing with these peace envoys has been an even tougher job. To be polite and sympathetic and patient in explaining for the hundredth time something perfectly obvious, when what I really want to do is to give utterance to whoops of rage and jump up and knock their heads together—well, all I can hope is that the self repression will be ultimately helpful for my character."[24]

Negotiations went on for a year after the president managed to intercede with the two empires. At times during the period, either Russia or Japan came near to walking away, but each was coaxed back. What they were trying to work out was a protocol for a climactic meeting, to take place sooner, Roosevelt hoped, rather than later. The location of the meeting fell to debate, Russia wanting Paris, Japan insisting upon Washington unless it be in summer, when they wanted to be in cooler climes, maybe Newport. Finally, Portsmouth, New Hampshire, was settled upon, and the diplomatic

hordes descended upon it on August 9, 1905. Roosevelt received some of the luminaries at Sagamore Hill several days before the meeting opened, having them sail from
Washington aboard the presidential yacht *Sylph*. Before he let the diplomats go on to
Portsmouth, the president pressed his case with them unmercifully in the midst of
lively family hospitality.

The president continued his pounding as the Portsmouth conference wore on.
Vulnerability in his performance was not invisible to the professional diplomats. Ser-
gei Yulyevich, also known as Count Witte, the Russian plenipotentiary to the peace
conference, had met with the president and the Japanese envoys aboard the *Sylph*
while en route to Portsmouth. The count remembered: "I represented the most powerful nation on earth. I knew we had been defeated. I was anxious that the Japanese
not be given precedence over us and told Baron [Roman] Rosen [newly appointed
ambassador from Russia to the United States] that I would not take it lightly if at lunch
on the yacht the president would first toast the Mikado and then our Emperor. I said
this because I was afraid that the president, having little experience and being a typical American, would commit a blunder by paying little attention to the formalities."[25]

Most of the diplomatic work had already been accomplished in the meetings in
Washington. A protocol had been devised. In New Hampshire the envoys and their
enormous staffs occupied an old summer hotel, but there was little mixing between
the Russians and the Japanese. The peace treaty was concluded at Portsmouth on
September 5, 1905. Russia's humiliation was less for it. The war was over. A victorious
Japan won the lands Russia had wanted for the Manchurian railway, gained several
crucial "leases" on Chinese soil, and was granted by Russia acquiescence to Japan's
territorial ambitions toward Korea. Russia paid no indemnity.

For the United States, mediation of the peace was a giant step into world affairs.
It was to win Roosevelt the Nobel Peace Prize. Only in later years would it be seen
that the treaty's results were not so positive, casting as it did the first seeds of Japan's
hatred of the United States and providing the opportunity for Japan's slow aggression into Manchuria. In Russia it hastened the revolution, for domestic dissent was
newly strengthened by soldiers and sailors returning in tens of thousands from Asia,
possessed by the revolutionary propaganda that had flooded them unimpeded on the
front but was forbidden to those at home.

Jusserand's assistance to Roosevelt had helped to bridge the lack of diplomatic
experience that John Hay's decline had posed in the Russian-Japanese negotiations.
Earlier in the summer of 1905, to be his last, a sinking Hay wrote in his diary, relative
to his own history. He had been in the diplomatic service well less than a decade. His
adventures before that had been by memorable happenstance. "I say to myself that I
should not rebel at the thought of my life ending at this time. I have lived to be old,
something I never expected in my youth. I have had success beyond all the dreams of
my boyhood. . . . By mere length of service I shall occupy a modest place in the history

of my time. If I were to live several years more I should probably add nothing to my existing reputation; while I could not reasonably expect any further enjoyment of life, such as falls to the lot of old men in sound health. I know death is the common lot, and what is universal ought not to be deemed a misfortune; and yet—instead of confronting it with dignity and philosophy, I cling instinctively to life and things of life, as eagerly as if I had not any chance of happiness and gained nearly all the prizes."[26]

He died just after midnight on July 1, 1905, as preparations were under way for the meeting at Portsmouth. The news, though somewhat expected, fell over the Washington diplomatic community heavily. Black crepe hung from the embassies and legations in Washington until well after Hay, in his rosewood coffin, was buried in Cleveland. Long lines of diplomats and government officials left their cards at the house on Lafayette Square. Memorials were held in the capitals of the world.

At the time, Adee was at sea returning from Europe, an early trip scheduled so that he could be present at Portsmouth. Word of Hay's death came to him first aboard his ship when it arrived at Sandy Hook, and a letter awaited him at home from Clara Hay. She said she was "paralyzed and numb" from her loss. He responded: "For me it was a hard blow to feel that the companion—may I say the almost brotherly affection of thirty-five years had passed out of my life and become a sacred memory to cherish until I, too, am called home."[27]

Roosevelt had thus moved in upon the operations of diplomacy as no other president before him. Hay's illness opened the way for him to call in Ambassador Jusserand to advise him on his mediation at Portsmouth. Even though he had turned the actual work of the conference over to professionals, he was nonetheless present behind the scenes, drawing the participants aboard the *Sylph* to participate in its ocean pleasures and then to the pastoral loveliness of Sagamore Hill and into deep conversation with himself. His secretary of state was already very low when in Roosevelt's State of the Union speech in 1904 the president outlined his corollary to the 1823 Monroe Doctrine, inspired by the continual worries in Venezuela that had so outraged Grover Cleveland a decade before him. Foreign countries, Roosevelt said, may not enter the Americas to settle their disputes. This responsibility was now assumed by the United States, to be carried out on its own terms.

Hay had died when the president, almost certainly in council with his friend, the admired Captain Mahan, came up with an idea that, while not exactly in the diplomatic orbit, nevertheless made a strong statement to all nations. It involved Roosevelt show business at its grandest. For twenty years Congress had been building modern steel battleships. About a week before Christmas 1907 the president sent sixteen of these battleships, with a sizable escort, out to sea from Norfolk, Virginia, to circumnavigate the world. Manned by fourteen thousand sailors, the mighty parade broadcast American power to the world for fourteen months. The convoy was named by the press—a name for which it was to be remembered: the Great White Fleet.

EIGHT
Massachusetts Avenue

The houses built along Massachusetts Avenue and, to a lesser extent, streets nearby, such as New Hampshire Avenue, Sixteenth Street, and Wyoming Avenue, were the most obvious and earliest expressions of the era's international pretensions. A large number of them survive today as embassies, hardly any still as private houses. They were finished before most of the monuments and great public buildings were, and some were in full operation while the McMillan Plan was still being discussed. Before the Mall was completed, they would be shorn of their original raison d'être and would struggle to survive by serving other purposes. Private houses built with private funds, they sprang up in the late nineteenth century and first decade of the twentieth. Unlike the public buildings, their appearance was unencumbered by governmental fetters. The result was an avenue of auspicious mansions that varied from small, finely built town houses to large, free-standing houses that without hesitation could be called small palaces, built for entertaining.

Very few were designed for full-time occupancy, but rather were built to serve the winter season in Washington. They remained closed for the rest of the year. Regardless of scale, most of them boasted European-style facades of brick or stone, stairs inside of stone or mahogany rising to several rooms in Louis XV or Louis XVI style, sometimes with a flavoring of François Premier or even historical touches from Britain or Spain. Beyond their tall casement windows, sister houses could be seen lining the avenue.[1]

The larger, free-standing houses, while fewer in number, boasted a skirting of greenery, but there were only a few that had what might be called gardens, and those were small. Such houses along the avenue provided the same comforts as their smaller contemporaries, the row houses, only they had more of everything. Both abounded in shiny white-tile bathrooms with modern fixtures, central heating by forced air or steam, kitchens with the latest ranges and iceboxes, steam laundries, elevators, and the latest domestic gadgets, such as built-in central vacuum cleaning systems. The big ones had ballrooms, conservatories, music rooms, billiard rooms, and comfortable guest rooms. The "salons" (*parlor* being passé) were gilded and primped with silk upholstery and hangings, fine rugs, glass chandeliers, and French furniture or variations on it, sometimes bright with gold leaf or painted and polished in a cream color.

Building lots on Massachusetts Avenue were small and costly. District records show real estate exchanges for single lots at a typical thirty-five thousand dollars, now and then as high as sixty thousand. For a large house sometimes several lots were combined. Even three or four lots together didn't make for much ground, a big house leaving little room for winding, tree-lined driveways or ambitious plantings, as one might have enjoyed in Cleveland or Brookline. Stables were fitted tightly in these properties, opening off alleys or side streets; some stables were handsome, too, with mahogany stalls and comfortable upper-story quarters beneath the mansard roofs for coachmen and grooms. More householders, however, kept their horses and carriages at livery stables rather than having stables of their own. Most, it seems, rented their equipage as they needed it.[2]

The houses set Massachusetts Avenue apart, then and today. Everything about them was fresh and fine and represented what the owners believed was the most superb modern European taste one could achieve by nourishing architecture with enough money to assure good taste. They were settings for the social performances of their owners. No confirmation of success swelled the satisfaction of a host or hostess more than when a duke or count or baron from the diplomatic corps sank into the down cushions of an ample French chair, looked about, and said, "If I didn't know better, I'd think I was in Europe."[3]

Along Paris avenues in the late nineteenth century, rich Americans admired the *hôtels particuliers* of bankers, merchants, and other businessmen, private mansions that reflected commercial and industrial wealth like their own. Houses to satisfy the French appetite for architectural academicism that sprang from the École des Beaux-Arts and dominated European architecture had been built in Paris over the past forty years by Ernest Sanson, J.-N.-L. Durand, A.-N. Bailly, and a dozen or more other favored "society" architects. In these opulent halls politicians and rich men mingled at a high level of fashion. On Avenue du Bois de Boulogne (Avenue Foch) in Paris, Sanson had built Palais Rose, a flamboyant chip off the Louis XIV block, for Countess de Castellane, the daughter of the railroad millionaire Jay Gould, creating a duet of French taste and American money that was perfect harmony to awestruck visitors from the United States.[4]

One American guest of the countess was so taken by the Palais Rose that she commissioned Sanson to design a house for her in Washington.[5] The resulting white marble mansion, built by the American architect Horace Trumbauer from Sanson's sketches, commanded a prominent, elevated spot not on Massachusetts but nearby on New Hampshire Avenue. It was renegade in a sense, burdened by scandal. The owner, Perry Belmont, once a congressman and a former American ambassador to Spain, moved there in 1906 with his wife, Jessie, never to be free of the storm of cheap publicity that had accompanied their marriage five years earlier. Mrs. Belmont's divorce from Henry T. Sloane, of the New York department store, had climaxed most shockingly in her surrender of rights to her children. Five hours after the judgment, she was married to the bachelor Perry Belmont.[6] Details of the Belmonts' romance were attached to the house like tawdry circus posters. At times, the couple lived there quietly, but they usually resided in Paris.

Sanson was the only architect with a big European reputation who designed a house in Washington during this period. The architects of the Washington avenues were more typically American practitioners, such as Glenn Brown, of Washington; T. P. Chandler, of Philadelphia; and Henri de Sibour, who practiced in New York. (French born, he usefully claimed descent from Louis XVI.) There were many more architects who left marks, some designing several houses, others only one. Americans elsewhere raised their versions of the great modern French mansions—on Belle View Avenue, in Newport, on Fifth Avenue, in New York, on Michigan Avenue, in Chicago and its suburbs—but in no place other than Washington did the houses, crowded together along the avenue, so closely parallel their human context in Europe. In Washington as in Paris, they were private houses built to share the exciting aura of power surrounding the government. Very few of the owners were a part of that power, like Belmont. Most of them came instead to enjoy the energy of the city at the time of year when it was the most potently expressed. It was the ambassadors and the ceremonies and other splendors attached to their positions and persons that made the Washington social season appealing to those from outside.

Use of the houses was attached to the political schedules of the day. The social season from December to Lent, and on sometimes to May, coincided more or less with the sessions of Congress. Most of the owners of the Massachusetts Avenue houses had no reason to remain in Washington otherwise. Even more or less permanent residents in this milieu, like the Pattens and Hays, left for at least the summer months.

The first of the houses was fully completed at about the time of Lord Pauncefote's accreditation in the spring of 1893. Built on an odd, triangular lot pointing south, it rather looked down upon Dupont Circle. Levi Zeigler Leiter, Chicago civic leader and former partner of Marshall Fields, built a large house with buff-colored brick walls trimmed in limestone. One architectural critic likened it to "a great, stratified dinosaur" of "overwhelming size." Others believed it looked a little like the White House. The south side of Leiter's house nosed up to the point on its triangular lot like a huge ocean liner, while the front was around the corner on New Hampshire Avenue, with a pillared *porte cochère*.[7]

Mary Theresa Leiter, daughter of a well-to-do banker in Utica, New York, was a beauty of note, but her open, somewhat whimsical ways had held her back from the social success to which she had aspired while living in Chicago. With three daughters approaching the marriageable age, she had no time to waste. Levi Leiter, uninterested

Levi and Mary Theresa Leiter's house on Dupont Circle, ca. 1900. *U.S. Commission of Fine Arts, Washington, D.C.*

in society, was a genial, private sort of man, a collector of books, manuscripts, and maps. As a boy he had walked the battlefields not far from his home near Hagerstown, Maryland, and as a man of middle age he had collected so much information about the Civil War battles that when one heard him discourse on the subject, it seemed as though he had personally participated. No pleasure to him was greater than to sit with a Union or Confederate veteran before a fire in his library and listen to the old man's memories. Returning to the scenes of his boyhood to enjoy them again was agreeable to him. For Mrs. Leiter, Washington held the prospect of fortuitous pickings in an orchard of eligible bachelors, not a few being diplomats with titles. The Leiters brought with them to their new house perhaps an acre of gilded furniture, statues, chests, clocks, and Leiter's significant collection of historical manuscripts.

Washington took a real liking to Mary Theresa even though Chicago had shied away, and she became an oft-quoted sort of corn-fed Mrs. Bennett, with girls to marry off and a penchant for making unintentionally funny remarks. For instance, when she returned from Europe with a sculpture of the hand of her eldest, Mary Victoria, she observed proudly that Rodin had made a bust of her daughter's hand. Departing from the ship another time, she expressed her joy at being back again on "old terra-cotta." After a funeral she asked the widow if she was having a good time.

John Hay, who admired her beauty and felt a scholarly kinship with Leiter, always defended Mary Theresa in public, saying that some of the stories everyone quoted were not true. In private, however, the Leiters sometimes aggravated him. "There isn't a natural note about either," he confided in a letter to Clara Hay. "They are very regular campaigners. They care for nobody except those who can help them into smart company." Yet somehow, Mrs. Leiter always redeemed herself with him. Aboard the RMS *Majestic* he overheard a rather grand British lady ask, "Are you not very rich?" to which Mary Theresa replied, "I have never been asked that question before and hardly know how to answer it." Hay could not conceal his delight with her response.[8]

Her little missteps, however, were trivialities beside her great triumph in the marriage of her daughter Mary Victoria to Lord Curzon of Great Britain. Although it could have been only a money match, this union was a love match, beyond question. The numbers of spectators crowding up to the streets between Dupont Circle and St. John's Church on Lafayette Square were compared to the crowds at inaugurations. Mary Theresa Leiter's daughter would one day be the vicereine of India.

The Leiter house at 1500 New Hampshire Avenue, built between 1891 and 1893, was the first of perhaps around forty big houses in that general neighborhood of the capital, most of others built after the Spanish-American War. A block northwest from Dupont Circle, on Massachusetts Avenue, Richard and Mary Townsend bought several adjoining lots in 1897 and 1898. Mary Scott Townsend had known Washington for years.

Her father, William L. Scott, from Erie, Pennsylvania, had become a millionaire through coal and had also been a member of Congress. As Mrs. Townsend, "Minnie" and her husband, Richard, had lived in Philadelphia, where he had been president of the Erie and Pennsylvania Railroad and upon leaving that position had become a stockbroker downtown, also managing their family money. When Minnie's father died and his fortune came to her, the Townsends, then in their middle fifties, decided to move to Washington, where they opened her father's house at 22 Jackson Place, mentioned earlier, on Lafayette Square.

Mary "Minnie" Townsend, ca. 1900. *F. J. Bassett GPN Collection, Erie County Historical Society, Erie, Pennsylvania.*

The row house proved too small and the neighborhood a little seedy, so they debated buying a house or building one. She wished to build, but they both feared doing so because of the belief that old people who move into a new house will die. Neither was much more than middle age, but both were superstitious. At last they decided to play it safe and bought a house, a three-story residence not quite twenty years old at 2121 Massachusetts Avenue, across the street from the Patten sisters, whom Minnie knew well. The house, however, was out of style, in the Napoleon III fashion of the old Department of Agriculture Building, its tall, purplish stucco walls and long windows conveying a past idea of elegance.

They employed the young architects John Carrere and Thomas Hastings, who would later design the Senate and House office buildings at the Capitol. This duo had recently left the drafting room of McKim, Mead & White to open their own practice in New York, with the enthusiastic blessing of their former employers, who may well have recommended them for this job. The architects and the Townsends met in deep discussion about remodeling the house on Massachusetts Avenue. Both Carrere and Hastings were educated at the École des Beaux-Arts in Paris and were conversant in the classic French architectural styles current in Paris, as well as houses built or in construction by French architects.[9] They were able to show the Townsends how the stucco-faced house could be entirely remodeled, swallowing the existing structure in the new one, while remaining well within their provision to keep the original building. Indeed, the architects provided a model in the Petit Trainon, the small palace on the grounds of Versailles intimately associated with the history and romance of Marie Antoinette. Minnie was sold on the idea. Plans were drawn for such a house, for which construction took place from 1899 to 1901.[10]

Mrs. Townsend's Petit Trainon took form quickly. Many old walls were torn out, while others, particularly external ones, were left on the street front and sides and sheathed with dressed limestone; the old purplish stucco was still visible from the alley, as if to confirm the Townsends' superstition. But the old house in most parts vanished into the new. The best millwork shops in New York sent handsome French doors and casement windows by rail to Washington and then by mule to 2121 Massachusetts Avenue. Oak flooring was laid plain in most rooms, but in the principal rooms it was laid in the "Versailles" chevronlike parquet and waxed to a sheen. When the decorators came, they stretched silk over some of the walls and set in place marble mantelpieces, all in the French classic styles. One particular mantel, in a narrow room overlooking the avenue, was white marble with columns like clusters of Cupid's arrows, a copy of one in Marie Antoinette's Petit Trainon bedroom. Edith Roosevelt approved the same model for the Blue Room at the White House.

Louis XV–style hardware and lighting fixtures, both sconces and chandeliers, were gilded bronze, the latter showered over with prisms and beads of clear glass. In the numerous white-tile bathrooms the faucets and sconces were nickel plated;

the porcelain fixtures, large scale and dazzling white. The house contained a modern laundry, rivaled in technical advance only by the hotel-size kitchen and a basement steam-heating system that could have served a luxury liner, the great boilers marvels in themselves. While there seems to have been no budget, as one might have in building most houses, it was the architects' job to keep costs down where possible. In the ballroom the paneled walls were a cold, porcelain white trimmed in gold leaf, but gold leaf only as high as one could reach, above which the more economical bronzing powder gilding took over. The centerpiece of the ceiling of that room was a circular allegory in oil on canvas, of the type turned out in Paris decorating studios for just such houses as this. Richly carved wood ornament in the dining room was in fact only cast plaster cleverly painted to look like polished oak. What appeared to be marble was likely to be the colored-plaster scagliola.

No one could deny that it was a beautiful house.[11] Minnie brought wonderful things to it, the latest adaptations of Louis XIV, XV, and XVI commodes, fauteuils, sofas, and cigarette tables, all gold or gold and white, the chairs and sofas fitted with deep down-filled cushions. A regular convention of marble statuary was assembled in the entrance hall, where a broad stair swept to the main floor above. John Singer Sargent provided a portrait in pinks of the one child, Matilda, a lovely girl of eighteen, whose name was revised to Mathilde, perhaps to better match the new house.

Minnie Townsend's Louis XV–style ballroom, 1902. *Library of Congress, Prints and Photos Division.*

As satisfactory as everything seemed, tragedy struck. Early in 1902 Richard Townsend was thrown from his horse in Rock Creek Park, broke his neck, and died. The precaution had failed. A proper Minnie Townsend went into mourning, along with Mathilde, black dresses, black veils. The requisite year of such costume and abstinence from social life, however, seems to have been too much for the widow, who appeared in society sooner than she might have, meeting tradition halfway, European style, by wearing mauve. She scheduled an open house, designed to be the most opulent Washington had ever experienced. There were considerations beyond herself. Mathilde was of marrying age, and Minnie wanted a European title to join the Townsend name. Minnie's social pace was not to slow down either. Within two years, the gilders were back to repair worn places on the doors and walls.

Across the street from Mrs. Townsend's first reception, her guests saw the beginning of another fine house, commenced in the year 1902 by Larz and Isabel Anderson, as engaging and lively a couple as ever enjoyed the Washington season. He was thirty-four, born a year after the Civil War had ended, and she was a "centennial baby," born in 1876, ten years his junior and participated in a fortune estimated at seventeen million. When the two married, the papers proclaimed the bride the richest woman in America. Indeed the whole romance of Isabel Perkins was chronicled in detail: The couple had met while he was secretary to the American ambassador in Rome. The *Boston Enquirer* reported, "She might very easily have done what so many other wealthy American girls seem to desire, to marry a bankrupt European or English nobleman, or some immoral and disreputable Prince, with castles in the air and a room full of mortgages. Miss Perkins will marry not for an empty title, but for the love which the husband of her choice from her own country can bring her with the proud title of an American citizen."[12]

Larz, too, was rich, only less so. Although reared in part in Washington, his family were prominent Cincinnati people, descended from pioneers of that city and still closely connected with it. At the time of Isabel and Larz's marriage, the *Boston Enquirer*'s account ran nearly a full page, describing Larz as "a splendid type of young American manhood!"[13] Besides the implied virility, his education and experience through travel, not to mention his money, made him extraordinary. After completing a large house in Brookline, Massachusetts, outside Boston, which they always called home, with a hundred acres of landscaped Italian-style gardens, the bride and groom decided to build a house in Washington, for Larz had ambitions to become an ambassador.

In Washington some years before, his parents had commissioned a house from the same Richardson who had built the double house of Hay and Adams. For all the similarity in its massing of brick blocks and pointed roofs, the Anderson's house was more pleasing than the Hay-Adams house, if only because it had more room around it. The young Andersons could have had that house, but it was fairly much out of style by 1902, and Larz's mother still lived there. They wanted a Washington house of their own for the season.

Larz Anderson wearing the court uniform he designed for himself, ca. 1915. *Collection of the Society of Cincinnati, Anderson House.*

Their house was built with one purpose, and that was to provide a setting for Larz's presence when in Washington. He and Isabel loved faraway places where they could learn new things; they loved camping in the outdoors and exploring rivers in their houseboat; they loved old houses and plants, animals and birds they had never seen before. Although never entirely sold on the American capital as a place to be, Larz would concede that the Washington diplomatic corps there was "not so much worse than anywhere else," especially when it turned out for gala events.[14] He scorned President Roosevelt's hunting as "terrible slaughter" of the wild animals that fascinated him and Isabel.[15] Society bored them, and they swallowed their local obligations like castor oil.

They never really seemed to love the house they built. The several lots they bought for it had belonged to the Patten sisters next door, who so disapproved of the couple's extravagance that they spied on them from the windows and listened to servant's stories, repeating all they saw and heard to Larz's aged mother, who was greatly upset by it and hastened to reprimand Larz.

The big house rose over a two-year period, a highly refined rendering in the *hôtel particulier* genre of Paris, French on the front, Georgian behind, finished in smooth dressed limestone over a modern steel frame. It was a house for a capital city and would not have been out of place in Paris, London, Vienna, or Buenos Aires, and had the context not been Massachusetts Avenue, the street facade might have been mistaken at first glance for an eighteenth-century building, although not an American one. A large annex provided for stables, garage, and servants' quarters, with an additional servants' home on the top floor of the house. The architect, an unlikely choice, was a family friend, Arthur Little, whose fame lay in an earlier era of the Queen Anne style in New England. What he produced for his friends Larz and Isabel outdid Minnie Townsend's house in baronial magnificence, but it had none of the playful quality that made the Townsend house appealing.

The big houses continued to appear. A block east of Admiral Du Pont's circle, yet another rival to Minnie Townsend's Petit Trainon was begun in 1901 atop a deep cellar. The builder was Tom Walsh, an engrossing personality, a risk-taker who had moved with his musical wife, Carrie, from a Colorado mountain residence they would always call home. He had made millions from a lively and successful career in gold mining. As roughshod and aggressive as the entrepreneurial Walsh was, he was also a gentleman in a western sort of way. In the newspapers the gregarious Irishman was sometimes styled "the Colorado Monte Cristo." He liked making money. Before the roof was put on his house, at 2020 Massachusetts Avenue, he sold his Camp Bird gold mine, preserving his money in low-yielding bonds. This giant nest egg he managed himself, rejecting the tempting trusts in which nearly everyone else with a substantial reserve of money put theirs. Tom Walsh did not like being separated from his assets.[16]

Walsh had come to Washington looking for peace and tranquility in the capital. Entrepreneur that he was, he soon threw this over and began buying and selling Washington real estate, especially investing in apartment houses. With cash to spend, he eventually cast his risks again to mining in the West and in Latin America. Although Tom and Carrie Walsh lived in Washington, they were there usually only in the winter, for they traveled in Europe about half the year, where he sought the company of other entrepreneurs. With these men he felt at home, claiming as a friend no less than the avaricious king Leopold of Belgium, who, crowned or not, was as hard-boiled and sly a businessman as the early twentieth century might have likely produced. Walsh's admiration for the king was so great that he built a suite for him on an upper floor of the Massachusetts Avenue house.

From the outside, Tom Walsh's house was a huge, round-cornered box, more analogous to a candy box than an ark, with its curving lines reminiscent of buildings of that time in Vienna. The light-colored, flowing, curtainlike walls, the fancy trimming, the curved window glass, the ornamental use of copper bore no similarity to anything yet seen on Massachusetts Avenue. The architect, Henry Andersen, who practiced in New York, had been trained and had worked for years in his native Denmark. Art nouveau was a style familiar to him, and Walsh's daughter, Evalyn, remembered that her father had told Andersen "just what he wanted."[17] On the ground floor, four main rooms flanked a central hall, all immense in scale and heavily decorated with architectural ornament. A grand stair ascended—or rather launched itself—from the center of the central hall, shooting up through the middle of the house. It was the first spectacle confronted upon entering. Yet all four floors were full of surprises.

Walsh's palace had an opera house glitter about it; colored marbles, gold leaf, silk wall hangings, rich chandeliers, and more were present in abundance. But it was the triumphal sweep of the stair, rising in a three-story open hallway crowned by a skylight, that gave the interior its energy. The speculation was that Walsh got the idea from seeing a similar stair on an Atlantic luxury liner. As for the interior decor,

Father and daughter: Tom and Evalyn Walsh, 1897. *Library of Congress, Manuscripts Division.*

Walsh had only one specification: no heavy curtains. He liked the open, airy feeling he had seen in European houses, so all the windows were fitted with ordinary starched white cotton curtains. The rest was left to Carrie Walsh, who engaged the services of Anna Jenness Miller, a local real estate agent considered the last word in good taste in Washington. When Carrie Walsh wearied of the task, Miller took over, traveling to Europe several times, poking about shops in Paris, London, Vienna, and Berlin, sending crates filled with furnishings of all descriptions back to Washington. Walsh was a generous client. A reporter from the *Denver Times* who happened to be in Washington looked in and wandered about. He marveled at the third-floor ballroom with its pipe organ, big enough, he believed, for a cathedral. The rest of the house he found almost unimaginably rich.[18]

The Patten sisters looked on quietly but finally could not help but observe that for all the chandeliers in the Walsh's new house, not a single one was as large as theirs, which was twelve feet tall, a colorful fountain of Venetian glass that their late mother had bought in Europe. Walsh seems to have been amused by that and other reactions to his house, which ranged from "amazing" to "ugly." To cap his approximately two-million-dollar expenditure on the interior, he designed and commissioned a gold-plated coffee and tea service spangled with raw nuggets of Colorado gold.[19]

Before the finishing touches were applied to the Walsh house, Herbert and Martha Wadsworth's less imposing house was started and brought to completion two blocks east on Massachusetts Avenue. Like the rest of the new houses, the Wadsworth house grew up in terra-cotta tiles around a steel and concrete frame. The external walls were clothed in glazed Roman brick of yellowish color, its architectural trim rendered in white tile, following a formal Georgian style the Wadsworths perhaps considered "colonial." This was a smaller house than the usual Massachusetts Avenue mansions. Some people compared it to a ship, pointing its bow to the narrow end of the lot on Dupont Circle. It had no portico. To find the front door one had to look twice, for there was no visible pedestrian entrance at all, only an archway through which carriages and automobiles might pass on an inner driveway. The entrance doors were within. Like the great *hôtels particuliers* of Paris, the Wadsworth house had no formal street door.

The Wadsworths never used the house except during the season. Home to them was a farm near the town of Geneseo, outside Rochester, in upstate New York, where Herbert Townsend's ancestors had settled after the American Revolution. Lands descending in the family included some fifty thousand acres, which were divided into several farms owned by different branches of the family. Herbert Wadsworth's cousin James Wolcott Wadsworth was in Congress when the Massachusetts Avenue house was built, having served some twenty years at that point. When Herbert was a small boy his father had died a hero in the Wilderness Campaign. Robert E. Lee had ordered a cease-fire while the remains of General Wadsworth were removed from the battle-field. Herbert and his brother, Austin, were raised with the family history, including the fame of their father, and they felt deeply for their mother, who was still living when Herbert and Martha built their Massachusetts Avenue house.

Herbert Wadsworth, tall, lean, and quiet, was fifty-one the year his house was built. An engineer, he took out patents from time to time, some of them on farm-related inventions, a better gate hinge, a better horse trough. Martha Blow Wadsworth, his small, red-headed wife, was thirty-nine and from a very rich pioneer family of St. Louis. Their wedding, fourteen years earlier, was a St. Louis social event that made national note, accounts of it claiming several full pages in the papers.[20] The couple called the New York farm, where they had built a rambling stone house, Ashantee, not to suggest the kingdom in Ghana but rather "a shanty," pronouncing the first vowel as a long *a*. Joking was more characteristic of the outgoing Martha than of the introspective Herbert, but he seems to have gone along with her. He devoted his labors to scientific farming, and she to horses, particularly hunters. With her brother-in-law Austin she became active in the Genesee Valley Hunt. As with everything Martha undertook, she entered this endeavor with dedication and passion.[21] She liked to take photographs. Old Kodak snapshots show her and Herbert and their beloved dogs, seeming players in some timeless happiness in the meadows on their farm.[22]

The house the Wadsworths built at 1801 Massachusetts Avenue seemed odd if you didn't know the Wadsworths, but not a great surprise if you did. Presenting a wide face to the avenue, the house nearly filled its roughly pie-shaped lot, having only a small terrace garden for plantings. The entrance was, in simplest terms, a hole through the building. A garage on one side of the passage inside was provided with an electric turntable for automobiles, to provide a turnaround in minimum space. Opposite the garage doors were glass doors to a paneled entrance hall with coat rooms beside it and stairs to the living quarters above. Except for the billiard room, which doubled for an after-dinner men's smoking room, the entire ground floor was given over to service, including an apartment for the resident housekeeper. The house was built for

Herbert Wadsworth with his dog, on a trail ride from Washington, D.C., to Geneseo, New York, ca. 1908. *Milne Library, State University of New York, Geneseo.*

automobiles, so the horses, which were ridden every day, must have been kept either at a livery stable or the Riding Academy, which Martha Wadsworth patronized. One could not readily imagine her ever being apart from horses.

Upstairs were ballroom, dining room, a round salon, and on above that were the bedchambers and maids' rooms. Heavy, dark-stained mahogany colored beams and woodwork characterized the open reception space that ran from the salon to the two-story coved ballroom, with its lilac and orange art-glass wall lamps and musicians' balcony. The salon was finished in the Louis XVI style and had French doors to a balcony, from which one could look down upon Dupont Circle and over to the Leiters' house. The Wadsworth house, like most of the others on the avenue, was not heavily furnished but was in fact a little sparse, perhaps to leave space to change it for the receptions, art shows, and dances held there.

From the Wadsworth's balcony, a very tall house of white marble could be seen between that house and the Leiters'; it was the Patterson house, which faced Dupont Circle. In its constricted setting, it was an abruptly tall palazzo-style building, all facade. Designed by Stanford White, of McKim, Mead & White, it was completed in the winter of 1903. The actual architecture took its design cues from several sixteenth-century Italian palaces. Like all of the firm's production, this was swathed by its designers in a whole litany of historical precedent, every detail a sure delight to the client. Following the cues of the Wadsworth and Leiter houses, this one occupied a similar pie-shaped lot, only wider, and White, abandoning the side entrance solution tried elsewhere, created a roughly Y-shaped building with the upper double arm, the V part, facing the point on Dupont Circle and crossed by a high, rather papal loggia overlooking Dupont Circle. When one entered the circle, the house was a surprise, seeming animated to jump, rather than having the anvil-hug of the ground that characterized its neighbors. One entered directly into the V of the Y.

It was built by Robert and Elinor Patterson, from Chicago, she heiress to the *Chicago Tribune*, owned by her late father, Joseph Medill. Medill had built the house for them, a project that ended in a controversy between him and the architect. Since Medill's death shortly before the house was finished, the Chicago paper fell under the editorship of his son-in-law Robert. The couple's new duties in Chicago made the Patterson house even more of a part-time residence than had been intended. It was seldom used for more than one month a year.

On P Street, just behind the Wadsworths and Pattersons, was a large, heavy masonry house that seemed to subside quietly within its orange-colored walls of glazed Roman brick. It was the house John Hay considered the finest in Washington. To most observers it had no real style, unless it might be Arts and Crafts, although there was a modern Germanic, maybe Viennese, quality to it, sometimes known in Europe as "Roman." And it was probably intended to be Roman and sort of Germanic. Here the Boardmans lived with two of their three grown daughters, the younger one, Josephine, and the older one, Mabel, the latter, it will be seen, being the most remarkable and indeed formidable Boardman.

~

The winter residents were in essence vacationers; home was elsewhere. The Hays had a residence in Cleveland, which Clara Hay always considered home. Tom Walsh gave his address as Washington, and he was in fact resident for a few years, but his heart remained in Glenwood Springs, Colorado, and he and Carrie eventually returned there, to be in Washington only during the season. For the most part these residents were middle-aged people. Those who had children who were through with school saw their young adults pass in and out of the city, thinking of Washington as a playground. The grown children who lingered in Washington were mainly young unmarried women, such as Mathilde Townsend, Alice Roosevelt, and Mabel Boardman; those in this group were somewhat older, into their early twenties, finished with such schooling as they ever cared to acquire, and returned home to live with their parents as their only recourse. Few of them went to school past the age of eighteen or twenty. They took for granted that they would marry, but the question that occupied their thoughts and filled their diaries was "whom?" The idea of taking a job or working was not even a consideration for these young women of means, even though there were exceptions, such as Vice President Taft's daughter Helen, who went to college to pursue a career in teaching, and Mabel Boardman, who was very serious about improving the world as she knew it, yet never imagined being a salaried employee.

The social season in Washington was largely an adult experience. For those privileged to participate, it was a busy time. Hostesses, social secretaries, and butlers walked the floors of the State Department to vie for dates available in Alvey Adee's open book. It was safest to secure the dates as early as possible for the entire season at once. Events that were registered were usually the large evening ones: receptions, dinners, dances, and special events, like weddings, which might involve guests from the diplomatic list or even the president. Members of Congress were often invited, but some, like Speaker Cannon, went with or without a "card" of invitation. A high official or diplomat would have considered such uninvited entry as crashing but had to respect such a gate-crasher's power as an elected representative of a segment of the American people. Diplomats were fastidious in replying to invitations. It was not usual to invite the president, but if he wished to attend, the host was warned in advance by his secretary. Straightforwardly sending an invitation to the White House was considered pushy and looked down upon.

The ambassadors brought along forms of entertaining copied from the courts of Europe, and social Washington was eager to comply. If one court was imitated more than any other in the capital it probably was Germany's. While court practices varied more or less in formality from country to country, Germany's rules of etiquette under Kaiser Wilhelm II were relatively new, and the players included newly titled industrialists along with the old aristocracy. Perhaps the inclusion of businessmen made German customs seem closer to an American approach, although Germany was not unique in expanding its aristocracy. During this period Britain elevated numerous businessmen to the peerage, so St. James's had a generous representation of the empire's newly rich.

When Larz Anderson took Isabel to London in May 1904 to be presented at court while in the city, he confided sarcastically to his diary: "You know I am really afraid that Isabel may be disappointed in the way in which Court Functions are managed here at St. James since she has had the privileges of seeing how things are done at the White House!" Yet he added parenthetically, "But truly it is to laugh when I think of that absurd vanity and see the real thing here, which, to be sure, is absurd enough."[23]

Early social forms at the White House had been suggested by what the diplomats had established in Washington long before. It can be no surprise that a social system, or protocol—that being a relatively new word in this application—was adopted by general agreement about 1900, when McKinley was president. This approach seemed appropriate, because it was obviously based upon international practices of diplomacy. Foreign diplomats knew the rules from their previous missions; in a professional sense they had grown up with them. Following these newly introduced formalities, Washington's hosts entered the social scene, staking their position in society by scheduled events that they sponsored. Every detail conformed to diplomatic usage. Rounds of private dinners and dances increased.

Public receptions were unique in American practice but also a familiar part of U.S. embassy life in capitals abroad. They were usually held in the afternoon to avoid evening conflicts. Receptions worked in several ways. The most democratic approach was to announce them simply by invitation placed in the newspapers. This sort was very familiar in Washington during the period in question. Some hosts, however, disliked open public attendance and restricted admission to those with invitations, which in some cases a stranger could apply for by formal note and receive by return mail. Invitations in the press or by card might refer to one specific date or extend admission for the entire season to a weekly or biweekly reception at the same time and same day of the week. Even an all-season event was supplemented by extra invitations sent out to distinguished visitors or friends who happened to be in town. A host or hostess did not actually have to know the guest, of course. An invitation sent through the mail was very pared down, engraved in black or dark blue on white card stock. Handsome baroque type in black seldom yielded to simple script or colored ink.

Mrs. Richard Townsend

At Home

2 P.M.

Thursdays

A response was mandatory in any case, but for an open, seasonal invitation received by mail, only one reply was necessary. The recipient of this open card could expect to be received any Thursday at 2 P.M. during the season. Probably half of the receptions in the season were public; the invitations printed in the *Washington Post* or the *Evening Star* showed text no different from the example above. Occasionally in the press such an announcement as this appeared on the society page: "Mrs. Walter L. Fisher will not receive today."[24]

When the general public was admitted, crowds lined up outside, stretching onto the sidewalk and along the street, awaiting the butler to open the front door. A mixture of guests could be expected, visitors in town, news reporters, groups of secretaries taking the afternoon off for this long-anticipated adventure, classes of schoolgirls in their teens there for the experience, and a general lot of people curious about the house or what famous person they might see. The public receptions Americanized the European counterparts by admitting all who were likely to turn up, providing that each caller dressed appropriately for the occasion, which could be a school uniform, a military uniform, or a business suit that said Sunday best. When Mrs. Roosevelt began to require diplomats to wear their official uniforms at the White House, for a while it became stylish for the diplomats to boast their gold lace, embroidery, and medals for receptions. Most diplomats hated the idea enough to stop the trend before it became customary.[25] At a public reception a guest could remain for most of an hour after passing through the receiving and still avoid the butler's cold stare. But to stay on past an hour was to risk having one's coat and hat brought forth. And clocks were found in the public rooms of the big houses in adequate number to assist.

Hostesses and the "house party"—house guests and friends asked to assist— formed a receiving line, which was usually in a hall or drawing room. In Europe, handshaking was not common in receiving lines, but in America it was, even with the diplomats. Except for those in the house party, men and women wore gloves; one glove was removed for the receiving line. All women wore hats, except the house party. Diplomats, knowing an army of hands awaited shaking theirs, usually wore a left glove and carried the right one, to avoid pulling off and on to accommodate the flesh pounding.

Men were rarely in a receiving line, unless it was a luminary like Admiral Dewey, hero of Manila, Professor Langley, the air flight genius of the Smithsonian, a cabinet member, or an ambassador. Such figures likely would have appeared as a favor to the hosts and hostesses sought to spice their public receptions with official luminaries. Men of the household usually stood apart from the receiving line itself, to be called by the hostess if someone wanted to meet them. In addition to wearing no hats, women in the line wore no showy jewelry, except for rings. Their dresses were of the "afternoon type," not ornamental like an evening dress. They were, after all, "at home," welcoming people into their domestic scene.

Young women did not appear in receiving lines unless they either had made their debut, or were a professional of note, or were married. Just when a single woman qualified is uncertain, but probably at midthirties in age, when she was considered a spinster. All rules about women were abandoned if a reception was given in a woman's honor. The Russian ambassador Cassini's daughter, Marguerite, nevertheless suffered censure from the diplomatic wives for presiding at receptions, even though she was her father's official hostess and her presence was perfectly correct. Whatever the nuances of regulation might allow, rules were not likely to be bent much when officials were to be present, for fear of confusion and embarrassment.[26]

Where a public reception might attract 200 to 250 callers or even more, a private reception welcomed from 60 to 100 guests. Private receptions tended to be smaller and later in the day, and they served alcohol, whereas the public receptions generally did not. Some of the company might come late and linger for dinner after the reception. These events were the main meeting ground for Washington's temporary community and the diplomats, who readily responded to this sort of invitation as part of their work.

Hospitality varied with both types of receptions. At public receptions fruit punch, coffee, and tea were poured, usually at a long table decorated with flowers. Cakes and sweets further filled the table, all to be put on small plates, which servants collected when empty. Usually a favor of some kind for ladies was provided at the door upon departure—a box with a special chocolate or a piece of sugared fruit, a pretty Japanese fan, a flower done up with silk ribbon. There was always music. At the Walshes the pipe organ thundered classics and popular European airs through the house. Mrs. Townsend liked violins. The Andersons might have a quartet. The Pattens thought it proper to have a piano and a soloist, recalling an earlier time when a daughter of the house provided the music, not a hired performer. During the composer and critic Reginald de Koven's two-year stint in Washington beginning in 1902, when he established the capital's first symphony, a heightened taste developed for music outside the musical theater and created a demand for professional performances at social events on the avenue. Mrs. Roosevelt's after-dinner musicales also were an influence.

Private receptions mingled the most important people in the capital for an evening. These occasions were more formal in arrangement, more flowers, more food, than the public receptions. Wine and spiked punch were on the table, although a male guest could request a scotch and soda ("charged water"), an act common enough for Americans; for diplomats, however, whiskey was still in the gray area of propriety. The dress code was more conforming if the invitation was for 7 P.M. or after, pushing the event into the evening. Men wore white tie and tails—the tuxedo not yet universally acceptable—and the women of the house party wore short trains.

Upon arrival, ambassadors and high government officials were taken directly to the hostess at the head of the receiving line. They felt no obligation to apologize or show reticence for such privilege to those they bypassed. When several dignitaries arrived at the same time, they were taken to the hostess in order of official rank. Butlers were familiar with protocol and likely knew more than their employers. For a large reception, the use of an announcer was necessary, to inform the host as well as the guests of who had arrived. The announcer stood at the door to the main reception room, called the name in full voice as the individual entered. The experienced guest paused to be looked over, then entered to join the other guests. When an official title was involved, it was used instead of the name, hence "the secretary of state and Mrs. Root" and "the ambassador of Great Britain and Lady Herbert." Mrs. Townsend and the Andersons sometimes dressed the announcer and waiters in powdered wigs, Georgian-style knee breeches, and buckled shoes, an effect universal in Europe, not unusual at elegant parties in New York and Newport, and fairly common at the embassies in Washington.[27]

Entertaining high-style in the capital of a world power was therefore complicated and wrought with pattern. Americans were fascinated by the ceremony of it. Parties and receptions made news; when made available, guest lists were published. For the hostesses the details were exhausting. Most of them hired professional English or Italian butlers through agencies in New York and London to manage ceremony as well as the operations of the house. A butler might serve part time at several houses for social events. By 1906 or so, as many butlers seem to have been African American as European. Perfection in everything was a foregone conclusion, for anything that was not perfect would be the gossip of the next day. Roosevelt's White House aide Captain Archibald Butt observed that the butlers planned guest lists and assembled dinner parties to such an extent that the host and hostess had no idea who was coming.[28]

Dinner parties were smaller and more intimate and naturally more numerous than receptions. Dozens of them took place every night during the season. Even a small dinner party for six or eight tended to be like an embassy dinner in form, and the smaller the guest list, the more lax the attention to the rules of conduct. Six courses were usual and as many wines, although serving three wines was becoming more acceptable. The presentation of dinner included large suites of silver and in some cases gold services, crisp white linens, flowers, and candles, in the highest fashion of the day.

Conduct on occasions not under protocol's thumb could be quite loose. The foreign diplomats' moral bar was considerably lower than that of the Americans. As long as personal activities did not become publicly embarrassing to one's country or to the diplomatic corps—remembering the delicate netting that diplomacy formed over the world—the diplomats were likely to overlook most transgressions. Hence the culture allowed Count Cassini's sham involving his wife and daughter, Marguerite, without the scorn that village society would have imposed. Mrs. Roosevelt, who did not approve of exceptions to social rules, seems to have been willing to overlook the count's situation, but she came down on others.

It can be safely assumed that the wives of congressmen and senators, judges, and lobbyists, as well as the permanent population of Washington, when they knew of a transgression, generally agreed with Mrs. Roosevelt, at least on the surface. To tolerate a difference between public and private morality was in theory unthinkable. In practice, however, it was overlooked every day. For instance, bigotry in matters, sexual, political, and racial was undisguised. Some members of Congress patronized Baltimore's brothels, and no scandal resulted; some politicians and statesmen took money under the table; the African American population was held down even in the capital, where it probably enjoyed the nearest to equality it knew in any numbers in the United States. Mary Theresa Leiter censured a friend for introducing one of her daughters to a Jew without prior permission.[29]

There was much talk in society about love affairs. A roguish remark young men made to one another was this: "I wish you would marry so-and-so, as I want to have an affair with her." Ambassadors tended to be frisky with the open, relaxed American girls, and the South American diplomats were particularly notorious, although advances

from the older men were not welcomed. One young woman, invited to a senior diplomat's *garçonnière*—as bachelor apartments were fashionably known—listened to
him plead, declaring "what bliss they would have together," to which she finally shot
back, "Mr. Ambassador you are out of fashion. We do not have affairs anymore in
Washington: masturbation on Thursday afternoons is now the chic thing. It has many
advantages—you will not be late for the appointment—you depend upon yourself for
pleasure and you will have no depressing snubs."[30]

The capital during the season was a matchless delight for a transient group of perhaps a thousand people, although the number in society is uncertain. Very few resident
Washingtonians were a part of this. So there was an outsider character to the whirl of the
season. All that held it to any one form or pattern was the schedule of the White House.
There what was known as the "made list" included Washington residents. Being included
on that list meant a great deal to the lucky ones. The list developed over time, beginning
as a resource for filling chairs at the president's dinner table. It defined local society. Old-
time Washingtonians, who called themselves "cave dwellers," were sprinkled through the
season's events but in a secondary way, for several reasons. In the diplomatic milieu, they
were not important to the diplomats' work. Diplomatic entertaining was business, and
only so many could be invited, so the irrelevant were eliminated. To be struck off the list
or overlooked was a curse visited upon a once-proud house.

Except for the White House schedule, however, the social season along Massachusetts Avenue was entirely separate from the season at the president's residence. It
was more closely attached to the diplomatic corps than the president's events of state,
which were also ultimately business affairs. Activities along the avenue promised good
times. Marguerite Cassini wrote, "Could there be a better place or a happier time to
have been a young girl than Washington at the turn of the century?" She remembered,
"The exciting new freedoms were coming in, but they had not yet crowded out the
graces of living. Cotillions, bachelors' germans with their intricate, graceful figures,
tableaux and lawn parties, beaux and flirtations—how deliciously daring we felt and
oh, how innocent we actually were!"[31]

The capital was a paradise of activities from which one could pick and choose.
At Fort Myer, for example, the Wright brothers tested their fascinating flying machine
before afternoon crowds. Washington theater was better than that in most other
American cities, and vaudeville was not too frisky for a public sort of individual to
enjoy. The Smithsonian held exhibits and lectures. Picnickers rode the boat to Mount
Vernon and spread their feasts on its grounds. Arlington cemetery and the Lee mansion were also popular resorts for young people on outings. Public dances were marginal but attended even by fashionable young ladies and their escorts. There were
many excuses to be away from home for a morning or afternoon or a whole day.

Marguerite Cassini's parents warned her, "Danger for young girls awaits on
the corners of every street!" Most dangers wore pants. Even so, Marguerite recalled

that being around "men all obviously so sophisticated and worldly" made it hard to remember the rules of conduct: "Never look into a man's eyes—that is bold; never allow a man to call you by your first name; never allow him to hold your hand; and never—the unforgivable—permit a kiss unless engaged."[32]

Central to the young adults was the president's daughter Alice. She had been reared most of her life heretofore with her father's sister Anna Cowles and the parents of her late mother, Alice Lee Roosevelt, in Boston. She left their household to join her father and stepmother at the White House. Only rarely had she lived with them before because of discord between herself and her father's second wife, Edith. Spoiled in a sense but feeling detached in another, she was seventeen when McKinley's death placed her father in the presidency. The advantages of joining her father were obvious. "In a way you will find this a hard position," Edith Roosevelt had written, "but in others it will be delightful." She continued, "You are being trusted with a great deal of liberty & you must be careful not to abuse it, & you must remember how unenviably conspicuous your position is."[33]

Alice wearied of her stepmother's persistent advice, but to please her father she tolerated it, although she tolerated little else she did not like. Otherwise she enjoyed her position very much. Not unlike her father, she made a point of being incongruous to the exalted position in which she found herself. Alice made being "first daughter" a wonderful context for cutting up. Life for a president's daughter was more carefree than that of an ambassador's daughter. Where other daughters left Washington to go to school or married and moved away, daughters who remained behind held card and tea parties, guided visiting dignitaries, and remained fairly busy helping their father. After their debuts, which were an official introduction to the adult world through a ball or perhaps a tea, they were considered eligible to accept invitations on their own and participate publicly in activities appropriate to their positions.[34]

Introductions to men were still restricted. A young woman associated directly with only those men whom she had met through persons she knew well. For the man to write to her or send flowers, permission was usually required from her parents to "address" her. Arrangements could be made for introductions, but little freedom was allowed otherwise. A woman's reputation was at risk if she broke the rules.

After their debuts, diplomats' daughters were required to fulfill the duty of calling, which meant they had to dress up and go out in a carriage to a number of houses, legations, or embassies and spend fifteen minutes, no more, sitting in a stiff parlor making conversation. This was considered a friendly courtesy. If the visiting daughter was lucky, no one was at home, so she was allowed to dog-ear her calling card on the left top corner and leave it, showing that she had come in person. This counted as a call. In the diplomatic community, calling times were usually announced, saying, for example, that this or that person was at home Wednesdays between two and four. So the call was made during that time. If it was known that the recipient of the call was out of town, the card was simply delivered by the coachman, received on a tray by the butler or doorman, and the call registered as having been made. To dog-ear a card delivered by a coachman was to imply a personal call even when in fact no such call had taken place.

Calling was one custom very much simpler in the diplomatic community because of set rules. To call at a house at a time different from the published hours was to be told that the lady was "not at home." An angry woman might have the butler tell a caller, "Mrs. _____ is not at home to you," but this was as rude as it sounds and one assumes rather rare. Private calling was much less a requirement during the Imperial Season than it once had been. The receptions that Washington had in such great number absorbed most of the lingering practice, except for calling in the case of a death or to greet a special guest. The flow of letters and notes was full and swift. Marguerite Cassini gave a portion of each weekday morning to this task, under the count's supervision. Being her father's official hostess, "Countess" Cassini used a title not yet recognized by the czar. Where it merely raised eyebrows with some in the Washington corps, a European diplomatic corps would have found it unacceptable.

Marguerite was required to hold receptions on Thursdays during the season, without fail. During Russia's difficulties and finally its war with Japan, Count Cassini, fearing the very obvious belligerence of the court in St. Petersburg toward Japan, decided to try to soften the appearance of the Russian rampage to Americans. Knowing that Americans favored the Japanese, he decided to hold a public reception at the embassy, so that ordinary people could see Russians mingling warmly with Japanese. Marguerite recalled his order that "whoever wished might come." It was unusual for him even to consider such an open house, for in Europe such a reception would be an invitation to chaos and considered inappropriate. In Washington public receptions were held all the time during the season, so the count put out his announcement. Marguerite reported, "The next Thursday a mob swarmed into the Embassy. From all sides and everywhere, even from out of town, they came, on trolleys, in carriages and herdics and on foot, curious people wanting to see the inside of an embassy and have tea with a countess. *Petit fours*, sandwiches, and bonbons were trampled into the rugs, tea was spilled, glasses, china broken, people squeezed in the crush."[35] The count never held such an event again.

One group of young women who were often together were Justice Joseph McKenna's daughter Isabelle; Louise Foraker, daughter of Senator Joseph B. Foraker, from Ohio; Alice and Helen Hay, daughters of John and Clara Hay, who had both married their brother Del's best friends early in the century; Alice Roosevelt; Cissy Patterson; and Marguerite Cassini. The friends rode sidesaddle along Rock Creek in early mornings. On snowy days their coachmen took them riding in procession by sleigh. At night more often than not there were dinners. They performed their duties and gave some effort to testing the rules otherwise.

They were at no loss for men. Quite a crowd of males in their twenties and thirties surrounded them. There seems to have been a rule set in concrete that a man had to be fun to be with, or they avoided him entirely. The girls made great sport of the beaux and occasionally met their match. In 1902 Nicholas Longworth joined the Congress. He was in his early thirties, a stocky extrovert of a man's man with an experienced eye for female company, be it high or low. The randy side of him was well-known among men, who even teased him about it, but apparently not so much among parents that he was kept at a distance. He called on most of the young women in society. Alice Roosevelt's father was not certain how he felt about Nick, finding the congressman a rival in dominating conversation and at times "vulgar" with his jokes.[36]

The girls considered him good company and brotherly and loved to hear him play his violin, at which he was quite gifted, according to the musical Bruce Cortelyou. Once settled in Washington, Nick secured a little nest of an apartment, a *garçonnière* with a fully stocked liquor cabinet, a fireplace, and, by implication, plenty of horizontal comfort. His late evenings at home became well known.

Charles McCawley, a major in the U.S. Marine Corps and the preeminent bachelor in Washington, was another member of the circle. His rank was brevet, in recognition of distinguished service in the Spanish-American War. He was thoroughly military. In his dress uniform, McCawley, a striking presence of a man with thick, waxed hair, was an ornament to the social aides group at the White House and a welcomed guest everywhere else. Though in his early forties and more the ages of the Pattens than Alice and her friends, they warmed to McCawley and considered him one of them. He was particularly close to Alice, whom he escorted often to evening receptions and dinners.

Another Charles quite as admired by females but not as dependable a character as McCawley was the French viscount Charles de Chambrun, in his late twenties. A direct descendant of General Lafayette, he was third secretary and legal adviser to the French Embassy. Chambrun had been born in Washington, son of the former Viscount de Chambrun, a well-known expert on American government and law, who had come to the United States as a diplomat during the Civil War and become a confidant of Lincoln. Returned to the French legation in Washington, he had remained and reared his family in Alvey Adee's neighborhood, about four blocks from Lafayette Square. He returned to France permanently near the end of his life and died at La Grange.

The Foreign Office in France, naturally aware of the fondness of Americans for the revolutionary war hero, had placed Lafayette descendants on official duty in America whenever possible as envoys or legation officials. A wise observer might nevertheless have wondered whether sending Charlie de Chambrun was a good idea. He was bright indeed, witty and good-looking, blue-eyed. A tussle of blond curls formed a deceptive halo around his noble head. Of personal polish and elegant form, he was also impoverished. Amorous and romantic by nature, he might present a lady with a poem of his composition to thrill her, but he was likely to appear before her wearing a dirty shirt and scuffed shoes. For a diplomat Chambrun seemed a bit outside the norm.[37]

Alice Roosevelt was captivated by him at one point. In her diary she wrote of "dearest Charley," "Darling Charley," "Adorable Charley," and "Angelic Charley." Later: "I am absolutely devoted to him." And at about that same time: "I am quite insane about Chambrun." Alice also recorded what Charlie told her one evening at Nick Longworth's: "He didn't find a lust for me anymore. Not that he ever really did—and when I am so devoted to him."[38]

The viscount was rather a pet in Washington society, stumbling into love affairs, sometimes with married women, speaking casually of his mistresses. Minnie Townsend liked most everything about him but his shabby habits of dress. She had no designs upon him as a husband for Mathilde but encouraged their friendship. When at her house he usually drank too much, so she had the two Italian footmen haul him upstairs and put him to bed, returning with his clothes, which they took to the large, modern downstairs laundry of the house. Next morning Charlie de Chambrun woke up to a big breakfast and a hot bath and found his clothes clean, pressed, and ready to adorn the man. He put them on, apparently hardly noticing the favor.

The erratic Chambrun was an easy target for jokes. Spencer Cosby, a young architect and "society man," son of the chief engineer who built the Library of Congress, got together with men friends and invented through perfumed letters a female burning with desire for Chambrun. He fell for it immediately and somewhat wildly, pursuing the phantom lady to the hilarious revelation anticipated by her sponsors. There were no broken noses, no black eyes; Charlie joined in the laughter.

Such was the light side of life in the mansions along Massachusetts Avenue, the street that imitated the capitals of the world before Washington itself began to appear a world-class capital.

NINE
Players

The season in Washington was a custom that had already developed as a local institution in the nineteenth century, but it was entirely different in the quarter century visited here. With the coming of the ambassadors it gained more glitter and protocol. The State Department's high level of involvement in shaping the character of private entertainments was unprecedented. Isabel Anderson wrote that the "old Washingtonians found it difficult" being displaced by rank.[1] In addition to the diplomatic work piled upon him at the office, Adee was involved more than ever in the planning of private dinners and receptions on Massachusetts Avenue. When asked, he helped with seating charts, receiving lines, music at receptions—every point of order and any detail that might impinge upon the sensitivities of attending diplomats. An error of appropriateness could easily topple a host's social crown, making that host the butt of laughter, even a subject of slicing comment in the *Evening Star* or the *Washington Post*. Among the diplomats, mistakes were forgotten only slowly.

In barren December the lights began to go up along Massachusetts Avenue. Congress was in session. Cards went out for the first state dinner at the White House. Just who was invited dominated conversation until the topic of Christmas usurped it. Through the winter, which in Washington could be either a tough, icy time or a cooler autumn, the activities continued: dinners, balls for the few, receptions and concerts for a bit broader number. Everyone was busy. The Capitol galleries and the Supreme Court provided performances like no other, if one had the patience to sit back and extract some dramatic form from the flood of words. Alvey Adee's brother, David, spent his days there, listening, taking notes, and making for his readership a certain music from the long deliberations. He and his wife, Ellen, and Alvey slipped away to go hunting at Yarrow, if the weather was not too cold.

Spring could be early in Washington. When it entered in its full glory, late in April, early in May, any semblance of a season came to an end, and the time of dogwood, redbud, and a million flowers was underway. The last garden parties were over by mid-May. Around that time the houses of the city were being stripped of rugs and curtains, which were packed away in cedar storage, and the furniture was refreshed with slipcovers, the floors with straw mats. All classes of society participated in some version of lightening the cold-weather load of their domiciles, to better welcome breezes and account for the inevitable sweat that accompanied a Washington summer.

In the mansions along Massachusetts Avenue, travel schedules were certainly finalized by the middle of May. By the time the *Magnolia grandiflora* began to bloom in June, most of the houses on Massachusetts Avenue were closed, their occupants having already passed through Union Station's great arches and vanished over steel rails.

Of the often self-described "stylish set," the Larz Andersons appear to have been the most mobile. For all the attention they gave to their entertaining, they always seemed about to leave for somewhere else. Each was a born wanderer, a born student. Washington was their workplace for his career. When in residence on Massachusetts Avenue they did what served him best. Anderson liked doing things the "old way," as he called it, dinner seated, with a footman standing behind each guest's chair in eighteenth-century-style livery and powdered wigs. He looked privately upon such entertaining rather as a sociologist might appreciate a cultural survivor from a lost time. His wealth, his opulent manner of life, and his own charm, he believed, assured him of a stellar diplomatic career.[2] While his life in diplomacy was to be marginal, he never gave up the image of the worldly diplomat. He liked the formal aspects of diplomatic service, once ordering a European-style diplomatic uniform for himself, even knowing that American diplomats did not wear uniforms.

The Andersons' lives were otherwise very private. If Larz may have had some trouble early on in forsaking bachelor privileges, his journals make it clear that he and Isabel were two souls melded together by the deepest affection and compatibility. Being without children seemed to draw them all the closer to each other. Away in the inner part of the house was a two-story room where they liked to stay, eating their dinner before the fire and sleeping in a balcony-like loft that extended over the room.[3] It was cozy and intimate and always available to them, even when the rest of the house was closed and in dust covers. And it was the only room in "Anderson House" that they claimed entirely for themselves.

They were not stuffy, at least after the parties were over. Having attended a formal event elsewhere, Isabel liked to cook a midnight breakfast for the interesting people she and Larz had encountered. The invitation was issued with a whisper. Carriages and automobiles wheeled in and parked along the short horseshoe driveway. Guests followed their hosts along the dark-paneled hall to a kitchen as large and nickel plated as any found in a first-class hotel. Isabel started the event by equipping the company with pots and pans, ordering that they begin banging them together as loudly as they could, and follow her in a noisy march past great chests and suits of armor that lined the lofty hallways and drawing rooms of the house, up and down stairs, then back to the kitchen. Preliminaries being over, Larz mixed drinks while Isabel cooked. She was a good cook; Larz praised her after-hours Welsh rarebit. Plates of eggs and bacon were passed from the stove, bottles of wine opened. Sometimes the talking went on all night, while on the top floor some twenty resident servants sought sleep.[4]

A more frequent scene of unorthodoxy in the orthodox world of Massachusetts Avenue was the Wadsworth house, where a couple a bit older than the Andersons presided in the winter. Herbert and Martha Wadsworth did their own good works. He funded Reginald de Forest's musical projects, which gave Washington a symphony orchestra and created a real appetite for professionally performed music in Washington, even at the receptions and teas on Massachusetts Avenue. Herbert Wadsworth was apparently a sort of troubleshooter for his congressman cousin James Wadsworth on various projects. Martha had her charities, many of which seem to have been put upon her by James's wife, Louisa Travers Wadsworth, an emphatic woman heard more on public issues than most congressional wives dared. Although Herbert and Martha's primary residence was in upstate New York, near Avon, south of Rochester, where he had his farm and she her horses, Washington was a place to have fun. Martha Wadsworth was old enough to big-sister the younger women in society, and they often came to her for advice. For the petite, red-headed Martha, age was a mere technicality.

Everyone enjoyed her entertainments. Her big cubical ballroom was often the scene of dances. Both Wadsworths were athletic, but especially Martha. When she danced, she did so vigorously, wearing her guests down with repeated waltzes, polkas, and sometimes square dances. Parties, she believed, should have themes. On one occasion she went about on the sly collecting baby pictures of the guests, which she hung gallery style to surprise them in an after-dinner show. In addition to being a photographer of considerable skill, she was a good watercolorist as well. She also displayed her own work for her

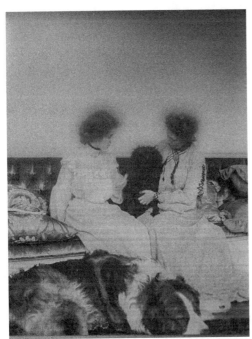

Martha Wadsworth showing her pets to her niece Helen (Nelka) de Smirnoff, 1903, in the round salon upstairs at 1801 Massachusetts Avenue. *Milne Library, State University of New York, Geneseo.*

guests in the ballroom and sometimes held competitions with other artists. Everyone involved in the competitions was invited to dinner along with guests who might want to buy the pictures.[5]

The Wadsworths had company nearly as constantly as anyone on Massachusatetts Avenue. For all the giddy occasions their friends were to remember in their home, dinner at 1801 Massachusetts Avenue could be as formal and dressy as any others in the capital. Martha received on Tuesdays during the season, open to all. The Wadsworths were generous with their family members. Having no children of their own, they gave every attention to their nieces and nephews. Martha's sisters and brothers came as house guests from St. Louis and Europe. Close at hand were Herbert's cousin James, the congressman, and his wife, Louisa; their son, Jerry, was a special favorite of Martha's. It was through a relative of Louisa's that Herbert and Martha knew Walter Gay, the famous "portraitist" of French interiors. He was married to Louisa's sister Matilda. While Martha claimed to be the architect of her house, in addition to the architect of record, named George Cary, of Buffalo, New York,[6] the Gays visited often from their home near Paris, and Walter's ideas may have had more than a little to do with the design of the Massachusetts house. Some of the rooms seem to spring from his paintings.[7]

The ballroom saw activities other than dancing and amateur art shows. At one period it was the stage for Martha's own brand of feminism, which held that a woman was likely to be able to do most anything physically that a man could do. She smarted when men referred to the "weaker sex," a phrase she thought was too often used by Theodore Roosevelt. In fact, the president seems to have annoyed her with much of what he said. In 1904, while Roosevelt was running for reelection, the famous Japanese jujitsu *judan*, or black belt, Yamashita Yoshiaki visited Washington, where at the White House he gave several vigorous demonstrations on the mat with Roosevelt. In the widespread publicity that resulted from the East Room performance, Roosevelt seems to have made some forgotten remark about women that especially aggravated Mrs. Wadsworth.[8]

Having already read about the Japanese art of defense with interest, she determined to show Roosevelt she could do anything he could do and contacted Yamashita at the Japanese legation. The professor, a princely-looking athlete of a very serious demeanor, had created a movement among women in Japan to take up jujitsu for physical protection against assault. He naturally was interested in an opportunity to extend his teaching to American women. When he met his Washington patrons he must have wondered how such a self-satisfied class might receive his life credo, "Always try to think of improvement, and don't think that you are too good."

Arrangements were made with the teacher and his wife, Fude, and the staff that had accompanied him. Martha sent out invitations to certain of her friends. When they arrived they were escorted upstairs to bedrooms where maids convinced them to change into pajama-like costumes with tunics; their feet were wrapped in linen.

Martha could do some strange things with her guests, so the women, amused, fell into line. Descending to the ballroom they were greeted by a similarly dressed Martha, who stood on the softened, mat-covered dance floor and introduced the professor, who in turn stepped aside for a demonstration of jujitsu by Yamashita Fude and a female attendant. Then Martha stepped forward, followed by the guests; a "society" jujitsu class was born in the Wadsworth ballroom. To the great pleasure of all, the class met off and on for two Washington seasons while Yamashita Yoshiaki commuted to Annapolis to teach at the Naval Academy.

The jujitsu classes appealed to Martha's more athletic friends, like Hallie Elkins and Grace Lee, but not to Alice Roosevelt or Marguerite Cassini. The latter were probably glad about how the class was described in an illustrated Sunday feature in the *New York World*, for their fathers would have called it vulgar. Remembered Alice, "I was brought up on the principle that 'nice' people didn't get their names in the papers except when they were born, when they married, or when they died."[9] Martha Blow Wadsworth nonetheless became widely publicized as being among the first women in America to achieve the rank of black belt in jujitsu.[10]

Martha was a loyal friend and one quick to act when needed. Marguerite Cassini never forgot how Martha came to her aid when the seventeen-year-old, in a fit of youthful despair, decided it was time to end her life. She had the coachman drive her from pharmacy to pharmacy, where she collected small portions of poison on the premise that she had to destroy her ailing lap dog. Once supplied, she consumed it all, then lay back against the coach cushions awaiting death. In agony soon enough, she cried out to the coachman to save her. Alarmed, he turned into the nearest familiar harbor, the Wadsworth carriageway. Borne upstairs by the coachman and the butler, Marguerite was stretched out unconscious on a sofa. Martha Wadsworth called the doctor, who said that Marguerite had only a very short time to live. Martha demanded a miracle. The doctor said that she could try for one: if the patient could be kept up and awake until the poison wore off, she might survive.

Marguerite was carried into the ballroom, laid on the bare floor, and Martha set to work. She slapped her, rolled her over and over across the room, punched her, walked her, dragged her; the hours passed through the night. The torment continued. Marguerite begged to be allowed to die. Martha was determined that she would not. When the first light of day came through the tall windows, Martha had won. Marguerite's tiny form, black and blue, lay on the floor sleeping soundly, but she was alive.[11]

Travel for most of the season's luminaries was a ritual never broken. Thus a large number of the seasonal residents of Washington had the opportunity to compare their American capital with the capitals of the world, because they saw European capitals every summer. They loved to travel, mostly to Europe but in some cases to Asia as well. Consequently an object staple in their houses was the steamer trunk. Of

Countess Cassini of Russia, dressed for a masquerade. *Library of Congress, Prints and Photos Division.*

the many types, the "wardrobe" trunk, a four- or five-foot heavy-duty case, sturdily hinged and provided with locks, was equipped with compartments and drawers and served for transport and as an object of furniture for the well-dressed on long trips. The owner's name and address were usually stenciled on the sides; the sides of a steamer trunk of a well-seasoned traveler boasted stickers from cities and hotels around the world.

Trunk and luggage storage rooms were usually on an upper floor, paneled in unpainted cedar boards, lighted by a skylight and a glass door or window facing on an inner room or hall, so that the natural light was useful but grayish dim, considering the room's purpose for storage. Portable storage was necessary in an age when all travel was relatively slow and Europe, Asia, and for all practical purposes Latin America as well were reached only by sea. What was thus a convenience for most people was an absolute necessity for those who planned to appear in society. Packing the trunks was an art. Wrapped in layers of tissue paper, the dinner and business suits, golf and tennis clothes, and hats all found their places. Drawers held collars, cuff links, and handkerchiefs. There were daytime dresses and frocks for evening, hats, scarves, furs, purses, shoes, swimming costumes, and ornaments for hair and bosom. With their carefully fitted trunks, those who traveled after the season went out from Massachusetts Avenue to the world.

Even much travel within the United States was by sea. Although one could journey from Washington to New Orleans by train, the sea journey was praised, served by steamers leaving and arriving at Baltimore. Such a trip from New Orleans was easily broken by a few days ashore, wandering the old streets of St. Augustine or taking it easy in Tampa, where luxury hotels awaited, the Ponce de Leon, the Tampa Bay. Havana, where friskier entertainment was available, was also a popular stop. Ships sailed regularly along the Atlantic coast to Maine and points in between. The president and his family sailed to Oyster Bay on the navy yacht *Sylph*, the vessel that had transported the Japanese and Russians in 1905 during the treaty conference. Going from New York to Newport by water was the best way to travel, whether by commercial steamer or private yacht. Ports all along the east coast were lively with business.

The Andersons had a yacht, a houseboat Larz designed himself, and a private railroad car also of his design. All three were enlisted extensively in their travels.[12] More typically for a trip by train from Washington to New York, those who could afford to reserved a "state room," which was a private room, ample enough by train standards, with sitting room, bedroom, closet, and a small, separate lavatory. John Hay traveled this way, unless a corporate friend such as Alexander Cassatt or Whitelaw Reid loaned his private car. Like the Andersons, a few of the other winter residents maintained their own private cars, but most were rented. George Pullman, of course, had a very grand car, as did George Westinghouse. Burnham traveled to and from Washington in a rented rail car, as did the partners of McKim, Mead & White. The railroads usually provided high government officials, including the president, with private cars when they called for them. The day of armed private cars had not yet come. There were plenty of private cars around, stored on spur tracks at Union Station.

Travel to Europe and Asia, which was of course only by sea, nearly all began in New York. Baltimore also had steamers and freighters, and some Europe-bound ships docked there, as they did in New Orleans and Mobile, but the most frequent point of departure for European travelers was New York. San Francisco and Los Angeles had major ports, where some travel to Asia embarked. Transatlantic service offered numerous ships. Only the grand ones are usually remembered, for example, the *Vaterland, Imperator, Lusitania*, and the smaller yet luxurious *Columbia, Auguste Victoria*, and *Elbe*. Many more lesser ships plied the Atlantic, kept to capacity by frequent sailings. The Massachusetts Avenue travelers presumably took their quarters in first class most of the time, as Alvey Adee nearly always did, but sometimes the convenience of scheduling outweighed the luxury of the legendary pampering that went with the most expensive ticket.

About thirty steamship companies served New York and the nearby New Jersey ports, including the Cunard Steamship Company, the Holland America Line, the North German Lloyd Line, the French Line, and the White Star Line. Booking a steamer to Europe was similar to making an air reservation today, in the sense that there were many options. The timing was less precise though, with travelers given a day to arrive and move aboard. Large areas of the ships offered various prices in second and third class. Steerage, or "cabin passage," was the lowest class, where passengers were considered freight, with only slight government regulation to honor their well-being. On a smaller scale, there were many mail lines and sailing ships. Schooners served all American ports in the early 1900s. Travel by sea was not a serious rival of land travel, given the immediacy of railroads, automobiles, and even in some cases horse wagons, but where there was no land to cross or land routes to shortcut, ships still ruled and they came in all sizes.

Now and again passengers to Asia went first by train to California, to avoid the long sail around Cape Horn, and embarked from Los Angeles, San Diego, or San Francisco. When Secretary of War Taft took eighty-three people on a goodwill mission to Asia in 1905, the party went by train to California, then sailed by steamer to Hawaii, the Philippines, and China. The Panama Canal would ease Asian trips, but not before 1914. There were no short trips, as one might understand the term today. Transatlantic passenger ships vied to be the fastest, but it took about a week to journey from New York to Southampton, and that with a fair sea. The sea journey, however, provided an orientation period that prepared travelers for the foreign countries, making them more receptive, more willing to be absorbed, than today's air trip of a few hours' duration can ever do. Sometimes the sea trip of a century ago might be compared to a process of removal, as shedding a heavy coat to better suit a new climate. However, most of the diaries and accounts of the Washington travelers indicate that they clustered together with friends on shipboard, as though they were still on Massachusetts Avenue.

The inveterate traveler Alvey Adee was recognized as a local expert on travel as well as diplomacy. He had decided ideas on hotels, food, and the best things to see. "If you go to Naples," he advised Clara Hay, "I suggest you put up at the Hotel Santa Luccia, on the bay-side opposite the Castello—It was opened in April of last year, only a few days before I went there, and is one of the brightest, most artistic, and well kept hotels I have ever tumbled into."[13] Extended travel, which was about the only form of ambitious travel, occupied part of every year among nearly all of Washington's temporary residents. Not that they were the only travelers, for others like Adee joined in, but the temporary residents were more certain to go because their money usually decreed that they could be wherever they wished to be. Generosity toward the diplomats during the season helped weave a network of interesting people to call upon and generated desirable invitations.

In the twentieth century's first decade, England and France remained the most common destinations for Americans, but Germany made a close rival. Had it not been for the language barrier in Germany, it might have been equal to France as a destination, where language differences were easier to overcome. For all its old and quaint parts, Germany seemed excitingly modern, and Berlin presented every attraction to the visitor. Under Kaiser Wilhelm II, as a relatively new great power, Germany seemed to have the best of everything. The German Empire's marriage of technology and philosophy, for all the dark side that would appear later, had no parallel anywhere else. Berlin life, as well as that at the nearby royal city of Potsdam, was polished to a high glow by major civic improvements, willed by previous generations, and brought to completion recently. Germany had achieved a state of modernity that any American who saw it could admire.

To visiting Americans, all of Europe seemed to prosper. In country after country they found areas reminiscent of the industrial United States, yet from Europe the postcard images sent home recalled the past, refined and mellow, old churches, other old buildings, and old towns. Understandably there were no postcards that showed the reality of a once-agricultural countryside now slashed by fast steam railroads or horizons pierced by the upward thrusts of smokestacks spewing dark plumes of exhaust from the factories below them, although such scenes were part of Europe as well. Americans poured across the ocean in seemingly endless numbers to see less the new Europe than the old one that lingered. If it was the old that defined Europe to them, they were nonetheless also impressed by the bustle of modern life and innovation, the modern attitudes, the urbanity.

Recognition by kings meant everything to Americans abroad. The roster of royalty was thick all over Europe, the thrones many. Courts had formal ceremonies of presentation. Where there happened to be no crown, as in France, for example, ceremonies transferred to the households of high nobility, whose rank, if it had no legal meaning to Frenchmen anymore, still had pervasive social power over them, and those who held titles were not uninterested in wealthy American visitors.

Court presentation in England was the peak of an American woman's social achievement abroad. To curtsy before Edward VII was to realize a dream, and the woman so honored would cherish the memory and tell the story for the rest of her life, how she wore the three plumes, how she had to move her train seemingly effortlessly. Rare was the rich man traveling abroad who did not take steps to have his wife and daughters presented at St. James's. The request, unless there was a personal connection, was first entered at the Department of State in Washington, filtered through Adee, and forwarded to the ambassador in London. Political power, however it may have been achieved, enhanced the request, which the ambassador presented to the appropriate court officials. If the petition was successful, the appointment was made. Neither hour nor date was negotiable. The women were instructed by highly paid consultants on how to curtsy, what to say. A rehearsal was orchestrated by the court chamberlain. As many as thirty women were presented on an occasion, each approaching the throne separately.

Naturally great attention was given to the dresses the women wore. They could be specially designed and made, or rented. The nine-foot court train, usually white, was detachable from the obligatory white dress, which could be simple or much-ornamented. Quite a number of these court presentation dresses must have been packed away in the mansions along Massachusetts Avenue. Certainly none was more elaborate than the dress made for Isabel Anderson for her presentation in the autumn of 1904. Larz encouraged the modiste Kate Riley in London to make it the finest dress she had ever made. When it was finished he called it "a lovely creation in white with embroidered pearls." Isabel, whose tastes were rather simpler, thought the dress perhaps "too rich" for her. But it was Larz who took over in the matter. The dressmaker fitted the gown to Isabel, who was short, and in a trial run stuck the three traditional ostrich

Isabel Anderson in the dress she wore when presented to King Edward VII, 1904. *Collection of the Society of Cincinnati, Anderson House.*

feathers into Isabel's hair; Isabel shrank from the mirror but then was persuaded that they made her look taller; she even came to like the dress for making her "look thin." Larz marveled affectionately at his wife in her glory. "I know it will be dear when she wears it," he wrote in his journal. "(Indeed, I might add that I know it is already 'dear' in the shop.)"[14]

Splendid it was: Isabel praised the heavy white satin and superb handwork of the seamstress and further described the outfit: "The sparkling trimmings, the long train falling from the shoulders was of silver cloth, and in my hair were the conventional white ostrich feathers. For jewels I wore an emerald and diamond tiara and on my corsage a big Indian emerald which a maharaja had once worn on the front of his turban."[15] The Patten sisters next door could not bear it when told about the costume and lost no time in telling Larz Anderson's mother that the dress cost over half a million dollars. Mother Anderson rewarded their efforts with a predictable gush of distress and embarrassment. Not a word of what the Pattens said was true, although the Anderson wealth made such a tale plausible. Convincing the neighbors along Massachusetts Avenue that the dress cost any less would have been a daunting task. Anderson didn't try, but his mother attempted to assuage any concerns he might have about the Pattens and their "gossip," writing, "I don't think they mean it unkindly, but it sounds so unlike Isabel to those who know her well."[16] Isabel was already occupied otherwise by the time the dress was back home, wrapped in tissue, and laid to rest in the cedar room.

~

While the party continued through the early 1900s, the destination of most if not all of the young women of the "set" was marriage. They seemed, for all their apparent and innocent rebelliousness, simply waiting for the event. To an outsider looking in, their lives, wrought with uncertainty despite the satin and silk, seemed at best a gamble.

In any case, they moved toward the future decreed to them. Immaturity, perpetuated in the manner of their lives, characterized them all, but Alice Roosevelt seemingly less so; her family tensions had given her a cynical edge that some mistook for maturity. In her diary and recollections of her friends, marriage was almost a preoccupation.

A prime example of how seemingly capricious marriage could be, Cissy Patterson, a slim redhead among the set, was among the first to marry. She lived in the large white terracotta house her parents had built facing on Dupont Circle, between the Wadsworths and the Leiters. The groom was the Polish count Josef Gizycki, whom she had met while in Europe with her parents and who then had followed her with little parental supervision from city to city. All of a sudden she was engaged to Count Gizycki. The *New York World* reported in 1904: "Society was startled when Miss Patterson made a round of visits to her friends and announced her engagement to the Count. Her parents were keenly annoyed, but hurried to put out a formal announcement." The Pattersons did not, in fact, like "Gizy," as Gizycki was called. He was demanding, an unabashed gold digger, and he was Roman Catholic, while they were Protestant; he would take their darling away to live in his castle in eastern Europe. Cissy was happy and unhappy at once. She listened to her parents and heard the ring of truth in what they said. To Marguerite Cassini she confided, "He does not love me. He loves the money I have and the fact that I am a virgin."[17]

Gizycki was a womanizing thirty-five-year-old with a crumbling palace in Poland he wished to restore. The thin, fashion plate of a count was perfectly manicured, his hair curled, waxed, and pressed, his suits perfectly tailored, his manner grand indeed. Witty and worldly, his aristocratic charm seems rather to have overwhelmed Cissy, for he seemed the sort of a man a rich girl should marry. Whatever the case, she wished to marry him and become a countess. Her parents made an agreement with Gizycki, reluctantly, to provide a dowry of something like five hundred thousand dollars and an additional twenty thousand dollars per year for the Pattersons' lifetime, at which time Cissy would inherit the estate.

The day of the wedding, events were about to begin, but no groom appeared. Cissy's brother Joe and some other men in the wedding party set out to find him and at last did, sitting calmly and primly in the railroad depot, ticket to New York in hand, valet and luggage nearby. He had learned that Mr. Patterson had not deposited the dowry money in his bank, and he had no intention of marrying Cissy before it was done. A deal was a deal. Persuaded with difficulty to return to the house on Dupont Circle, he agreed at last and was shown by Cissy's father proof that the deposit had indeed been made. The marriage took place. Count and countess boarded a private car for New York. As the car rolled out, Mrs. Patterson shouted tearfully, "Darling, remember, you can always come home."[18]

Two years later Alice Roosevelt married Congressman Nick Longworth in the East Room at the White House. They had been friends, part of the crowd of regulars often together during the season. Marguerite Cassini in later years insisted that she had been Nick's preference. Rejected by Marguerite on a snowy sleigh ride, Longworth found his way to Alice. She was quite taken with him for a while. But in the full light of reality, the president's daughter never seems to have been sure that she loved Nick Longworth. "One of the reasons I married," she said in later years, "was because I felt I had to get away from the White House and my family."[19] She was encouraged to give Nick a chance: "My father considered Nick Longworth a very good match." Even though Roosevelt did not approve of Nick entirely, he had shown real promise in Congress, perhaps encouraging most presidents' dream of a dynasty; his Cincinnati background and connections were impeccable; he could well afford Alice; and factoring in the money she got from her mother's side of the family, they would be able to do as they pleased.

In her diary at the time of the courtship, Alice appears smitten. "Oh Nick, I love you passionately Nick—What are we going to do tomorrow. I havt see you," and "Nice old Nick, very sweet. Oh if it only would last. How much do you love me Nick?" Earlier beaux had gone. Beginning in 1904 the crowd had thinned. Marguerite Cassini left in 1905 to return to Russia with her father, not to return to Washington for thirty years. Charles de Chambrun departed Washington and the pages of Alice's diary ahead of a scandal. His affair with a married woman may have aroused only a discreet whisper among the diplomats, but it assured his rejection at the White House. This is doubtless the reason he left. Marguerite Cassini reported that his lover left her husband and followed him to other missions, where she and Charles lived together for a time before he began his remarkable ascent in the diplomatic service of France.[20]

The perennial eligible bachelor Charlie McCawley had begun visiting a widow fifteen years his senior, Sarah Helen Frelinghuysen Davis, daughter of the former secretary of state Frederick T. Frelinghuysen. Her husband, wealthy Judge John Davis, of Washington, had died suddenly. McCawley's romance was kept quiet. At the time, he was still very much in evidence at the White House as the chief social aide, even lending his dress sword to Alice to cut her wedding cake, and by no means did he vanish from the social scene elsewhere in Washington. On July 24, 1906, when he was recovering from a near-death battle with typhoid fever, he and Sarah revealed their secret very suddenly. They called a small group of friends to his flower-filled room at Providence Hospital, where Mrs. Davis stood beside the bed with the vicar. The marriage took place on the spot, the groom, according to the press, "too weak to rise even during the brief ceremony."[21]

Capping off the reports of notable marriages in those years was the extensive publicity that accompanied the brief wedding trip of Nicholas and Alice Longworth and later their tour of Europe. The broader world received them almost as royalty. They attracted cheering crowds in England and were presented at court before Edward VII and Queen Alexandra. Newspapers were filled with Alice and Nick until 1906 had come to its close. It seemed that privacy would never be theirs, and to an extent it was not, nor apparently did she want it.

~

The panic of 1907 appeared abruptly, at least to people who knew little about economics, which was most people. Rich men of the time—those of second-generation wealth or those who had made great fortunes more or less lump sum—nested their money in trusts and received their incomes from the managed security. The trust companies were either of banks or investment management companies, and the accumulation of many clients gave them great financial power. Through investments of the money they held, the trust companies oiled the economy to a fast pace. Bitter memories of hard times in the panic of 1893, which was not eased until the second half of that decade, seem not to have made trust officers any less cautious. They eagerly supported new businesses. They financed the absorption of many companies into one. They hungrily bought stock in coal companies, railroads, and, a particular favorite, copper companies, for the spread of the telephone created a powerful demand for copper wire. Even wise investors thought ventures in copper were as safe as speculation could get.

The sort of bank trusts that wealthy people like Minnie Townsend made use of paled beside the speculating corporate trusts, often caricatured as an octopus reaching out and taking everything in sight. Suspicion of the dangers of speculation was not new to Congress, although the Sherman Antitrust Act of 1890 seemed little more than a too-costly ideal when the '93 panic struck. It had been enforced weakly since the earlier panic, as the nation's economy slowly recovered. One of the prime objectives Theodore Roosevelt set for his presidency was to curb the worst features of trust economics. In his speeches he expounded on the evils of great wealth. His efforts, for all their merits, created a wave of discomfort concerning the national economy.

Trust executives have been described as stock-market cowboys. Freed from the restrictions that kept banks in line, they took loans with stocks and bonds as security, at face value. Standing on egg shells, as it were, the trust companies were unable to combat the apprehensions of the public. Withdrawal of funds began on a small scale in the winter of 1907, but on March 25 a panic entered full-swing, with hundreds of people lining up at the various trust companies and banks, attempting to retrieve their accounts in cash. In October came a crash.

Reasons for the panic of 1907 were many and interlocking. Some insurance companies, for example, which operated as corporate trusts, were hard hit by external forces unrelated to the economy. For example, a number of these companies had to pay some five hundred million to seven hundred million dollars in settlements as a result of the San Francisco earthquake. This knocked the props from beneath them. The real root of the panic, however, was not unexpected disaster but rather the creation, spread, and ultimate collapse of the card-castles built of poorly secured loans. When the stocks fell in value, a void resulted in the supply of money. The leading financier, J. P. Morgan, first saved the day by bringing the banks together and, through cross-loaning, stabilized the system. The need for cash returned soon enough. Again summoned, Morgan turned to the federal government to close its eyes while he concocted a more radical remedy. Secretary of the Treasury Bruce Cortelyou agreed to ignore a blatant violation of the Sherman Antitrust Act to halt the failure of one company and enlarge others. The panic ebbed and the seas calmed. The American economy was rescued from collapse. Some already large fortunes, notably Morgan's, became vast. Very many more shrank. As to whether fate preserved one person's or another's, the answer was that the winners naturally were those like Tom Walsh, who managed his own money and did not entrust it to others.

Hardly a household along Massachusetts Avenue missed the impact of the panic of 1907. Mrs. Leiter blamed the reduction of her income on Roosevelt and his "trust busting," and she was not alone. The president was not held in good odor by many another rich person. House building fairly well stopped, at least for the big houses. Not all of those in progress were finished until later, some by new owners. Apartment building increased. The season in Washington was not to be so brilliant again, although neither it nor its worldly customs were discontinued.

Old patterns prevailed where it was possible. Tom and Carrie Walsh, for example, continued to be in Washington only for the season, usually departing for their home in Colorado in early spring and not returning to Massachusetts Avenue until October or November, after an interim in Europe. But with the Walshes, misfortune that had nothing to do with money all of a sudden clouded their lives forever. In the summer of 1905, when they were occupying a rented house in Newport instead of going to Europe, their son, Vinson, was killed when he lost control of an "electric" he was driving. Evalyn, the daughter, survived but was thrown out and seriously hurt, spending months in recovery. Carrie and Tom's grief was naturally great. Carrie found eventual peace in Christian Science. Walsh, himself a Catholic, did not seek religion but concentrated upon business. Both doted upon their surviving child, Evalyn, to the extent of seeming to compensate for Vinson's death. She would one day name a son for Vinson, and the child would die also as the result of an automobile accident, another curse in Evalyn's often tragic life.

Among the figures of note in the heyday of Massachusetts Avenue, Evalyn shines in her earlier years. Others would leave Washington. She, Alice Roosevelt Longworth, and a few others of their generation remained and at last called it home. Evalyn became the wife of Edward (Ned) Beale McLean. No other couple was destined to so completely characterize the unhappy side of Washington's winter community of wealth than these two. They eloped in the summer of 1908 to avoid a storybook wedding they knew they would have to endure otherwise. Soon they were off to Europe, making no plans to return and sending repeated telegrammed requests to their parents for money. Bride and groom were twenty-two years of age. Their madcap lives seemed to have not had a serious moment. Socially and financially, Ned was a good catch. Otherwise Evalyn's parents had reason to worry. Evalyn would one day write of Ned's newspaper publisher father, "Old John R. McLean was the oddest hybrid of gentle friend and fierce monster that I have ever known."[22] Residents of Cincinnati, with a house also in Washington, the John McLeans owned the *Cincinnati Enquirer*, and in 1905 McLean purchased the *Washington Post*. In 1907, McLean, a tough businessman, had two purposes in his life: the first, to help rescue from the panic the American Security & Trust Company, in which he had a large interest; the second, to enlarge his Washington residence of twenty years into a huge neo-Renaissance-style house, rather more an art museum or a world's fair–type exhibition building for entertaining than a home.

Emily Beale McLean, John's wife of many years, had been reared with one foot in Washington and the other in California, hence the capital's attraction to her. She and her brother, Truxton, had been reared both in her parents' home on Lafayette Square, in the venerable house built by Commodore Stephen Decatur, and on General Beale's immense Tejon Ranch, in California.[23] The Beales were a prominent Washington family. The general, in his adventurous youth, had crossed the continent disguised as a Mexican vaquero to bring the first samples of California gold to President Polk. From that time on, he took advantage of every opportunity his measure of fame had opened

Evalyn and Ned McLean on the terrace at her parents' Massachusetts Avenue house, 1912. *Library of Congress, Prints and Photos Division.*

up. John R. McLean, in contrast, cared not a fig for Washington but had agreed to having a residence there because of the capital's relative access to New York. The McLean family were usually in town only from Christmas to Lent.

Emily McLean was a quiet, motherly little woman who had spoiled Ned almost beyond imagination. "Neddie," her only living child, was perfect in her eyes, and as he grew up she cushioned him to the extent of tipping his playmates ten or fifteen cents to let him win at baseball, checkers, or any sport he played. The resulting man was lazy concerning work, unpredictable, and from a young age developed an affection for liquor and drugs. Ned was not without gifts of his own, but he lacked the ability, if not always the inclination, to set useful goals. In short, he lacked gumption. He and Evalyn met at the age of eleven. A laughing, teasing sort of friendship intensified in the period when he comforted her on her brother Vinson's death. Suddenly they were in love.

The honeymoon was a disorganized trip from one grand hotel to another: Paris, London, Rome, Cairo, Prague, St. Petersburg. Ned's mother wrote to Carrie Walsh, "John says I came into his room from 3 A.M. on & say I wonder where the children are & what they are doing—but seriously I *have* been wondering whether there is as much sickness in Russia as the papers report—do you think we had better cable them to be careful?"[24] Parental concern heightened to yearning at the news that Evalyn was pregnant. Ned's father sent a telegram to Tom Walsh, who was at home in Colorado: "On account of Evalyn's changed condition they do not want to come home. To remain in Europe would be a bad mistake. This year will mean much to their future. Ned is too young a man to have no occupation. A year of idleness in Europe might change their whole life. Hope you and Carrie agree with Emily and me. I can think of no greater mistake."[25]

Ned could be responsible for short periods, giving time to the newspaper and some obligatory civic endeavors, but never for long. His father continued to run the *Washington Post* with valued lieutenants. In the early years after their marriage, Ned and Evalyn became now-and-then residents of Washington, living usually in the Walsh house on Massachusetts Avenue when in town during the season or at other times in his parents' country house, Friendship, located rather away from town on Wisconsin Avenue, several miles above Georgetown. They were nearly always in Europe in the fall. Summer found them in Bar Harbor in a big house Tom Walsh had given them. The parents, particularly Emily McLean, had hoped for achievement and fame in their lives. "I have been sleeping very badly," she wrote to Evalyn only a week before the elopement, "your 'Pa in law' says it is because I lie awake wondering how I can put you & Ned in the White House! My dear, that sounds [like] a very good joke, but with all you both have, added to a life of high ideals & a determination to win, there is no reason why you should not attain that end very easily and have plenty of fun getting there too."

She continued, suggesting between the lines the awful pressure that had accompanied the jocose Ned as he grew up. "Believe me, child, there is lots of fun in being a success, and only heart aches in being a failure—keep Ned at his business, which is his importance, and you will both be happy."[26]

The young McLeans seemed to all who looked in from the outside as free as birds. Travel, collecting, partying, the accumulation of jewels, such as the Hope diamond in 1912—all came to little. Boredom soon wore upon them. The first habit they had to overcome was alcohol. And they tried. First they both became Catholics, a conversion that took place in Rome. Then in Denver in the summer of 1908 they "took the total abstinence pledge—for life."[27] This may have helped Evalyn, but it did little for Ned, who eventually graduated to narcotics. In the end, abuses took their toll on him, and he was institutionalized. Evalyn, toward the end of her long life, divorced from Ned, summed it all up: "I often wonder what he would have been, what he might be, if he had never had much money. But we had the money, or rather it had us. We were held fast in its clutches. . . . Indeed, I think that is the way to say it: We were the slaves of an infernal habit. This habit stole our will, subtly metamorphosed our point of view, thwarted our creative powers, and quite constantly made us the victim of such awful shapes of greed as would defy the fancy of such persons as we Walshes were."[28]

Alice Roosevelt Longworth, the one of the crowd who would have the last word on the era, remembered those raucous days. "I never drunk my fill of an evil side of life—and then never had the patience with the impossibility of comparing the average man with the nice [ones]. . . . I once was a 'nice young girl[,]' my instincts and desires were at least half in that direction. I always wanted to know everything—personally— from my own experience—for if I didn't inquire I could not be any too absolutely certain. I've been contented, but sometimes furiously happy."[29]

~

In addition to the declining displays of private wealth along Massachusetts Avenue after the panic of 1907, life became notably more serious in other ways as well for some people. A harbinger of this shift, an event reflective of the changed thinking to come, took place on September 29, 1907, only days before the crash, when the cornerstone was laid for the Washington Cathedral. An ambitious project it was, entirely in private hands, a dream for a mighty church to stand on a high hill overlooking the capital. A Celtic "peace cross" of stone had been erected on the hill at the close of the war with Spain, nine years earlier. At that time the envisioned cathedral complex consisted only of the cathedral's girls school and the boys school under construction.

Some thirty-five thousand people attended the cornerstone ceremony on St. Alban's Hill, out on the avenue well beyond Dupont Circle. The carriages of high clergy and major politicians were identified by tassels of purple ribbon tied to the coachmen's whips. The American ambassador to Britain, Whitelaw Reid, rode along-side the British ambassador to the United States, James Bryce, their trim white beards making them look almost like twins. The elegant equipages of the Boardmans, Walshes, Andersons, Leiters, Mrs. Townsend, and others not only added to the day's color but also suggested their generosity to a project especially loved by the winter community. Theodore Roosevelt gave a thrilling oration. The bishop of London conducted the formal, high-church proceedings. That day the Church of England and the Episcopal Church warmly joined hands. And, symbolically at least, they were never to disengage in this holy place.

The Washington Cathedral was to be central to a close containing the high schools and facilities necessary to operations and activities of a great national church. For the design of the cathedral itself, Daniel Burnham and Charles McKim had been brought in as building committee members. They attempted to take control, invoking L'Enfant and the idea of a national church, but in no measure could they dissuade their fellow committee members from Gothic as the style of architecture. Both architects naturally wished the cathedral to complement the "classic Renaissance" of the federal buildings on the Mall, as espoused in the McMillan Plan. But classicism was entirely too secular. They suggested a rich Venetian style as an alternative. The history the committee wanted, however, was English. Bishop Henry Yates Satterlee, his vision and heart fixed on a building that embodied the British and earlier American traditions of the church, loaded the scale toward Gothic, and there the discussion stopped. Already he had convinced several of the big donors that a Venetian sort of Renaissance style was not appropriate.[30]

From the pulpit, Satterlee, a dynamic man and one of those "building" preachers, readily condemned the people of Massachusetts Avenue for their opulence. None of them seems to have noticed, for he suffered no bruises among them raising money for his cathedral.[31] His coffers filled and emptied quickly. As for details of what the new Gothic house of worship would look like, his ideas were firmly set. He was in regular touch with the architect in residence at Canterbury Cathedral. An acquaintance in the Holy Land had suggested pulling limestone for the proposed Jerusalem altar from the original quarry of King Solomon. Satterlee sought biblical and Anglican relics. The bishop had pictures of a score of churches he admired, every one of them of Gothic architecture. Against this man's strong will even the powerful Burnham began to step back, writing to him weakly, "It is perhaps true that most people love Gothic work, but that does not seem to be reason enough for a choice. . . . In this country we need to correct our tendency to settle things on the basis of our own private feelings."[32] The bishop's preference stood firmly based upon church culture, not design.

He toured England and France, met with churchmen and architects, and was convinced that the best practitioner working in the Gothic style was the London-based George F. Bodley. Perhaps stung a bit by the objections of Burnham and McKim, Satterlee was determined to hire an English architect familiar with Britain's Gothic buildings and able to copy them. Bodley, and, upon his suggestion, Henry Vaughan, had begun studies for the Washington Cathedral earlier, in the fall of 1906. Two more perfectly tailored Britishers could hardly have been contrived than Bodley and Vaughan when they appeared before and captivated the committee in December.

Meeting with Satterlee frequently, the architects gave his national cathedral an intellectual context. Roman Catholic origins of the Gothic would be adapted. American history would replace the holy iconography in stained glass and statuary that had been cast out of the English church by the Tudors. The Washington Cathedral, although of the Episcopal Church, was to be a cathedral for all religions of the nation.

The setting of the cornerstone marked a new day for Bishop Satterlee. A day that had started out dark and threatening suddenly turned sunny just before the ceremony. In describing it, the bishop wrote to a friend that when the skies began to clear, he observed an American eagle perched high in the heavens. "One could almost see the Archangel and his hosts hold back the clouds in answer to the prayer of God's people."[33]

With the cornerstone of the Washington Cathedral, the international city gained a new and different symbol. For all the solid faith and nationalism of the bishop, the cathedral's political meaning is crystal clear in retrospect but was less so at the time it was begun. America's relations with Great Britain after the discord in the Cleveland administration, really from the point of John Hay's peacemaking in 1896, had, like Hay's life itself, wholly changed. Diplomatic spats between the United States and Britain had indeed occurred, but friendship, more like kinship, between the two countries had strengthened in spite of them. Steps were already being taken to celebrate a century of Anglo-American peace less than a decade from then. The relationship between the two nations expressed in the rising cathedral was to strike a reverberating note in events yet to come.

TEN
Commitment

When William Howard Taft was elected to the presidency, the voters expected his political future to be a continuation of the Roosevelt administration. This was not to be the case. Taft's style of management was different from Roosevelt's, more businesslike and often more innovative. His personal feelings were well hidden, unlike Roosevelt's. In fact, later in Taft's presidency, Roosevelt would shower him with a cold rain of abuse, but in the early days Roosevelt was relatively quiet about his politics, in part because he was far away on a big game hunt. Taft actually enjoyed great popularity when he took his oath on March 4, 1909, in the worst blizzard the capital could remember.

So many new issues surrounded life in 1909 that Roosevelt's administration seemed a distant history very soon after Taft took office. Perhaps a new president was needed to open people's eyes to the country's changes. Despite being that needed agent, Taft suffered from the start, because, unlike his predecessor, who was able to convey ideas as he entertained his listeners, Taft was all business. There was no drama to the man, and his brilliance was often simply not enough. Every element in the capital naturally sought to learn how to gain his favor. No exception were the adherents of the McMillan Plan, who saw a powerful need to achieve reassurance from the new president.

In truth, the changes of this time moved quickly beyond the construction of classical architecture in Washington to new, more universal things. A prime illustration of these broader transformations was the very obviously changing status of women. This frightened some people, while others welcomed it. Women were now appearing in public, alone or in groups, suggesting for many a freedom of movement they had not known before. No one could explain it. How had it happened? The change was ascribed to everything from the new style of clothes to the advent of the automobile, which a woman could drive as well as a man, unlike a team of horses, usually a man's work. Women patronized restaurants, conducted their own business, and took political stands, although they did not yet have the ballot except in a few states. The change with women in the public eye was not radical but very subtle, even natural. It came much like a new state of mind, an attitude that dawned on women and to some extent men. Some women came forward to demand change; for others, change seemed simply to come quietly, as from the clouds.

Amid the architectural renaissance of Washington and these sociopolitical changes lived two particular women who mirrored the period. They were activists working in widely different contexts and with different personal approaches. The first, Mabel Boardman, whom we met earlier in this story, made changes outside the view of the public and by working within the system as it was; the second, Alice Paul, stepped to the fore to play a major part in achieving a significant change to the system: the vote for women.

~

President Taft found his warmest welcome in Washington at the Boardman's. He was a familiar guest at their massive pile of a house on P Street, only a few steps from Dupont Circle, placed formidably behind the Pattersons. Mabel's father, William Jarvis Boardman, had made his wealth in the law and banking. By the time he followed the flow of political power from Ohio to Washington, he was already known as a charitable man. Public service became an avocation for him, as it was in the Taft circle. Within the two families, Taft was closest to—indeed, rather a soul mate to—Mabel, the eldest and most intimidating of William's three daughters.

The Boardman family was a quiet, intellectual one, consisting of William, who was seventy-seven when Taft took office, his wife, Florence (known as Flossie), their three daughters, and a son, also named William, who remained in Cleveland to run the family bank. Two of the daughters, Florence and Josephine, married politicians, while the third, Mabel, remained single and very much heir to her father's noblesse oblige. "Will" and "Nellie" Taft moved into the Boardman's house in February 1909, following his election in November 1908; the third floor was adapted for their use. The Tafts enjoyed every convenience Bill and Flossie could supply. From the warm hearth of the Boardman family, they journeyed by motor through the snow and ice to the White House on March 3, the day before the inauguration, obliged to accept the Roosevelts' chilly invitation to dine and spend the night.

By 1909, the elder Boardmans had turned over the entire management of their house to Mabel. She was on the threshold of fifty, a proper lady, and a serious woman. Photographs show handsome, richly embroidered or jeweled dresses tailored to her substantial form. Her wit was quick, and she was bright and strong, yet softened by sharing the kind natures of her parents. Like Taft, she had a compulsion to make things better. Born to a conservative viewpoint, she also resembled Taft in her inclination to make changes through redesign or remodeling rather than through replacement. Yet she was a woman of strong opinions and, if usually reserved, exploded occasionally in bursts of impatience with those who might not share her commonsense views.[1]

Mabel Boardman, ca. 1912. *American Red Cross, Washington, D.C.*

Personally Mabel Boardman was the outdoor type, an avid golfer who had boldly opened the golf course to women at the Chevy Chase Country Club, forcing a "ladies' day" upon the unwilling male board of directors. She never tired of pursuing seemingly inconsequential changes like that. Seeing her coming, other clubs trembled with apprehension. She had proudly accompanied her father on the course in Augusta since she had been big enough to hold a golf club. No one seems to have dared question her presence. She might be seen as a feminist, but she would have disliked the label. Her triumphant battle against U.S. Customs for its "undignified" manner of physically examining all classses of women entering America was waged not for the sake of women per se but to end a process she felt was embarrassing and crude. Miss Boardman was in fact wary of public crusades and liked to work behind the scenes.

Her personal acquaintances were legion, and she had not been short of suitors early in her life. In her twenties, when she had lived in Germany with her uncle, William Walter Phelps, United States minister to the court of the kaiser, she had the attention of many young men, including Theodore Bingham, then a military attaché to the legation. She loved Germany and German customs. In Washington her servants were German. Guests arriving at dinner for the first time were asked if they spoke German, in the hope they would free the hostess to conduct the entire evening in that language. The table was filled with traditional German dishes, and the butler poured German beers and wines. Even Miss Boardman's dogs were addressed in German.

Several diplomats wrote to her for many years from their various missions around the world, remembering her hospitality when they were assigned to Washington. The texts of the letters were reservedly affectionate at the opening and quickly fell to diplomatic subjects, relating details of news from abroad. Many of these she folded away and kept. She loved politics and was an astute observer of goings-on at the Capitol. The years of young womanhood for Mabel Boardman had passed into middle age, happily but not momentously. When Taft was elected president, her lifelong friendship with him became a political association. The president was only three years her senior, being fifty-two when he took office.

Member of a prominent family in his own right and an Ohio jurist of note, Taft was one of McKinley's many appointments from that state, relocating from Cincinnati to Washington in 1900 to chair the commission for establishing a civil government in the Philippines. He then served as governor-general residing at Manila and, from that seemingly innocent eastern perch, observed the rest of Asia. Back in Washington in 1902, he served the Philippine interests for President Roosevelt, who then made him secretary of war just before Roosevelt's second administration began. This cabinet position gave Taft an official connection to the Red Cross Society, an organization about which both Congress and the president had developed serious concerns in recent years. The situation was a bit of a hot potato.

Central to the problem was the leader, Clara Barton, who had founded the Red Cross in America in the early 1880s. Having a Red Cross in peacetime America seemed important to the lawmakers at the time, so with the blessing of Congress the society was founded as a private organization. But also during this period, Congress debated whether or not to adopt the Geneva Convention. Even its humanitarian sections generated fierce argument before the convention was adopted, and Barton's prestige as the "angel of the battlefields" of the Civil War made her voice a significant one in the contest.

The great worth of the Red Cross to the military had been demonstrated most recently during the war in Cuba, but its inefficiency had also been revealed on the battlefield and later in the bungled management of the Galveston storm's aftermath. In an attempt to improve the situation in 1900, Congress chartered the American Red Cross, thus making some federal participation and control possible, which took the Red Cross and its issues to the desk of the secretary of war. Taft immediately recognized that the organization was a problem in need of a solution.

Clara Barton was one of the most respected women in the country, but she was eighty in 1902, and she failed to understand that it was time to step down. In spite of her age, she seems to have lost none of her pluck. She made every effort to seem younger than she was, from dyeing her hair to touching her cheeks with rouge. She held tenaciously to her authority, rising against any criticism with her credo: the nation needed volunteers on call, not only for war, but also for disasters. No one objected to the idea, but up close there were problems with the management of the organization. The limited details of Red Cross business that Barton was willing to unveil were revealed to only a close circle of people under her control. Congress was alarmed and was warned by the military that more lives could have been saved in Galveston had the Red Cross been more efficient.

At Taft's request, Mabel Boardman joined the board of the American Red Cross as a troubleshooter. She was received as yet another benign socialite member. The existing power structure might have known better. The siege began with her first meeting as a board member. Chaired by Dr. Julian Hubbell, Clara Barton's lieutenant and companion, the board assembled in 1902. The icon of charity and womanhood herself was provided with an easy chair up front, set well apart from the room full of people. When she entered the meeting room, well after all others were present, the group stood up. Barton was striking to see, handsome, if not beautiful, high cheek-bones, her shoulders carefully draped in a fringed shawl that fell over a long, full, bell-shaped skirt, a relic image from the Civil War years, the era that had been hers.

No one spoke but Dr. Hubbell. The meeting had all been rehearsed as usual. He hurried through several subjects, inviting no comments. Mabel Boardman and several others began interrupting with questions about the bookkeeping and financial accounts. Hubbell could hardly answer, for Barton kept all accounts, received donations, and approved or disapproved the outflow of money. On closer inspection, much of the banking was traced through her personal bank account, including deposits and donations. The new board members' questions, which some considered brutal, were directed at Dr. Hubbell, always with a side glance to Clara Barton, who sat quietly by, barely able to conceal her astonishment, then annoyance.

Boardman was no hero for her effort. One of the regulars at Red Cross meetings wrote to Clara Barton afterward, "I shall be deeply grieved if you consider one single one of the parties who arranged themselves as an opposing force in that hall yesterday." Dr. Hubbell "stood there defending himself" against the "infamous attacks of Miss Boardman."[2] Reports leaked out from both sides, and the newspapers soon carried the story. Clara Barton read "many unkind and untrue statements" about herself and her management practices in the *Washington Post*. She was accused of not acknowledging a gift of ten thousand dollars for the relief effort at the Johnstown flood fourteen years earlier and for accounts poorly documented, with unlikely or even questionable balances. Barton and Dr. Hubbell cultivated the support of friends while taking steps to purge the Red Cross of those who defied Barton.

Barton had long believed that Red Cross business should be contained within a small circle of people. She had written in her diary a decade before: "I believe the plan of letting *any* outside person have any management of our National Red Cross is a complete failure. They get into fights, then make up, walk off arm in arm and leave the wreck of their battles and all its rubbish with us to clean up or live in. They next turn and admonish us to *peace* when we have never opened a lip from first to last."[3]

In the spring of 1903 the executive committee ordered the board members by memorandum to cease their questioning. Mabel Boardman immediately took up her pen—and she wrote very well—to denounce the memorandum in strong language. So many letters began to flood into her house that she employed a secretary, A. E. Trumbill, who was paid by the letter and envelope and profited nicely. Mabel was dismayed by the attitudes of some of the board members. One wrote to her, "I fear I am disposed to look rather upon the humorous than upon the serious side of the subject."[4] *Humorous*? A Massachusetts woman said that the fight reminded her of the local "Round Table Club," which was "a woman's club here in which a few generally boss over the majority in a most lordly way & the majority weakly submit and even adulate their rules."[5] *Woman's club*? Mabel Boardman, though somewhat amazed, was pragmatic enough to admit to the truth in the analogies. Such letters, which she kept, seem to have helped her shape her objectives.

On orders from Clara Barton, the executive committee suspended twenty errant board members, including Boardman and Anna Cowles, President Roosevelt's popular sister. Their crime, as charged by Barton, was calling public attention to the private business of the society. This hit the papers with quite a splash, not necessarily in favor of the recalcitrants. Secretary Taft probably did not have to urge Boardman to respond as she did, for she had got in fighting fit. She published a pamphlet quoting the relevant correspondence and declined to honor Clara Barton's edict.

An ailing Levi Leiter, her neighbor, wrote in a wavering hand, thanking her for sending him the pamphlet "touching upon the affairs of the Red Cross Society—now so prominently before the public." He went on: "To those who know you, a vindication of your actions by means of this publication was not necessary—but to them who were not so fortunate—this publication makes it clear that your actions were impelled by the highest & most generous motives."[6] An earlier correspondent wrote that Clara Barton's conduct "appears to me so absurd as to lead to the suspicion that there must be something which the committee is desirous of covering up." He asked that his letter be kept "strictly confidential."[7]

Taft continued to encourage Boardman and Anna Cowles as "arch conspirators" in Red Cross reform for the "new Red Cross Society." Boardman called the controversy the "Barton problem."[8] In March 1903 she asked Hubbell for a list of the names of members of the new board elected at the secret meetings. Ignoring this, Hubbell wrote a flattering letter for a press release, "Some Facts concerning Clara Barton's Work," to help reporters articulate the lady's greatness.[9]

In the wake of Mabel Boardman's dismissal, others of the board formally resigned. Alvey Adee remained but revoked the proxy Clara Barton had wrested from him and the others in 1900, when the American Red Cross had been chartered by Congress. As a friend of both Mabel Boardman and Clara Barton, Adee probably sensed a dog fight coming and wanted to be in control of his position.[10] When the reconstituted executive committee voted to sue the local newspapers for libel, the press began to call for Barton's resignation. Meanwhile in February and March 1903, Barton made many public appearances before grateful crowds, talking of her experiences in the Civil War and in Cuba.

But Clara Barton's crown had toppled. What Mabel Boardman could not achieve, her friends did. Taft was by now in Manila; he turned the matter over to the Department of State. Alvey Adee, acting for the absent Hay, took over the project and requested a list of the board members and officers. According to the dictates of the charter, the Red Cross had to comply. As he doubtless expected, Clara Barton ignored the request, so he suspended her. In explaining her removal, Adee's official report did not mention her dismissal of the State Department's request but did discuss the need for an investigation of the irregularity in her "methods of distributing relief funds and accounting to the committee from whom received."[11] Clara Barton had no alternative but to accede and save face as best she could.[12] Adee wrote to congratulate her: "I deeply regret the stress you have undergone in the matter of the Red Cross and trust that the situation will soon be less trying, now that you have directed an impartial examination of the administrative records."[13]

Barton's was an unhappy ending to a distinguished career. In 1904 the Senate ordered an investigation of the business practices of the Red Cross. Clara Barton yielded at last to pressures to resign but insisted upon waiting until the Senate had cleared her name, which, predictably, it did, and then she did resign.

Congress revised the charter, reorganizing the Red Cross under a board of governors consisting of congressional appointees, citizen members, and members elected from the various regional chapters. The mission was clear: The Red Cross was to be the coordinator of an extensive volunteer resource that was vital to the nation. It was to function ahead of and in cooperation with the more complex government agencies in relief work, including plagues, natural disasters, and, almost secondarily, wars. The Red Cross was to be ready to act at a moment's notice.

Mabel Boardman entered the renewed organization as a volunteer committee member. Very soon she became wholly absorbed in the mission of the Red Cross. Except when she was in Europe, with her family at the summer home at Manchester-by-the-Sea, or on the links at Augusta, she reported daily to Red Cross headquarters, a room in the State, War, and Navy Building, not far from Adee's, where her desk was lined up with those of other volunteers and the few paid employees. She became an effective, whip-cracking chief executive officer who never held a title or was paid a salary.

Boardman was a woman succeeding a woman in command. After the revisions to the charter made by Congress in 1905 and 1906, however, the Red Cross was a far more transparent organization than it had ever been before. She made it her life and, already in 1906, showed her ability in the great success of her and her colleagues in serving the victims of the San Francisco earthquake, one of the worst disasters in American history. It was not that she ran or commanded the organization outright; she never would consider being its "director." She was a volunteer within the system, powerful and a hard driver at times. The organization grew, and its structure changed. Yet when one thought of the Red Cross for the next thirty years, the first name that came to mind was Mabel Boardman.

∼

Feminism and *feminist* were words not known until the 1890s, but by the second decade of the twentieth century both were applied to a movement to achieve the same legal rights and freedoms for women as were held by men. Mabel Boardman's philosophy centered in the individual, demanding that a woman have the power to do absolutely anything she wished. She believed that for practical and administrative reasons it might be best for a man to appear to hold the authority, hence her insistence that a man always head the Red Cross, although she clearly ran it.

There were many degrees of feminism. The extreme for the time was represented by Alice Paul, whose singular objective was to achieve the national vote for all women. "Alice Paul," wrote an observer of the time, a ladylike silhouette artist named Marietta Andrews, "is something of a fanatic, if devotion—absolute devotion—to a cause is fanaticism." She was "the sort of ethereal, inspired-looking little girl that a motherly older person wants to take home to feed upon eggs and cream. . . . She has great, thoughtful eyes with the expression in them of hunger for better things than are the share of her own generation."[14]

Alice Paul moved to the American capital in 1912 at the age of twenty-seven, fired with ambition to achieve voting rights for women. The pretty, petite Paul, reared a Quaker with strong convictions about the equality of men and women, was a social worker by training, and while in England serving an apprenticeship in Liverpool, she had made the acquaintance of Emmeline Pankhurst, the widow of a member of Parliament and the premier figure in England espousing the vote for women. Captivated by the articulate and committed women dismissively called "suffragettes," Paul joined Pankhurst and her two daughters in public acts of protest. They and others carried posters, overturned mailboxes, heckled leading politicians, and threw rocks at windows, anything to shock people into noticing and possibly even considering their voter cause. She marched with suffragettes, lived with them, and went to jail with them, at last returning to America, excited about carrying the lessons she had learned to the women's suffrage movement already started in the United States.

While taking postgraduate courses at the University of Pennsylvania, Paul joined the National American Women's Suffrage Association, an often quarrelsome group established four years after the close of the Civil War. For most of its years the NAWSA had been under the direction, and indeed the thumb, of Elizabeth Cady Stanton and Susan B. Anthony, both of whom had since died, their places taken by women of the new generation. Appointed head of the national legislative committee, Alice Paul moved to Washington with two young friends, Crystal Eastman and Lucy Burns.

Paul was utterly committed to her cause. The NAWSA, which had headquarters in New York, was not totally focused on suffrage but had a plan to achieve it state by state, a movement already well along in many states. Its members were not militant in the ways of Pankhurst, for they realized that Pankhurst's approach would probably not succeed in the United States. Once Paul and her friends grew accustomed to Washington, they took note of the ease with which they were graciously received by the senators and congressmen and federal officials. They realized that their power might well grow from the respect they were shown. It was clear to them that the government sphere was the place to make their mark most effectively. The high objective they set, and to which officials of their organization raised eyebrows in disbelief, was to seek an amendment to the Constitution. The plan was to speak loudly and be heard, not to speak harshly and be dismissed. And though their approach served them well at times, their work was not done. They would have to wait nearly a decade for the ratification of the Nineteenth Amendment.

~

Publicly Taft found Theodore Roosevelt's presidency a hard one to follow. After the general excitement of having a new chief executive waned, it was clear that the former president's glamour left a void that was filled soon enough with tension and unrest. Taft continued the White House procedures established by Roosevelt, changing only a few details. For instance, instead of descending the grand stairs to trumpets, as Roosevelt had done when he entered on state or public occasions, Taft descended quietly in the elevator, and the music began softly as he walked down the hall to join the guests. This variation was reflective of the different personas of the two presidents. Sensitive about his weight and mindful that, if not cautious, he could easily be perceived as pompous or silly in ceremonies, Taft avoided all circumstances where he might appear foolish. The flash Roosevelt had brought to the White House dimmed in a hurry.

Outgoing President Taft and incoming President Wilson in high spirits on Inauguration Day, March 3, 1913. *Library of Congress, Prints and Photos Division.*

Beyond considerations of public face, Taft's was a positive administration. Despite the relatively unimportant differences in their ceremonial demeanor, however, the political differences between Taft and Roosevelt were sometimes in sharp contrast. For example, though both feared an all-out war between the world powers, Roosevelt's idea of precaution was the thundering, glorious challenge of building American power so that the United States could overcome any confrontation from the war machines building up in Europe. In contrast, Taft believed that the United States already had the power to withstand any aggression from Europe and that what was necessary in foreign relations were treaties to keep conflicts from happening. His orderly, legal mind rejected Roosevelt's compulsiveness. But Roosevelt's simpler approach, for example, in rich versus poor, was easier for the public to understand. From the new Oval Office, which Taft built, the new president reorganized and organized more than any president had before him. This president liked the details of management as much as Roosevelt disliked them.

Taft's part in the transformation of the Mall and the City Beautiful was more enduring than Roosevelt's, although both were devoted to the concept. Taft's wish to institutionalize the McMillan Plan was well known. Roosevelt had been interested in a similar legal context. To encourage the new president, the architects cooked up an event to illustrate the romantic heritage of the plan with a strange ceremony that took place in Taft's first year.

Glenn Brown and his fellows at the American Institute of Architects staged the reburial of Pierre Charles L'Enfant, designer of the city, from a graveyard in rural Maryland to Arlington National Cemetery. L'Enfant had been promoted continually as the enduring spirit of the revival of the original capital plan. Of course the original plan had been Washington's as well, in that he had approved it, but L'Enfant was its architect, which signaled a special poignancy to the sponsors of the reburial event. Taft's approval of the idea seemed to seal his approval of the City Beautiful.

Moving the remains of famous men to new, symbolic locations had become almost a universal state agenda, inspired in 1840 by the French, who moved Napoleon's remains from St. Helena to Les Invalides, in Paris. The rest of the Western world looked on in fascination. In 1906 the U.S. Navy had moved the remains of John Paul Jones from Paris, where he had died in 1792, to Annapolis, where he was reburied at the Naval Academy with great pomp.

More had been left of Jones than was found of L'Enfant. Those who dug down where he had been buried in 1825 retrieved only some discolored earth to provide evidence of his long-decayed burial site and to serve as his remains. This earth was transferred to a new hermetically sealed coffin and sped back to Washington, flag-draped, in a modern motor hearse with full military honors, to lie in state in the Capitol rotunda.

Next day, the coffin and its contents were buried on the crest of the hill that sloped down from Arlington House, overlooking the panorama of "L'Enfant's city."

President Taft made the main address, followed by politicians, artists, architects, and planners.[15]

Taft's enthusiasm for public building projects was well-known. The question was, to what extent would he promote acceleration of the McMillan Plan? As it turned out, the president started the process with politics, playing a conciliatory role between Congress and the architects in achieving permanency of the plan. Roosevelt had seen the need for some sort of meeting ground between the two, which he had hoped to settle several months before leaving office with an executive order creating a thirty-member fine arts "council." It took only one meeting of this oversized body for Congress to object, thinking it a usurper of congressional power. Taft discontinued the council but lent his support to institutionalizing the effort through another body, the Commission of Fine Arts, which was created by Congress in 1910. Carefully structured as advisory only, the presidentially appointed, seven-member committee of experts was to guide the president and Congress on building design and the locations of new buildings, fountains, statues, and other fine art in Washington's public areas. The commission was to suggest architects and artists for federal work and advise, if asked, on any matters relating to art in public places. Taft wisely assured suspicious lawmakers that the commission was intended not to take power from Congress but to help in its deliberations.

Daniel P. Burnham became the commission's first chairman. On Burnham's death in 1912, the sculptor Daniel Chester French took the gavel, followed three years later by the indomitable Charles Moore, who stood fast and tough in the job for more than two decades, persistent champion of the McMillan Plan well into what would seem another age.

Notwithstanding the misgivings of Congress about visionary schemes and, to some of its members, the presumptuousness of the McMillan Plan, Washington was acquiring public art along the streets in substantial quantity. Earlier, in the previous century, representative sculptures had been placed in the Capitol and outside it, notably the toga-draped *Lieutenant General George Washington*. Polk had placed a statue of Jefferson in front of the White House in 1846; Grant had moved it to the Capitol in 1873. The principal abstract monument of the city, first commenced in 1848, had been the Washington Monument, so long in construction, followed seven years later by the portrait sculpture in bronze of Andrew Jackson on his rearing horse Duke, put up in Lafayette Park. An equestrian George Washington was put up in Washington Circle in 1860. Thirty-three more statues had been placed in Washington—military heroes, patriots, explorers, scholars, and the poet Longfellow—by the time the Commission of Fine Arts was established. These commemorations of national heroes gave Washington more the look of a capital than had the once-barren spaces they occupied.

The statue building continued. Roosevelt complained that there were too many, that they littered the city. Sculpture stood in the centers of circles, like that of Admiral

Du Pont, at intersections, and in the squares—all portraits of men aside from the few symbolic or figural groups, such as *Emancipation*, set up in Lincoln Park in 1876. None received as much attention or international notice and acclaim as the four monumental bronzes placed at the corners of Lafayette Park between 1891 and 1910. These represented foreign heroes and kingdoms key to victory in the American Revolution.

The first was General Lafayette (1891), at the southeast corner; General Rochambeau (1902), the southwest; General Koscieuszko (1910), the northeast; and unveiled a month later in the same year, General von Steuben, at the northwest corner. They were envisioned as a salute to America's rising international importance. Those who had seen the first installed, such as Colonel Bingham, would have been amazed to see the changes in the nation's world position by 1910, when the last two were unveiled.

Each was dedicated in an important ceremony, the diplomats swarming in full uniform with dignitaries, including many guests from Europe, seated on bunting-draped grandstands, with the flags of the countries the statues represented flying overhead and long orations vowing eternal friendship between the United States and those countries. The four different unveilings elicited the admiration of all who experienced them and were glowingly reported both in the American and the European press.

The Commission of Fine Arts promoted the McMillan Plan vigorously, particularly after Moore took the chair. The plan was a Ten Commandments of capital city design. Proposals for statues, fountains, and memorials of many kinds were encouraged to fill in the blanks and flesh out the plan in small details not specified. As it happened the commission worked in harmony most of the time with the Army Corps of Engineers. No such battles took place like those in the days of Colonel Bingham, now a retired general.

One major work that was to be the ultimate verification of the McMillan Plan loomed unrealized: the memorial to Abraham Lincoln. On February 7, 1911, Congress finally appropriated two million dollars to build this critical feature of the world capital. Victory for the planners came nine months after the creation of the Commission of Fine Arts, and the memorial became the commission's first major undertaking, with the happy blessing of Congress. The memorial was the apex of the McMillan Plan, completing the symbolic triad of the American story: on the east, the Capitol, the living voice of the people; in the middle, the Washington Monument, commemorating the man who created the nation; and on the west, at the end of the Mall, the Lincoln Memorial, to the man who saved the nation intact. The idea seems to have originated with Glenn Brown before the City Beautiful movement began in Washington, although he has never received full credit for his ideas. The concept was so widely adopted by proponents of the McMillan Plan, however, that it would be difficult to pinpoint any one source.

Burnham, as chairman, was in failing health, yet his influence on the format on the Lincoln project, together with his decade of debate in shaping the idea, made him

a major figure in the design. He had made many sketches himself, all with colonnades, one even round in footprint. The various ideas on paper that went into creating
the monument provided quite an extensive archive for the planners when the actual
designing began. Like all the architects of the time who were concerned with raising the level of professionalism and opportunity, Burnham believed in architectural
competitions. The Lincoln Memorial, however, was too important to him to chance
its design in a competition. Anyone as familiar as he was with public works knew the
unhappy realities of coping with politically advantaged competitors. Of course inter-
acting with people whose work one knew, be it contractors or architects, was always
better. It was easier to go to bat for a certain contractor than an architect, however,
because of the negative attitudes of legislators toward what architects had to sell. The
Lincoln Memorial Commission sought guidance from the Commission of Fine Arts,
which resulted in the selection of two architects of exceptional gifts and knowledge
of neoclassical architecture to make proposals for various versions of a memorial to
Lincoln on several different sites. These were Henry Bacon and John Russell Pope.

The two worked separately and brought their projects to the memorial commission's office during the winter and early spring of 1912. One projected a circular
building; the others, long colonnades; each had an ambitious landscape design, offer-
ing several alternate approaches to where the memorial might be situated. A bold
pedestal for the memorial was the crest of Meridian Hill, where Mary Henderson had
wanted to build a new White House. At last Henry Bacon's project won, a colonnaded
housing for a statue of Abraham Lincoln, to be built on the Mall.

When on February 12, 1914, the ceremonial first stone was set in the Lincoln
Memorial, it was a special triumph for those who had awaited this keystone addition
to the world capital for more than thirteen years.[16]

~

Taft forged ahead with other changes. He was the first president to appoint a
woman to a high federal position, naming Julia C. Lathrop as the director of the Federal Children's Bureau, which was founded during his administration. About women's
suffrage, he was not convinced that the majority of women wanted it, and he said so
when he addressed a NAWSA convention in Washington in the spring of 1910. To
his astonishment some among the female audience hissed. If this was a bold expression of objection to the administration, it joined other subtler ones rising within the
Republican Party.

The president urged Congress to pass the first income tax since the Civil War.
His was a tax on corporations. Significantly, records of the corporations were to be
considered public information. He urged the reduction of tariffs. With swift strikes
he sought to respond to bloody attacks by bandits along the Mexican border and
met there in person with Porfirio Díaz, the venerable president of Mexico. To a large
part of the public, however, the administration seemed to be drifting. This viewpoint

weighted the ballot boxes in the congressional election of 1910, and the GOP lost control of the House for the first time since 1894. The Senate emerged Republican in 1910, however, but not safely so, for a coalition between Democrats and Republican insurgents stood poised to collapse the majority.

Taft met with little praise in the press. Of greater interest to the papers was Roosevelt's African hunt and his trip through Europe. Larz Anderson, then minister to Belgium, was embarrassed by the former president's conduct: "Roosevelt is going down the ages as one of the greatest charlatans of all time: if the papers over here report truly, he has certainly passed beyond the line and is no longer to be respected for even the high places which he has more or less unfortunately, filled in the past." Reveling in the apparently universal public affection he loved, Roosevelt seemed to Anderson a "boor."[17] And it is true that only Mrs. Roosevelt's admonitions restrained the ex-president from wearing his Rough Rider clothes before the host kings and queens who received him in their courts. However little a stiff diplomat might think of this and Roosevelt's other apparent disregard for protocol, the ex-president was an amazing performer. The world looked on, delighted with the diversion he provided.

Roosevelt returned to the United States in rip-roaring form, appearing in public frequently, a parody of what he had been as president but full of political commentary. Even an attempted assassination did not slow him down. In the presidential election of 1912 the Republicans ran Taft, the Democrats ran Woodrow Wilson, and Roosevelt styled himself the candidate of the Progressives, proclaimed as the Bullmoose Party, calling to his camp the dissatisfied and, in no small measure, the nostalgic. It was a regular country fair of candidates running for the big office. In addition to these three, two socialist candidates and a candidate from the Prohibition Party ran. Assuming Roosevelt's votes would have gone to Taft had Roosevelt not been on the ticket, the former president split the Republican vote. Wilson, the Democrat, won by a large majority of both the popular vote and that of the electoral college.

As Wilson's inauguration approached, Alice Paul and her colleagues discussed making a public statement. They had grown to dislike Woodrow Wilson between the convention and his election. He had courted advocates of women's suffrage to get support, only to drop the issue entirely after he was nominated. These advocates were already frustrated by the lagging political process. An early bill had left from the Senate to the House in 1887 only to languish in a desk drawer; the climate had changed but little in over twenty years. No attention had been paid to the issue at all since 1896. Alice Paul decided her group had waited too long, that it was time to make a public demonstration for women's vote. It was not the sort of public act the NAWSA was comfortable with, but the zealous Paul and her associates broke away and proceeded anyway, striking out on a new and more militant course than the suffrage movement had yet known in America. After discussions, they decided to stage a great parade and tableaux the day before Wilson's inauguration, which was to take place on March 4, 1913.

Alice Paul, champion of women's right to vote, 1902.
National Woman's Party, Washington, D.C.

The idea took on a life of its own very quickly. Women from seven states convened in Washington. In designing the parade and the tableaux that were to climax it, Alice Paul worked with Lucy Burns, with whom she had been jailed for a time in England and who had moved with Paul to Washington. They enlisted the help of Alice Pike Barney, an artistic, rather dramatic divorcée, whose Spanish-style studio on Massachusetts Avenue was the busy center of activity for those of the seasonal residents inclined toward painting, sculpture, and acting. Had Martha Wadsworth not disapproved of women voting, doubtless reflecting the vociferous condemnations of her nearby Wadsworth kin on the subject, she would surely have lent a hand to her neighbor Barney.[18] Instead, apparently, she may have supplied a horse for the parade. Eight weeks were left for planning after Paul ground out approvals from the unsuspecting parent organizations.

Given the gentle name the "Woman's Suffrage Procession," the demonstration was a numerous parade beginning at Capitol Hill and moving down Pennsylvania Avenue to the Treasury Building, where the concluding speeches and tableaux were to be performed. An estimated eight thousand women took part, marching beside twenty-seven floats, ten bands, and six horse-drawn chariots styled to honor the six states that had already granted the vote to women. The plan called for a trumpet-bearing herald to lead the parade. Inez Milholland, the famous track star and magazine writer, also noted for her statuesque beauty, stepped forward to become "herald" of the parade, but there was some discord over the choice, the more ardent sponsors believing that having such a beauty in the fore was pandering to men, diminishing the real meaning of the event. Milholland did as she pleased, however, and cantered from a side street to the head of the parade, a superb rider draped in filmy white, crowned by a gold diadem, astride a silvery white horse called Gray Dawn. This lit a flame of excitement that invigorated both marchers and onlookers.[19]

Glamourous protest: Inez Milholland leading the suffrage parade, March 3, 1913. *Library of Congress, Prints and Photos Division.*

Even before it took place the women's march was the talk of the town. Ellen Maury Slayden, wife of a Texas congressman, hurried through her duties at home with her cook: "Mattie and I stuffed eggs and made sandwiches enough for fifty people, and have everything ready for lunch" for her husband's committee meeting. Then she and friends hurried to the Gibson Building to see the suffrage parade. "We almost fought our way into the room, which we found steaming hot and smelling of printer's ink, and then had almost to fight to stay there. Most of the space was rented . . . and they thought it a part of our 'unwomanliness' to keep one small grimy window open so we could breathe. It was a mild afternoon with bright sunshine."[20]

From their window they looked down on the street. The moment came when Inez Milholland suddenly appeared on Pennsylvania Avenue. She was a vision at once magical and bizarre, and behind her marched an orderly procession of thousands of women in a solid, rippling, moving carpet of humanity. The parade slowed and eventually dispersed before the majestic portico of the Treasury Building. There Alice Barney's goddesses of liberty and a host of other symbolic figures awaited in togas to form dance figures and sing of the glories of nation and freedom. "In spite of everything the parade was inspiring," Ellen Slayden confided to her diary, "and I was ashamed of the self-consciousness that kept me out of it."[21]

As the female surge moved forward, some small clots of men among the half a million spectators were provoked by what they saw. They began yelling, then broke into the parade. Marchers recoiled in fear as men lunged at them, pulling their hair and pushing them to the ground; the women were also spit upon, slapped, and cursed. Boy Scouts, who had volunteered to hold the lines along the sides, were helpless children. Metropolitan police intervened, supported by a detail of cavalry from Fort Myer. The marchers persisted with their parade and with performing their tableaux at the Treasury, but some would say later that the soldiers' defense of them was

192 THE IMPERIAL SEASON

half-hearted. Many were the torn garments, cuts, black eyes, and bruises suffered by the marchers.

The frightening scenes that accompanied the parade, described for days in the newspapers, probably did more than the pageantry itself to stir support for women's suffrage. The public read uncomfortably of the insults to decent women peacefully expressing their views, of the flight of Helen Keller, who, positioned prominently on a float, sensed the chaos of the riot and cried out in terror for her companions to take her away to safety.[22]

A common tendency at the time to see the women's movement as a joke changed, if not wholly to unqualified support, then certainly to a measure of sympathy. This did not mean that everyone changed his or her view, but very many more now took the movement seriously and were thus less detached. From the day of the parade on, the movement, which, like most revolutions, was started largely by upper-class and well-educated people, became focused on one objective: the vote for women. Its adherents gained a new dynamic on the day they marched. Alice Paul, moving forward in a style akin to that which she had learned from Emmeline Pankhurst, broke her group permanently from the NAWSA and formed the National Woman's Party. Headquartered in Washington, where it attracted activists from all over the country, the NWP would give the new president, Woodrow Wilson, many a headache in pursuit of its goal.

~

Presidential households have always seemed to lend their character to the general picture of capital life. In the years between the arrival of the first ambassador and the Great War, five presidents presided in turn as administrators over most of the capital's permanent population, as well as being head of state for the nation. Cleveland and his youthful bride lived with their children mostly in the suburbs, using the official house only for business; the childless McKinleys, only in their fifties, seemed ever so much older. Roosevelt had broadcast his optimism and love of life from his remodeled White House; Taft was all business. He made little publicly of his smart wife and children, encouraging them all to be what they were as individuals. The first lady, Nellie Taft, and their daughter, Helen, both interested in the vote for women, had been seated in the Treasury Building reviewing stand to watch the Woman's Suffrage Procession. No first lady before Mrs. Taft ever gave such bold public support of so controversial an event.

The Woodrow Wilsons did little to arouse those who looked on. No one knew a whisper's worth of information about the Wilsons' personal lives. Even when a snippet of news escaped, it was seldom interesting. If Wilson was said to be a witty and delightful companion one on one, little evidence of it showed publicly. Certainly he was not a familiar face at the receptions on Massachusetts Avenue, unlike most of Washington's other political figures who flocked there. He scorned such activities. Nor had Wilson beforehand known many people in the capital personally. A notable

Alvey Adee with his bike, 1914. *Author's collection.*

exception was Alvey Adee, who had bicycled with Woodrow and Ellen Wilson in 1895, after a chance meeting in Scotland. Whether they remained in touch afterward is not known, although there was a cordial relationship between Wilson and Adee during Wilson's presidency.

In Washington, Wilson put forward no particular enthusiasm for the city's ceremonial development. Except for a love of musical theater, he was a homebody. Among his domestic circle were the small, dreamy-eyed wife, Ellen, an artist of some gift, with good connections among East Coast painters, and the three girls, the eldest, Margaret, a musician and independent woman of her time; the middle girl, Jessie, the very picture of golden-haired sweetness, marriage, and motherhood; and Nell, the least interested in books, the best-looking, and always eager to have a good time. The Wilsons thus brought their own circle with them when they came to Washington. It consisted largely of family and a small huddle of advisers, all preapproved and encouraged by the savvy Ellen.

To know Ellen Wilson was in a sense a good way of understanding Wilson. Behind the domestic front she was a wise and perceptive woman upon whom he depended intellectually. She knew his strengths and weaknesses like no one else, perhaps even better than he. Of his brilliance she had no doubt, and she welcomed and encouraged any friend or adviser who might compensate for what he lacked, stepping back to allow their friendship and communication. She loved him, wanting nothing for herself but everything for him. She supported and probably aided him in every aspect of his work, but most of all she understood.

Professor Wilson, as many were still inclined to call him, even though he had held the title of governor in New Jersey since his professorial days, assumed his presidency as an almost holy mission. He went to office, he believed, to correct years of Republican mistakes both in particulars and in points of view. Wilson believed he was the first true Democrat since James Buchanan, disregarding Grover Cleveland, his Princeton neighbor. Sometimes a thrilling orator, though not attempting the platform burlesque traditional to political speaking, he nevertheless probably seemed too intellectual for the average American's taste. He realized commendable domestic success in most of his two terms, making changes of his own and carrying through innovations started before his presidency. Only toward the end did his presidency seem to fall apart when as an individual he became obsessed with his self-defined mission of forging America's great power and prestige into a tool to bring peace to the world. He considered himself the key to achieving this, yet with no experience in diplomacy to prepare him.

Not much about the Wilsons was social beyond the quiet dinner parties they held nearly every night. One observer wrote that Wilson reverted to the old way of presidents: to accept no dinner invitations at all except to the homes of cabinet members. Even some traditional White House receptions were not held. Two of the daughters, Jessie and Nell, were married in pretty White House weddings, Jessie to a handsome young engineer, Francis Sayers, Nell to Treasury Secretary William G. McAdoo, a domineering, worldly man twenty-five years her senior.

Perhaps more than any president in a long time, Wilson warmed to the idea of social forms. He liked rules. Yet society itself had no interest to him at all, and the diplomatic community, in which Roosevelt and Taft took delight, was also of no interest to Wilson. The Woodrow Wilsons stood well apart from the capital's temporary community as well as its permanent residents. The change of party had seemed to bring a change of style to the national capital. Many were the jokes about how boring Washington had become. International Washington was less a consuming topic. Action had moved to Europe.

～

Intensifying relations between the European nations was the topic of conversation in the State Department. William Jennings Bryan, whom Wilson had appointed secretary of state more by political obligation than by preference, was something of a renegade. A pacifist, his views could not have been further from those of his predecessors, who had an understanding he did not share of the complexities of the tense European situation. The British ambassador Cecil Spring-Rice observed that Bryan was "unlike any other Secretary of State or Minister for Foreign Affairs that has ever been known." His personal agenda included treaties that he considered "his children and the sheep of his pasture." However, to be fair, the ambassador added for context, "Remember that in this country all things are personal and that Christ, if he had been an American, would have run for the Governorship of Judea with the Sermon on the Mount for his platform."[23]

Nearly a hundred years had passed since the Congress of Vienna cast its diplomatic net over post-Napoleonic Europe. The net had been frequently mended with alliances, intricate diplomatic patches, and reweaves. In a general way the Congress had succeeded. There had been no major wars in Europe; generally speaking, in the years since the Congress of Vienna the nineteenth century had been a century of peace. But by the twentieth century the cast of characters had changed some. A once-obscure, fragmented Germany had emerged unified, as a major power; the same was true of Italy.

In 1898 the United States had joined the world powers through expansion over the ocean, notably in occupying the Philippine Islands, which were more or less in the scope and region of that newer power, Japan, the most distant from the other great powers. The application of technology to war machinery implied horrors not lost on the leadership of the different countries. Efforts, if weak and ultimately futile, to establish world arbitration courts to ward off war had helped point up the mass destruction that could lie just ahead. Official Washington knew about this possibility and discussed the dangers. America the arbitrator called upon past experience in that role, attempting to assure peaceful settlement of international disputes through "pacts of peace." Alvey Adee either wrote or edited all of the documents. In a few years he would remember the pacts of peace like a deck of blank cards he had shuffled.

The Senate, taking a strict interpretation of its power to "advise and consent," was the arch enemy of nearly every effort on the part of William Jennings Bryan's State Department to make the pacts. The Senate would not approve bills that granted general authority to make pacts or agreements. Two bills were required in every case, the first setting down the program, and the second binding the first to a specific situation. Anything beyond that was judged an effort by the State Department or the executive branch to take power that belonged to the Senate.

Secretary Bryan believed the arbitration approach too strong, even threatening. State Department officials were as uncomfortable as Bryan's political colleagues with the "treaties of conciliation" they had to hammer out. The secretary of state edited their work heavily, then took his plans to the cabinet. Some of these were received more favorably than others. The visionary idea for an international committee of five, for example, granting power to mediate between nations in dispute, was eventually endorsed by Bryan. He summoned thirty-six resident diplomats to the reception room at the State Department and presented this idea to them. Reaction was polite, but the diplomats judged Bryant naive. Still he would not yield and in due course brought twenty-six of the nations under signature. For the diplomats he ordered a stock of paperweight plows made out of old swords he had located in military storage. With each came a message from Isaiah: "They shall beat their swords into plowshares."

When the European war erupted in August 1914, treaties and alliances were called into action, yet like a string of firecrackers Europe exploded. The news arriving daily from late July through August drew the State Department's few employees in town that summer into the telegraph room to catch the latest information. The reports were electrifying. August 6, the day Austria-Hungary declared war on Russia, Mrs. Wilson died at the White House. Only the president himself had insisted that death would not come. Struck hard, he placed her body on a chaise lounge with a cover draped around her, as though she were merely napping. The bulletins and news from Europe piled up on the table in the hall outside the door. At length he rose from his painful absorption in grief and scheduled the funeral in Georgia. Returned from the service, Wilson took up his duties in Washington, calling for the nation to behave as the neutral power it was.

Meanwhile, Alvey Adee was one of thousands of Americans vacationing in Europe that summer who were captured in the chaos of the beginning war. He had joined his friends and frequent fellow cyclists, Eleanor and Alexander Thackara. Alexander was the American consul-general in Paris.[24] They were biking in France, talking of going home when a State Department telegram ordered Adee to proceed to Kristiania (Oslo), Norway, to represent the United States at a conference to determine ownership of Spitsbergen.

Adee's burdens at the State Department had been, in theory, lessened in 1909 through a reorganization by Secretary of State Philander P. Knox. The overburdened department run by Adee was one of the first that Knox addressed. In addition to all other departments reporting to Adee, the continual labor of correspondence and counsel to the Secretary of State on diplomatic issues fell to him. Secretary of State Knox refashioned Adee's job as that of a general adviser. The paperwork went to another department, as did supervision of department heads. Adee was to be available to all but was assigned in particular to the secretary, with the title "third secretary," which he had usually held during his career. The work load was distributed but not lessened very much; the State Department simply could not do without Adee. So when he received the instructions in Europe during his bicycle vacation, Adee, now at the age of sixty-seven, when most men were retired, could not have been much surprised.

Spitsbergen was in a Klondike-style boom, thanks to coal mining. The island was suddenly appealing to Norway for annexation. In August, from the Victoria Hotel in Kristiania, Adee wrote to Eleanor Thackara, "I haven't seen a star since I got here! The young moon don't set, it describes a circle in the mixture of twilight and dawn. But the nights are beginning to grow darker—I cannot now write in the open at midnight as at first. As for temperature, this place is accursed. Eighteen hours of cloudless sun have baked the city red hot." He was bored and eager to take flight on his bike. What he called the "spit box conference" dragged on and on. "There are no signs yet of the conference coming to a close and not much chance of its doing anything."[25]

Ten days later Adee found himself in the chaos of thousands of Americans rushing to cross the Atlantic. Lights were out at night. Cafés were closed. Hotels were filled with military men. Long lines at the crowded train stations frustrated people, even frightened them, and Adee saw angry faces everywhere. He reached Copenhagen by ferry. To Eleanor Thackara, back in Paris, he wrote, "Not much use in trying to send you anything, now that Europe is boiling with war. In companionship with about 60,000 American tourists I am trying to get away, and I may be trying for a month." Adee hoped to take a ship from Denmark to England, then sail from Southampton to

New York. Everywhere he went, in London as in the north, he found utter confusion, especially among the stranded Americans. Their money was no good to them. Gold was all that counted. Adee, even pulling strings, had to take what ship he could get. He had to travel ever lighter, discarding first his trunk and last, and doubtless most painfully of all, the bicycle that he had always maintained as though it were of sterling silver. Now who would have his treasure? Adee boarded his ship to America without it.[26]

~

In the midst of war's rage overseas, the grieving widower at the White House fell in love. One afternoon after golf, he had a chance meeting with the comely widow Edith Galt, sixteen years his junior. Edith Bolling had been the wife of Norman Galt, the owner of Galt's Jewelry Store, a cherished Washington institution since the early days of the capital. Although the Galts had never been part of the political or diplomatic circle in Washington, they had a certain worldliness, having traveled extensively in both the United States and Europe. The fashion-conscious Edith was not politically ambitious like Mabel Boardman and Alice Paul, but her whimsical personality may have been one of her appeals to the president. Wilson, an amorous man, saw what he wanted and wasted no time.

A romance heated up "in about ten minutes," according to the social secretary Helen Bones, who was present when they met.[27] The couple became inseparable, the talk of Washington. Their casual conduct raised eyebrows, the president staying alone with her at her house until midnight or after and, while walking home with his guard, pausing on a streetcorner now and then to sing and tap dance one of the vaudeville numbers he imitated quite well, but heretofore in private. The imaginations of onlookers required no boost, nor does ours, reading their letters a century later. Still the public was happy for the president, who had seemed so dejected. They were married in her parlor just before Christmas in December 1915. Edith Bolling Wilson, whose life had seemed doomed to loneliness, now walked from the house she had shared with Norman Galt to share the world's stage with a man she idolized. It was a fantastic, romantic dream for them both. Wilson, in love, was alone no more and felt stronger on the eve of his confrontation with several hundred years of unyielding European history.

ELEVEN
The World at Last

The German ambassador Count J. H. von Bernstorff heard of the assassination in Sarajevo while he was having lunch at the Metropolitan Club with the Spanish ambassador Juan Riaño y Gayangos. Bernstorff remembered that day in August 1914: neither diplomat was "for a moment in doubt as to the very serious peace-menacing character of the incident." But he further observed, "We found little interest in the matter among the Americans in the club, who, as always, regarded European affairs with indifference." Back at the German Embassy, staying close by the tele-

Johann Heinrich von Bernstorff, ambassador of Germany, 1908–17, ca.1915. *Library of Congress, Prints and Photos Division.*

graph, Bernstorff received no word of the assassination of the Austrian heir "either officially or through the Press."[1] When he finally received the news officially, it was through a State Department telegraph, which officials had allowed him to use after discovering that German communication to America had been cut off by the British.

The situation was quite different for Constantin Dumba, the Austro-Hungarian ambassador, who found his Massachusetts summer residence in Manchester-by-the-Sea besieged by reporters from Boston and New York when the European news first arrived. Nor did reporters leave his side when he

Constantin Dumba, ambassador of Austria-Hungary, 1913–15, ca. 1915. *Library of Congress, Prints and Photos.*

returned to Washington in the fall. They clustered on the sidewalk outside the embassy and even in rain could be seen awaiting a story beneath shiny domes of umbrellas.[2]

When Bernstorff found no excitement in Washington, he assumed that the way was clear and called at the State Department for his passport, eager to sail home to Germany for his summer vacation. Back in Germany he realized that the edifice of peace, the aged network of the Congress of Vienna, had at last begun to fall to ruin. After World War I was over, he wrote of having heard "the muffled beat of drums announcing mobilization" on his first night in his lakeside retreat. "The dark forebodings with which the sound of the drums filled me have fixed that hour indelibly in my memory."[3]

Ordered to Berlin the next day, Bernstorff was instructed by his foreign office to return to America at once with the objective of selling the German point of view to Americans. When he arrived in New York, he found that the British had virtual control of public opinion. He saw that the New York daily newspapers "did all they could to spread anti-German feeling. . . . Outside New York the Press raged against us, particularly in New England and the Middle-Atlantic States. In the South and West we were also hated by the Press, but with considerably less intensity."[4]

In vain he tried to stem the tide, remaining in New York, giving interviews, writing letters. Back in Washington and once again resident in his embassy on Connecticut Avenue, he was on an island in a changed capital. Crowds gathered on the sidewalk staring at the German outpost, sometimes shouting insults. Surveillance by the Secret Service was less than subtle, their cameras constantly fixed on the embassy windows. By the rules of diplomacy the ambassador could neither speak to nor acknowledge good friends who represented enemy countries, such as Jusserand of France and the now ailing Cecil Spring-Rice of Britain. Responses could not be sent to invitations from the legations of enemy countries. Bernstorff could not penetrate the wall of silence, except in backstairs contacts, which were perilous.[5]

Dumba perceived his fellow diplomats in Washington perplexed by the situation in which they found themselves.[6] Europe was at war, yet in America the diplomats of the warring powers were surrounded by peace—no soldiers, no arms, no signs of war. They all knew that the scales could be tipped toward whichever country America chose to favor. American power was vast and untested; some in Europe had feared its potential so greatly that, for example, Kaiser Wilhelm II had at one time suggested that the European powers ally against America early on, to curb undesirable possibilities that might emerge if the New World giant chose to cross the ocean. When war came, the British ambassador Spring-Rice believed the Germans had a plan to invade America and became almost paranoid on the subject, to deaf ears in Washington.[7]

At the State Department, William Jennings Bryan was an engrossing presence, filling rooms with his roar. His staff members, whether they admired his ideals of peace or feared his inexperience in diplomacy, were trapped in his shadow. He traveled over the country making speeches, riding all-night trains, seeming to be everywhere, addressing crowds in churches, courthouses, town squares, theaters, and any venue large enough to accommodate his show. Women clustered around him admiringly in public places. He spoke more or less freely to the press, making no secret of his antiwar sentiments, which were as much a part of the man as his silvery voice.

In the diplomatic community in Washington, the president was more prominently represented not by his secretary of state but by his personal friend Colonel Edward M. House, the most intimate to Wilson of the presidential advisers. Heir to a fortune originally based in the wholesale grocery business, House had become involved in Democratic king making in Texas, his home state, in the beginning years of the Texas oil boom, from which he made great profits. On the national scene, wholly independent financially, he had attached himself to Wilson and remained as a freelance aide, handling high-level inquiries and even originating them behind the scenes. He was a mystery man, a man of few words, and the diplomats soon learned that he easily slipped between them and the president on almost any matter he chose. So it was House, not Bryan, whom they found the most frustrating and learned to address with care. No rules of diplomacy limited the colonel.

House made it his business to become intimate with the most important ambassadors of the time. A frequent companion of Bernstorff, he was equally at home with Dumba. Personable and interesting, House envisioned an international program for world peace not unlike that envisioned by the president. Wilson was commonly quoted as saying House spoke for him, although the president cannot have meant the extent implied in the statement. Colonel House had an agenda. He readily slipped back into the shadows after he might have sought the spot light, and he carefully maintained a web of useful associations out of sight. The extent of his power is hard to gauge. Without question, he was very able deal maker and much in the know about foreign affairs.[8]

In the press Adee was quickly established as Bryan's "righthand man" at the State Department. Secretary Bryan and at times the president were in need of the assistant secretary's talent and his astonishing recall, for the content of his institutional memory was rivaled only by the paper archives so carefully maintained at the department. Reorganization and expansion in the department had given Adee a staff of six. By 1914 he was called the second secretary instead of the third, indicating he was only one step removed from the top. In fact, "second secretary" was an archaic title reserved for Adee, for in the changes of 1909 assistants became "councilors." (The title would become "undersecretary" a decade later.)

Adee could perhaps have felt side-railed if he had been less devoted to his job than he was, but in practice his actual role changed little. The title in itself likely meant little to him. In theory he was to write treaties and notes; in practice he remained the source of last resort for very many issues at the State Department. Adee's place in the government was well-established. The clerks especially sought his advice and approval at junctures in drafting texts, trying to bypass the embarrassment of his red pencil. Nearly all social questions still came to him. The second secretary was a patient man but so intolerant of laziness that on one occasion he responded to a clerk's stupid question by smacking him in the face with his luncheon slice of apple pie.

A young matron who knew him well as a family friend had memories of a gentle, self-effacing man, whose formidable position in the Washington scheme people might overlook, until some experience reminded them. She wrote that he was "very deaf" and had "an impediment in his speech" that "no doubt augmented his discretion, since his words were few, and hardly articulate." His handicap did not diminish his position. The same young lady went with him to a White House reception: "I found myself immediately among the chosen few who do not stand in line, but are at once shown to the 'presence chamber'!"[9]

At home, in the same house, only his niece Lucy was left. His brother had died, as had Ellen, his sister-in-law. For a time after their deaths he continued his enjoyment of their Maryland farm, Yarrow Brae, but without the two of them for companions on his bird hunts and other country amusements, the farm had meant less, so he eventually sold it. At times Adee still slept on a cot in his office. And he was ever the athlete. "To what do you really attribute your good health?" asked a news reporter. "To outdoor life," he responded. "I stay in the open air all I possibly can." He continued, "I do not believe in excessive eating. I never saturate myself. . . . I believe in temperance in all things." Not least, he concluded, he avoided tension. "I simply will not allow things to disturb me and worry me."[10]

A man experienced with the relations among nations since the 1870s, however, cannot have been comfortable with the apparent shortcomings among his colleagues. Even as the European war built up steam, the most pressing international alarm at the State Department was not about Europe but about Mexico. American troops, dispatched by the president, had been made a joke by bandits, whom they chased unsuccessfully across northern Mexico. It was often difficult to tell who was chasing whom. Where Europe was concerned, the American government simply emphasized its neutrality. The diplomats knew that Colonel House had journeyed abroad, consulting with Britain. Because of his rather extraordinarily informal status, the presence of Colonel House troubled the diplomats, just as the president's irregular practices in diplomacy were a prime topic of private discussion when they spoke among themselves.

Wilson remained a puzzle to the diplomats. Those of long duration in Washington found the president distant and missed Roosevelt's and Taft's friendly visits to their dinner tables. For the most part, the diplomats had little but hearsay upon which to base their personal opinions of Wilson. It was clear enough that he thought little of them. The diplomats thought Bryan a dangerously placed daydreamer. He took personal fees for making speeches that should have been part of his job. Among the diplomats he ignored procedures. His showy moralistic behavior was symbolized by his refusal to serve wine at his official receptions and dinners; gossip held that he planned to begin pouring sweet milk. But it was Wilson who was the greatest enigma of all. The journalist John Reed, who had seen the Mexican situation firsthand, wrote in frustration that Wilson was "more interested in principles than policies."[11] The context of his statement was Mexico, but it reflected a general opinion current among the diplomats in Washington that the president was impractical and at times even unrealistic.

Continental Europeans reported to their foreign offices the inordinate warmth that Americans extended toward Britain. Count Bernstorff's embassy, according to the British ambassador, was "extremely well informed by some mysterious source."[12] The count quickly learned that when the British cut off America's direct communications with Germany, that contact could be made only circuitously by wires threaded via Greenland. German reporting on the European situation was largely blanked out. For the time, Bernstorff maintained use of the State Department's telegraph and was a lone voice home.

The Washington Cathedral, as yet in process of building, saw the completion of a chapel. High Anglican services were held there with Ambassador Spring-Rice in notable attendance. All manner of public events were staged by the British ambassador to underline the blood kinship between the United States and Britain, overriding the enormous German heritage in America. There were discussions now and then about how George III, advised by lawyers, had lost America for the British Empire. This was called a great wrong.

The centers of German propaganda as it related to the United States were in New York and Washington, while the pulse of Britain's anti-German projects beat most significantly at the British Embassy. Anti-German feeling was stirred tirelessly by the British and often directed at American citizens of German descent, projecting the unfounded scenario of hundreds of thousands of Germans in the United States waiting to rise up against their adopted country. In Washington, fear centered on the diplomats and their foreign agencies standing upon "foreign soil," as embassy sites were reckoned. Government security pitched right in. Cameras mounted in street trees were now fixed on all of the embassies representing the Central powers. Where else might sabotage planning originate? To one who made a study of the sidewalk traffic on Connecticut and New Hampshire Avenues and on Fifteenth and N Streets, plainclothes agents were not difficult to spot. The men among them wore business suits or various signature work clothes; the women, stylish sun frocks or rags. They lingered, seeming to have no destination.

The comings and goings of individuals from the embassies were noted and reports filed at the War Department pending action. And for good reason. Count Bernstorff worked in closet collusion with Count Dumba. Their associate in New York, Franz von Rintelen, directed a "Liebau Bureau," a so-called job agency, which behind closed doors nourished espionage and issued fake passports. Von Rintelen supervised a spy ring, assisted by several key attachés to the German and Austrian Embassies in Washington. Altogether their mission was to inform their government of goings-on in America and especially any American contact with the Allied powers. They generated plans to destroy ships carrying military supplies. Ammunition and dynamite storage at the Black Tom docks in Jersey City was blown up in the summer of 1916, with an effect similar to that of the San Francisco earthquake of a decade before; the tremor, registering 5.5 on the Richter scale, bent parts of the Statue of Liberty and shattered window glass all the way to Philadelphia. Spies were arrested in different towns, particularly along the coasts of the Atlantic and the Gulf of Mexico. Most other terrorist plots were exposed before damage was done. All were blamed on Germany, and an ugly image of blood-thirsty Germans rose ever more threateningly in the popular imagination.

Espionage was a reality, however, and the press hungered to satisfy an anxious and curious public for news of it. Facts were embellished, as in the Spanish-American War seventeen years earlier. In his memoir, Count Dumba praised William Randolph Hearst, father of the yellow press of the Spanish war days, as being among the few publishers who tried to be fair. In Count Bernstorff's memoir he insists, "I myself was never a partner to any proceedings which contravened the laws of the United States. I never instigated such proceedings nor did I consciously afford their authors assistance."[13] Official records indicate otherwise.[14]

In the winter of 1915 Germany announced the decision to pursue submarine warfare in retaliation against Britain's tight blockade. War in France had become centered in a standoff twenty miles from Paris. Already, through U-boats, Germany had taken aggressive steps at sea against British shipping. Submarines were still relatively new weapon bearers. *Neutrality* was the public word in America. The president proclaimed the United States a neutral power, to remain free and clear of Europe's problems but available to arbitrate. With Wilson's blessing, Secretary Bryan planned a pan-American convocation in Washington for the twenty-nine countries of Latin America.

Groundwork lay in a longtime effort to unite all Americas through the Pan American Union, which had been represented architecturally since 1908 in one of the finest of the Beaux-Arts expressions in Washington. Built on the site of the old Van Ness house, the Pan American Union stood facing Seventeenth Street at its corner with Constitution Avenue, across from the Mall. Of white marble, its elegant, high-arched design echoed Union Station and honored the McMillan Plan. With its palm court, with splashing fountain and live parrots flying about, the building also conveyed a romantic Latin American flavoring in the Beaux-Arts neoclassical context, popular at the time in Mexico City, Buenos Aires, Santiago, and the other capitals of Latin America.

William Jennings Bryan gave nearly full time to planning the convocation. The pacifist secretary believed that a successful union of all American nations (excluding Canada, which was not the requisite republic) would provide a model for Europe to follow, an example of how America could manage a cooperative agreement to keep peace. Spanish-speaking Adee assisted, although a greatly enlarged staff was also at the secretary's command. Bryan's and the president's hopes to use the Pan American Union as a symbol of unity and cooperation for the world, however, were not fulfilled.

Reflecting other less vaulting endeavors, the effort with the Pan American Union was only an ambitious example of the secretary's wide sweep of ideas. The department's expansion and the energy of the man himself revealed Bryan to be the busiest secretary of state who had ever served. Accommodating the man was not easy. His working patterns followed no order whatsoever, wild freshets rushing over plains of diplomatic custom historically smooth and seamless. The great orator's presence during office hours was never guaranteed, for he was often away. On the platform he pressed his personal views favoring the prohibition of alcohol and vehemently opposing war. He expounded in tirades that did not reflect well on his cabinet position. His antiwar speeches were like Old Testament forebodings of doom. Adee, upon whom many sensitive matters were still laid, can only have found him a trial. Bryan's speeches went without Adee's red pencil, to which even presidents had submitted. The gracious and accommodating relationship between President Wilson and "Dear Mr. Adee" perhaps lightened the load the secretary of state hoisted upon the State Department's employee of longest service.

Where the war in Europe had been only of mild interest to the American public when it began in 1914, its unfolding events reported in the press greatly exercised general opinion. Ambassador Dumba wrote of two camps in America in 1914, one pro-German and the other anti-German. The debate between them rose and fell on a sea of anger until the spring of 1915, when the two camps largely united in hostility toward the aggressions of the kaiser and Germany. On May 7, 1915, the British passenger liner *Lusitania* was torpedoed and sunk by a German submarine fifteen miles off the Irish coast, at a cost of over a thousand lives, 124 of them Americans. Church bells all over the nation called hundreds of thousands to memorial services. Walter Hines Page, the American ambassador to Britain, wrote of the disaster to President Wilson: "A profound effect has been produced on English opinion in general regarding both the surprising efficiency of the German submarine work and the extreme recklessness of the Germans."[15] Although President Wilson sent a strong diplomatic note to Germany in June 1915, protesting the sinking of the *Lusitania*, he urged the American people to keep to the path of neutrality. This time the Americans were not to be appeased. A newly inflamed press carried the public's anger even higher for the *Lusitania* tragedy. Wilson's calm words were offset by war propaganda. Sentiment for neutrality turned to outrage. After the *Lusitania*'s sinking, Colonel House wrote to Wilson that diplomatic relations with Germany might be broken: "I can't see any way out unless Germany promises to cease her policy of making war upon non-combatants."[16]

Wilson's note to the Germans, which followed a milder one sent by Secretary Bryan a month earlier, aroused Bryan as being too strong. In June he resigned, a decision he reached on his own, fearing the portent of an announcement by the president that the United States would bear arms if necessary. "Hurrah!" wrote Edith to Woodrow, "old Bryan is out!"[17] Wilson's increasing impatience with Germany had also disturbed Bryan. Like most everyone else, Bryan probably failed to fully grasp the seriousness of Wilson's overriding vision for a postwar system to perpetuate peace. Historians since then have traced and studied the thread of Wilson's thinking. At the time, the vision was less obvious than the turmoil surrounding it, leading up to the war. Bryan was replaced by Robert Lansing, who better suited the situation as a less indelible character and one more under presidential control. A former attorney general, Lansing was "Mr. Wilson's legal conscience," in Count Bernstorff's view.[18] Lansing was not opposed to Wilson's ever stronger notes to the belligerents through the State Department, nor was he committed to neutrality.

International pressures built in the capital, turning usually serene and orderly city life into confusion; disparate voices cried out. Seasons of the year, once marked so significantly in the capital's ways, blurred into one, overwhelmed by what was happening in Europe. The war movement was challenged by pacifists. Public demonstrations on both sides shaped general opinion to an extent, with a current of patriotism rising powerfully against the antiwar factions, which notably included the socialists and a peace-party branch of the women's movement. Any public events that involved the diplomats usually attracted protest demonstrations of one sort or another. It was a difficult, even frightening time. Europeans, a century removed from the chaos of the Napoleonic wars and beneficiaries of the long years of freedom from all-out war that followed the Congress of Vienna, had gone to war without the level of caution that Americans would have perhaps shown, though an ocean away from the problem. But America could not simply wish away the international position it had gained over the nearly twenty previous years. Events brought the war closer. Time came when the country's involvement in it was inevitable.

The president's reasons for finally committing to war are evasive even now, but by the time he did commit, the American people were ready. For all the pledges the fighting nations made to peace, to a "league of nations," the war in Europe grew ever more devastating. Wilson made the idea of the league public in December 1916. Opposition sprang up immediately in Congress, largely as a result of the fear that Wilson wanted to sacrifice some of the power and integrity of the United States to a foreign collaborative. But, for the time, war mania outshouted the quiet logic of the protest. In January, Germany broke its brief moratorium on submarine warfare.

Curiously, Count Bernstorff continued to be permitted to use the State Department's telegraph, to bypass British interference. Repeatedly the German ambassador stood outside Adee's office and watched the department's telegraph operator tap out his plea beseeching his government to hold off in its aggressions that so stirred the Americans, only to report to Secretary Lansing within a few weeks that his appeals fell upon deaf ears. In February, the "Zimmerman letter" was intercepted, wherein the secretary of Germany's foreign office, Arthur Zimmerman, offered the civil-war-torn Mexican government support in a declaration of war against the United States and an invasion of Arizona, New Mexico, and Texas, to reclaim those "lost provinces." The general outcry across the American nation matched that over the *Lusitania* two years earlier.

On the evening of April 2, 1917, President Wilson delivered his war message. Antiwar protestors in the thousands had crowded around the Capitol all that day and jammed corridors of the House and Senate offices; they broke through doors. They pressed in to see the shambled meeting room that a terrorist had blown up in the Capitol, walls of raw brick and rubble, swept up by then in some ruinous order. Making the scarred shell neat did not erase the awesome ugliness of a sort of scene already common to Europeans but new to American eyes. The American demonstrators chanted; they sang their protest; and they threatened violence. Scorned by the press as "belligerent pacifists," they formed a human chain blocking the steps the president was to climb on his arrival that evening. When Senator Lodge stepped from his car, a hostile group of pacifists assaulted him, pelting him with their fists. The number of guards was doubled and tripled. Secret Service men were called in from out of town, joined by postal inspectors and a full contingent of police. When during the afternoon the government's barriers seemed to weaken and the protest crowd swelled, mounted troops of the Second Cavalry rode in. The Capitol was cleared; the doors locked. Sharpshooters stood in strategic windows. By the time the president was to appear, it was impossible for "a disturber to get within pistol shot of the Capitol," according to the *New York Times*.[19]

When time came for the president's speech, Ambassador Spring-Rice was there: "I shall never forget a rainy evening in April when I drove down to the Capitol. The Capitol was illuminated from below—white against a black sky. United States troops were collected round it, not for a parade, but for defense—and necessary—and the President came down. I sat on the floor of Congress. The President came in, and in a perfectly calm, deliberate voice he recited word by word, deed by deed, what Germany had done. At the end he said: 'I have told you the facts. We have several courses to take. One course we will not take, the course of submission.' I shall never forget the cheer I heard at those words. The die was cast." A colleague who later read this description remarked that the British ambassador "must have said to himself that, come what might, his mission was accomplished."[20]

In the period of neutrality, when the word was *preparedness* and the war seemed so far away, Washington felt its presence more than any other city in the country. Because of the very visible activities of government and the orbits of activity surrounding preparedness, the events in Europe seemed not just distant news items, but close at hand. Count Dumba believed that the balance between the public's pro- and anti-Germany stances had tipped tenfold in favor of the Allies. "The neutral diplomats naturally went from one camp to the other. Hardly a dozen houses remained open to us."[21] Much the same was true in New York, where he went with some frequency, creating as little notice as possible.

American energy relating to the European war during the neutrality period, which lasted two years and eight months, had first been seen in private and quasi-private programs for war relief on behalf of Britain, Belgium, and France. Women would not be denied, so their participation was conspicuous. They made bandages and clothes and raised money. Sarah Bernhardt, while touring America gathering up funds to aid French war widows and orphans, was coaxed to join a large group of ladies invited to Alice Barney's studio on Massachusetts Avenue. The faded stage star, at seventy-two years of age, had suffered amputation of her right leg and legendary ill health that left her "faint and suffering." She entered the studio seated on a gilt chair held aloft by four strong men.

Carried up the stairs to Barney's private theater, Bernhardt was lowered to the floor while the assembly of women looked on in silent awe. Barney had designed one of her tableaux, with a special script that imitated in flattering terms the acting style of Madame Sarah. The young female performers, all amateur, wore filmy robes and plumed headdresses. The tableau so pleased the famous guest that she ordered several of the performers to come before her, touched them gently, and praised their talent. When the hat was passed, the widows and orphans of France did well. At the conclusion, Bernhardt, lifted high in her chair, bid a gracious farewell in French and floated away, her clear, bell-like voice, undiminished by age, resounding through Alice Barney's studio.[22]

By the time war was declared in 1917, the people of the capital seem to have been less shocked by the idea of an international conflict than other Americans, because they had been closer to its effects. Washington itself, unprepared, suddenly became the focus of all attention, as a new sort of outsider came to exert his influence. What seemed a human tide of soldiers, volunteers, opportunists, news people, businessmen, and officials rushed upon the capital. At Union Station people slept on benches or atop their luggage on the floor, battling for place in the human swarm. The four-hour train trip to New York never went that fast again, often taking six hours, sometimes nine, with standing room only.

Government office buildings filled up. New commissions, boards, councils, and agencies called for space, which quickly exhausted available rental properties and inspired the quick construction of line after line of temporary wooden buildings on the north side of the Mall, facing the Washington Monument and housing hundreds of offices. Only two of the planners of the City Beautiful, Glenn Brown and Charles Moore, were alive to regret the intrusion on their monumental city. Other concerns overshadowed the passions that had inspired the international capital. Streets were crowded. The old gentility that had for so long characterized Washington as a city seemed to vanish as the good and the bad moved in. Crime increased, and the military became involved in its prevention.

The crush for space soon had officials looking at apartments unused or empty, then private houses. Residents were encouraged to divide their houses into apartments and to let as many rooms as they could. Through the first summer of the war the capital underwent a reshuffling of its familiar patterns and a feeling of suffocation brought on by the appearance of huge numbers of people. Soon enough government officials turned to the big, closed-up winter houses on Massachusetts Avenue. Many were commandeered for war purposes, becoming headquarters of various kinds or "government hotels." Men and women on official war business in the capital bunked in the fine French-style rooms as well as in the unoccupied upper-floor servants' quarters.[23]

Carrie Walsh, widow of Tom, still occupied their big candy-box house on Massachusetts Avenue, which she and her increasingly civic-minded daughter, Evalyn, willingly opened to war work. Women volunteers gathered in the drawing room to make bandages and pajamas from bolts of cotton cloth. Mrs. Walsh took an active role in the aid of Belgian war orphans, recalling her husband's friendship with King Leopold. She gave a lot of money and worked hard funding orphanages and securing adoptive parents in America. Both Evalyn and Ned worked on war projects for European relief.

Before Mabel Boardman left for Europe to work with the International Red Cross, a transition motivated at least in part by her well-known German sympathies, she came forward with characteristic vigor to do her part. President Wilson told his wife he needed a thirty-minute nap before meeting with her.[24] Boardman thought up the idea for the Washington Refreshment Corps, summoned Isabel Anderson, and ordered her to organize it. Anderson handled the job masterfully, appointing five committees: commissary, cooking, recruiting, uniform, and intelligence. The work was carried out in Isabel's kitchen at Anderson House. Supplies were stored in the great gilded rooms. Army titles were given to the volunteers, Isabel a colonel. When the troop trains arrived, the corps was ready a month after war was declared. At the close of a year the Refreshment Corps, at its little rolling canteen beside the tracks about a mile from Union Station, had served nearly two million men. This success extended them into an unofficial catering service for the military. The Refreshment Corps learned to feed the many—army brass dinners at Fort Myer for fifteen hundred, lunch at another place for six hundred. With justifiable pride, Anderson later wrote a book about her war work with the canteen ladies.[25]

Everyone wanted to play a part in the faraway war. Martha Wadsworth, true to her character, designed a role for herself while back home at her husband's Genesee Valley farm. She wished to apply her horse-training skill to the cavalry mounts. A woman's conviction that she could perform such a task made the generals pause, but Martha had dealt with doubting men before. Drawing the relevant officers and officials to her Massachusetts Avenue house, Mrs. Wadsworth wined and dined her way up the ladder to proper approval. To dramatize her project, she repeated a similar experiment she had first carried out a decade earlier in response to yet another of Theodore Roosevelt's quips about women's shortcomings: that women lacked men's stamina on horseback. To convince the generals, she selected horses, all hunters, from her farm and from those of relatives in the valley, and transported them by railroad to Union Station. Early in May 1917, before summer's leaves had begun to shade Massachusetts Avenue, a trail ride began at the Wadsworth house, the selected participants, including some key cavalry officers, headed overland to Genesee Valley, New York. Chuck-wagon stations along the way provided food and drink. Martha outrode the best of them and made her point. Her ensuing war work in training cavalry horses made her the most famous horsewoman in America.

Washington naturally saw a parade of important guests beside which the diplomats who had dazzled the winter residents in days gone by simply paled. Early in the war Theodore Roosevelt was in town seeking permission from the president to raise a division. "He had been in communication with men all over the country who wished to serve him," wrote Alice Roosevelt Longworth.[26] His family was all behind him, merrily teasing him for his devotion to the idea, proposing the dodo bird as emblem for his battle flag. Congress gave its blessing, but the president and the secretary of war turned him down, claiming weakly that such a volunteer force would interfere with the draft. Woodrow Wilson had little use for the man he referred to as "Teddy."

Roosevelt's visit, which kept Alice and Nick's house full of visitors and callers, was soon followed by the arrival of the Allied missions—Marshal Joffre, from France;

Vivian Balfour, from Britain; the Prince of Udine, from Italy; and Boris Bakhmeteff, of the new Kerensky government of Russia. Harry White opened his doors on Sixteenth Street to Joffre and his staff. Allied officers came as instructors for the training camps. Parades accompanied the appearances of the Allies, long, exhilarating marches from Union Station down Pennsylvania Avenue. Never did Burnham's granite railroad depot seem more properly a city gate than when flags fluttered, bands played rousing anthems, and lines of mounted and marching soldiers poured into the plaza before it.

In the uproar of the world war, the high spirits building a world capital turned elsewhere. Work on the Mall and other civic projects was halted; the rush to build was over. The social season stopped. The Washington of the ambassadors, the international city that had been taking form, the Washington of Burnham and Theodore Roosevelt and Taft, simply fell silent. Wartime Washington was another sort of place.

The openness among people ceased. When war began in Europe, most doors were closed to representatives of the Axis powers. Cissy Patterson (Countess Gizycki) and her mother, Nellie, like Mabel Boardman, loved Germany. If they did not support it in the instance of the war, they still loved the country and its people. Their friend Bernstorff was entertained in both houses until anti-German feelings attracted protesters outside their walls, and Cissy Patterson and Mabel Boardman no longer felt they could invite him or his colleagues. When they finally quit entertaining the Germans entirely, they also ceased their other social activities. Soon the Germans and Austrians had gone home.

The heat of war intensified in 1918. News from Europe was filled with tragedy, even as Allied victories mounted. American casualties came in great number, ultimately more than a hundred thousand, and in the winter of 1918 the terrible extent of it was sinking painfully into the public awareness. Newspapers announced American deaths in battle, burials on the battlefields, deaths from sickness, sacrifices in every form to the world's conflict.

But death claimed fewer victims of the sword than of the Spanish influenza, a deadly disease that ravaged the battlefields and everywhere else. In March 1918 the first case of influenza in America appeared at Fort Riley, in Kansas, and in weeks the disease was spreading fast. The "influenza" panic hit Washington in the summer. An emergency city ordinance, impossible to enforce effectively, made it illegal to walk along the streets and sidewalks and imposed fines for those caught sitting on their porches. Citizens were to stay behind closed doors. At first some shops closed and the streets were vacant; people avoided being in range of the breath of others. White mouth masks were a common sight on those who had to move about.

Tens of thousands died at a rapid pace, several thousand in Washington alone. Funerals were few. Most victims were taken to the graveyard, many without the deference of a coffin. At St. John's Church on Lafayette Square, the bells tolled every day, and the interior, worn and seedy, had empty pews. Theaters were naturally closed, as were the dance pavilions that had been so festive with soldiers and their girls. One saw mourning when one saw people: left-arm black bands, black veils, wreaths on doors. The symbols could represent death from war or from influenza; the source mattered little, as the stream from both seemed to pour together like a molten lava of agony. Even thoughtful editorials were tempted to imply that America was being punished with mass death for participating in a war that was really Europe's and not her own. For many a preacher, this opinion became a handy text.

The harshness of the war, the mystery created by its distance and unseen clashes, created a tension among Americans and not least those in the capital. Activities of a social character that had made the capital unique seemed almost irreverent to continue. With sadness all around them, the diplomats were starved for distraction. Only one house left its doors open to all foreigners. Minnie Townsend welcomed the isolated foreigners into her home on Massachusetts Avenue. Her house presented no rows of ugly typewriters and file cabinets. The Townsend house was as it had always been. From whatever country they might represent, the diplomats would remember her graciousness to them when they penned their memoirs of the war.

Once Townsend's guests entered among the statues of her crowded entrance hall, they could retreat into a memory, something that somehow had spilled over and lived on. Although the influenza kept most other people away, the diplomats, cut off anyway from the churning world, attended with delight. Sad things that had come with the war remained outside the iron grilles of Minnie Townsend's front door. Beyond it, covered in diamonds, she welcomed them all as ever before. Guests ascended to the ballroom, the dining room, the airy galleries, where champagne was poured and memorable dinners came up from the kitchen below. Teas, musicales, balls, and dinners attracted the noble titles Minnie loved, but now in addition there were generals and admirals from the Allied powers with their sharp young aides. Interesting people came from everywhere. But mainly, as always, it was the diplomats she loved to entertain, especially those with titles.

Even Townsend's house must have been closed against the influenza for a while. But by Christmas 1918 the worst of the epidemic was over. After that, it might be said that she emerged rather much alone, the last of those great hostesses who had adorned the international capital. And what of the elements other than the society of the great city, the elements that had been devised—the monuments, the mirror of Europe, the international ideas, the causes that took people into the streets? Was the impulse to resume their pursuit all dead and gone?

In a word, yes.

The first news of peace broke the waning influenza quarantine, and several hours of dancing in the streets stopped short when the report was announced as false. Next time such a report was heard—this time against the fall color of November, on a date to be called Armistice Day—the guns actually were silenced, and thousands of people resumed their victory dancing. Everyone, it seemed, poured into the streets. The terrible grip of world events relaxed. America had won, as Americans were to say of World War I from then on.

President Wilson had already laid out the work ahead toward the last act of his great plan that would redeem the carnage and end all war. It boiled down now to the vehicle of diplomacy. The president determined to go to Europe in person to help design the world's future. He had shared his plan for perpetuating peace, asked for opinions of the league of nations he had proposed. None of this was secret. He elected to undertake personally the role of principal negotiator, one traditionally played by experienced diplomats. Because Wilson had no personal experience but was equipped with the power of the presidency, his approach to the peace conference was unusual. He believed that by being on the spot he could convince the war-torn Old World how obvious his plan was for the perpetuation of civilization.

Wilson's gifts as a diplomat were not to match his gifts as a convincing politician, American style. His usurpation of diplomatic functions—like Roosevelt's before him—had concerned the State Department as well as the diplomatic community for some time. So the prospect of his going in person to Versailles to negotiate with tough, expert diplomats seemed at best unlikely. Even Roosevelt had remained at home, sending his diplomats out to confirm whatever international work he had assumed. McKinley had personally negotiated the protocol in the Spanish-American War in his own office, but he had remained on his own turf, sending experienced diplomats to Paris to negotiate the treaty itself. Even though the American presidency represents a combined head of government and head of state, Wilson seems to have reasoned that he would exercise his administrative role to negotiate the treaty, thus would function as prime minister in taking the American part. What worried the diplomats was that he could not simply leave at home the other role of the presidency, head of state. No others of that rank among the world powers were to be present.

The peace meeting at Versailles was to be the moment of truth for the international United States, as the war itself had been for Washington's pretenses to an international capital. With the horrors of the world war, American public opinion had drawn back from internationalism. Over a hundred thousand Americans had died and been buried on foreign battlefields for a war that offered no immediate benefit to the United States. Congress reacted to international participation negatively, as Congress always had. In the House and the Senate, powerful enemies of Wilson's plan were hard at work against his world views: yielding American power was unacceptable to them, and the case was not difficult to present to the people. The document Wilson brought back from France demanded a surrender of some national perogative in the creation of his League of Nations. Moreover, the president left the peace tables at Versailles too soon, with plans for the future of war-torn Europe unfinished. When he returned to Washington, the political context was quite different from what it had been before he left, and Wilson stood largely on the outside.

In retrospect, the night he left Washington for his journey to Europe might seem a tragic foreshadowing, but since no crystal ball was available, prospects seemed positive at the time. It was December 4, 1918, cold, with rain falling. He and Edith sat back in the lead automobile of two, the only cars on the street, rolling hastily out the White House gates to Pennsylvania Avenue on the way to Union Station. Behind lines of mounted soldiers, spectators pressed forward, cheering in places, silent in others, all straining for a glimpse of his sharp-nosed profile through the rainy windowpane. It was dark; Edith Wilson remembered the faces in the pools of light that surrounded the electric street lamps. Precautions had begun twenty-four hours earlier, so that the protest disturbances of twenty months before would have no chance to be repeated.

Added to the regular Pennsylvania Express to New York was the *Ideal*, the Pennsylvania Railroad's finest private car, set aside by the company for the president's historic ride to the ship that was docked and waiting at Hoboken. This was to be the first of two journeys to Europe, both for negotiating the treaty. At Union Station, President Wilson stepped out of the car, and beneath black umbrellas held by aides, he and Edith faced the crowd. They seemed happy. He raised his high silk hat. There was no speech to make. Rain rolled in silvery clouds through the sheltering sheds as they walked silently to the train car that spirited them away, and with them an era in the national capital.

CONCLUSION
Ember Days

By the close of the Great War, the Washington way of life that had been fashioned in response to America's emerging world position was gone, the great stage planned for its performance, unfinished. Forces of change came once again from outside, not from within. World War I turned Americans against internationalism. With the city now divested of the romantic appeal that internationalism had carried with it before the war, the re-creation of the capital to relate to other capitals of the world had little meaning. The capital's reinventors had labored to mold it into an American version of the capitals of Europe, in architecture, ceremony, and social customs. Of their efforts only a few buildings and the master plan remained, to amble along through the twentieth century, adapted, reshaped, but still not fully realized as it had been intended.

The all-encompassing war, the climax of a century of relative monarchial calm, turned Europe upside down. Crowns fell. Tradition was challenged by upheavals from all angles and echelons; voices were heard that, if not completely silent before, had never been so forceful. National power was not the real victor in this case; rather, the idea of democracy was. Princess Eulalia, the infanta of Spain, whose American visit in 1893 had caused such joy, prefaced her memoirs of royal life before the war, saying, "I am democratic in my sympathies. The world, as I see it, is peopled by one big family. We are all brothers and sisters; let us know one another better."[1] In theory at least, Americans had always felt that way, if only about other Americans.

Yet the McMillan Plan itself was kept alive, an icon from an ever more distant past, if only because it was the lone plan at hand. It had never been official. The splendor it projected looms over Washington planning even today, a century-old presence with influence and a title but, like the postwar kings, with little real authority. The transformation of Washington into a capital, in the sense of its being the combined governmental and economic center of the country, never happened. It is, of course, the apex of government in America, but unlike Boston, New York, Chicago, New Orleans, and San Francisco, for example, Washington contains little emotional sense of a city that fires its soul. The patchwork of neighborhoods and communities that L'Enfant appears to have imagined for the permanent population was already filling up in the period addressed in this book, but today Washington's sprawl is merely a continuation of that proliferation, reaching far beyond the original city and possessing only a dim magnetism.

The visual domination of the Mall defines Washington as a symbolic place. But no city center lies beyond it. Government construction realized some very ambitious public buildings in the 1920s and 1930s, but the overall monumental civic ambitions for the capital fell by the wayside. Huge office blocks characterized most of the building in the 1920s. Temporary wooden wartime buildings remained on the Mall for decades, greatly increasing in number during World War II. The last were not removed until 1970, when President Richard M. Nixon ordered them pulled down.

The spirit of the McMillan Plan, however, raised its head proudly in the Jefferson Memorial, ordered up in 1934 by President Franklin D. Roosevelt, who had lived in the capital before World War I and was determined that the memorial, so long in the planning, be neoclassical, like the buildings of the City Beautiful movement he admired. In spite of criticism from modernist architects, who by the time of Roosevelt's presidency rejected the Beaux-Arts ideals of their schooling, the memorial, completed during World War II and mirrored in the Tidal Basin, also created then, has been a popular one, built on land filled early in the century. The 1960s saw a commendable rebirth of the open Mall concept, as well as a revival of Pennsylvania Avenue, which in some areas had fallen into shameful neglect. The avenue experienced solutions in urban landscape, architectural restoration, and some new buildings, many of which uncomfortably await the judgment of time.

The capital, like any other, is the place where the business of government is conducted. In the formal aspects of its appearance, it is meant to symbolize power and the best the country has to offer. In the vastness of the modern environs that spread out from the District of Columbia into two states, Virginia and Maryland, and then into two more, West Virginia and Pennsylvania, one can easily see in the midst of it all, like a picture in a frame, the monumental capital, an island central and essential to the identity of the barely definable sea of settlement. Most of those who populate Washington's vast complex of places are there because they are part of the government, directly or indirectly. Control buttons are still pushed largely by outsiders, who come to the capital to give the government its lifeblood.

The city's transformation into something more than a governmental center—a city, in other words, like Paris or Vienna, Budapest or Rome—was probably a pipe dream in the first place. Those cities are alive with the energy of time, of lives lived and epochs past, with art and commerce as well as government. Such places are not simply built but grow with history over centuries, keeping part, replacing part. Yet the dream of achieving the same through a hurried metamorphosis was vivid during the quarter century between the arrival of the first ambassador, on April 11, 1893, and the departure of President Wilson for Europe, on December 4, 1918.

When the war was over, traditional American suspicion of the Old World was rekindled: anything European reminded the populace of who had caused the war. Besides, with the dissolution of the royal courts went the capital ceremonies the Americans had tried to match. What was left in Europe to imitate? The way of living in some European capitals was also gone; trees had begun to grow on the slate roofs of Potsdam, and the counterpart houses in Paris were subdivided into offices and apartments. Real estate agents likewise hung up signs outside the Massachusetts Avenue houses, and those big, European-style houses were bought by embassies and legations, the only tenants whose unique requirements fit the "social" side of these houses. After all, who else needed a ballroom? The "Embassy District" of Washington today was the Massachusetts Avenue of this book.

Since this account of the era is based upon the characters who lived it, what happened to some of them may be of interest to the reader. The Lincoln Memorial rolled on to completion. To dedicate it and celebrate a member of their own ranks, the American Institute of Architects presented the gold medal to Henry Bacon for his design and construction of the great memorial. The torchlit evening ceremony at the Lincoln Memorial on May 18, 1923, could have sprung from one of Edwin Austin Abbey's murals. Robed in a long Renaissance-style garment of crimson velvet, Bacon stood on a barge, which was rowed the full length of the monument's reflecting pool by tunic-clad architectural apprentices, who were flanked on the shore by costumed flag bearers with tall banners. At the memorial, the gold medalist climbed the long marble steps, where President Warren G. Harding waited among architects and distinguished guests to loop the medal's ribbon around Bacon's neck.

Most of the architects principal to the McMillan Plan and the Mall were dead by the war's end. McKim, Burnham, and Carrere were dead; Hastings continued to head the successful office in New York. Most of the architects died in their beds, although Carrere was killed in a car wreck, and the Patterson's architect, Stanford White, was shot, famously, by the husband of one of his lady friends. Glenn Brown, who continued in practice, surely had a hand in the gold medal presentation to Henry Bacon. Mary Henderson, whose name belongs with the architects, died in a nursing home in 1931, spunky at ninety, having proved her right-headedness in a court suit brought by an avaricious relative and retaining her fortune to bequeath to whomever she chose.

Of the diplomats, Count Dumba returned to Austria and died in the year the United States entered the fray. Count Bernstorff went back to Germany, where he was an active supporter of the League of Nations; in the 1930s, at odds with the Nazis, he moved to Geneva, where he died in 1939. Jules Jusserand served as ambassador in Washington for twenty-two years, one of the most successful diplomats France has ever sent to the United States. He returned to France in 1924 and died in bed in 1932,

A legacy of the Imperial Season: the Lincoln Memorial being built, in 1917, the year the United States entered World War I. Earth was mounded to cover the basement once the structure was complete, five years later. *U.S. Commission of Fine Arts, Washington, D.C.*

at the moment of death dropping the pen with which he was writing his memoirs. Charles de Chambrun straightened up and had a stellar career as a diplomat, climaxed as France's ambassador to Italy during 1933 to 1935, where he married the author Marie de Rohan-Chabot. Elected to the Académie Française in 1946, he died in 1952 and is buried with his wife and all the Lafayettes in Picpus Cemetery, in Paris near the spot where many of his ancestors died on the guillotine. Jules-Martin Cambon was ambassador at Berlin when World War I broke out. He remained active in diplomacy, becoming a strong influence on the views of the French delegates at the Versailles conference. He died in Switzerland in 1935 at the age of ninety.

John Hay's widow, Clara Stone Hay, spent little time in Washington after Hay's death but kept the house in Cleveland open and there assembled her late husband's correspondence and literary remains. She seems to have had a mission, for she censored sentences in a number of the letters and diaries and corrected the grammar. Her approach suggests that some of the material may have been destroyed. All the letters in her possession were copyrighted in her name, and she commissioned from a group of these she had assembled in 1908 a "personal" biography, not an account of his public life. The two-volume work, by the well-known historian William Roscoe Thayer, was published in 1915, one year after Clara Hay died in New York at the home of her daughter Helen Hay Whitney.[2] Minnie Townsend continued the life she loved in her Petit Trainon, at 2121 Massachusetts Avenue, until her death in 1934. Vacant for some years after her tenure, the house was sold to the Cosmos Club, which it serves today. Mrs. Townsend herself is still elegantly housed, now with Richard Townsend, in a magnificent Doric-columned mausoleum in Rock Creek Cemetery, not a long walk from where Henry Adams was laid to rest beside Clover in 1918. All that greets one in the Adams plot is a bench and the somber bronze statue that Adams commissioned from Augustus Saint-Gaudens in Clover's memory. There is no epitaph, or names, or dates.

Nearby is the mausoleum of Evalyn Walsh McLean, where also entombed are her parents, Tom and Carrie, and her husband, Ned. Ned died in a nursing home 1941, trapped in alcoholism and bankrupt in the 1929 crash, in which he lost the *Washington Post*. Evalyn died in 1947, weary of the awful glare of publicity that had accompanied her since she came into possession of the Hope diamond, with its bogus legend; this unwelcomed notoriety violated her privacy and masked the extent of her kind heart and charities. Despite her qualities, her life was sad, braced in low times by morphine. A dispersion of their possessions under the hammer took place the year after she died. The auctioneers announced with huckster gloat, "To relate the stories concerning the articles to be liquidated would encompass a full catalog."[3]

Martha Wadsworth emerged from World War I and enjoyed her fame as a horsewoman. Much decorated for her war efforts, she was praised as an innovator in the fading art of training military horses and decided to forgo Washington and remain in her kingdom, the Genessee Valley of New York. She and Herbert never returned to Washington to live. The Massachusetts Avenue house was left closed until they turned it over to the Red Cross, probably under threat from a governmental condemnation for military use. Herbert died in 1927 and Martha in 1934. When the Red Cross abandoned this Washington house and left it standing vacant, their back-door neighbor, Mabel Boardman, rescued it by founding the Sulgrave Club, a women's membership club of a kind rather new at the time, patterned on men's in-city eating clubs. Mabel Boardman remained in her fortress of a house for the rest of her long and productive life, which ended there in 1946, in her eighty-sixth year. Mabel Boardman is buried in the Washington Cathedral. She built a memorial there to all her kin, situated across the nave from Woodrow Wilson's sarcophagus.

Larz Anderson, minister to Belgium and ambassador to Japan, has the grandest memorial of all. After his death in 1937, Isabel built St. Mary's Chapel in the Washington Cathedral. Her ashes joined his there in 1948. She left their large estate to charities and trusts for the benefit of her servants and their families. She gave her and Larz's palatial Anderson House on Massachusetts Avenue to the Society of the Cincinnati as its national headquarters; the society has since added a research library and opened the building as a historic house museum. The formal rooms are kept much as they were when the Andersons knew them. Anderson House and the

Palais Rose–inspired house at 1618 New Hampshire Avenue, where Perry and Jessie Belmont had lived sometimes, are the only survivors that remain furnished as they were. The Belmont house is preserved as the International Temple of the General Grand Order of the Eastern Star.

Countess Cassini returned to Russia with her father in 1905. The czar summoned her to his presence and conferred upon her the title "countess," which she carried for the rest of her life. She was happily married to an Italian diplomat. Her son Igor was an author and writer of the widely read Cholly Knickerbocker column in the Hearst papers; he refashioned "café society" as the "jet set." His brother Oleg was the fashion designer. Countess Cassini died at seventy-nine in New York, in 1961. Her sprightly memoir, *Never a Dull Moment*, which almost certainly benefited from the literary skills of Igor, is the best social account of young people in diplomatic society during the Imperial Season.

Alice and Nick Longworth moved to Massachusetts Avenue in the 1920s, and she lived in their small limestone *hôtel particulier* for the rest of her life. Always a performer, her funny, sometimes pithy remarks were frequently quoted in the press. Her marriage to Longworth was not a happy one for long. Nick seems not to have been the marrying kind. They had one daughter, who died young, herself leaving a daughter. Nick became Speaker of the House; for a while in the 1920s Alice played Republican politics, writing letters and columns and at last a memoir, *Crowded Hours* (1933). She died in 1980, at the age of ninety-two, a widow for nearly fifty years.

The Patten sisters, holdouts on Massachusetts Avenue, sold their mother's towering brick house in 1944, surrendering to a Washington that had changed around them. Most of the contents were auctioned. A businessman from the Midwest bought their mother's huge Venetian glass chandelier, of which they were so proud, for his restaurant. The Pattens found more convenient quarters on the other side of Dupont Circle. Demolition crews moved in after the house sat vacant for a year, but it continued to sit resolutely, like a granite bulldog. The *Washington Daily News* reported, "Wreckers have been working on the old house for nearly three weeks. . . . They figure it will take at least two months more to finish the job."[4]

Their neighbor up the street at Sheridan Circle, Alice Pike Barney, painter and creator of tableaux, emerged from the war years divorced and happy to be. While she kept her residence and studio in Washington, she was soon residing full-time in Hollywood, in her element, where she lived for a while with a young husband, grew old, admired, and ever-more powdered and rouged, sponsoring and designing plays in her own theater. According to her wishes, on her death in 1931 she was buried in her family's plot in Dayton, Ohio, with this epitaph to elevate her from lesser relatives: "Alice Pike Barney, the Talented One."

Alice Paul's great quest came to its climax February 18, 1920, with passage of the Nineteenth Amendment to the Constitution, granting women nationwide the right to vote. She remained busy with the work of the National Woman's Party for many years, living in its Washington headquarters near the Capitol. She and her colleagues were not entirely pleased by the manners of the new-age "women's liberationists" who came to join up in the 1960s, finding them a touch unladylike. When she retired, she left it all behind, returning to the New Jersey countryside where she had been born and dying there in 1977 at the age of ninety-two.

Bruce Cortelyou, who left government when Theodore Roosevelt left office, moved with his wife, Lily, back to New York, where he went into private business as president of the New York Gas Company. Ever devoted to music, when the gas company's board of directors decided to build their new office structure on the site of New York's old Academy of Music, on Third Avenue, Cortelyou scheduled several days of free public musical performances there to bid farewell respectfully to the old hall he had loved as a penniless young man. Cortelyou's had always been a special touch. He died at seventy-eight in 1940.

Theodore Roosevelt, having pronounced, in true TR style, that Taft was so fat he would not live long after his first term, died at sixty in 1919, and a lively Taft became chief justice of the Supreme Court, dying in 1930 at the age of seventy-two. Roosevelt served as an editor on the staff of the *Outlook*, for which he had written over a long period of time in the past, but his real wish was naturally to return to public service in some big way. In spite of his efforts, this was not to be. Unable to cope with the death of his youngest son in action in the war, he declined rapidly. During his last days in the hospital, newspapers noted among his callers was General Theodore A. Bingham.

Mrs. Roosevelt survived her husband by many years, until 1948, when she died at eighty-seven. Edith Roosevelt suffered the loss of a son in action in World War I and another from illness during World War II. A private person, she nevertheless published accounts of her travels. She restored an old New England house and garden in the 1920s and lived between it and Sagamore Hill, the house Roosevelt had built for his first wife, Alice's mother, and shared with Edith for the thirty-two years of their marriage.

Former president Taft proved a helpmate to the president during the war, supporting Wilson's idea of a league of nations. His return to the bench was the fulfillment of his fondest wish. The Supreme Court Building, across from the Capitol in Washington, was designed by Cass Gilbert under Taft's careful supervision and would please Burnham and McKim greatly.

As is well known, President Wilson suffered a stroke during his campaign for the League of Nations, after his two trips to Versailles. Edith's tendency to isolate him came into full power with his illness, and she did so, ever claiming that she had no part in any important decisions required of him. But she did decide what was important for him to see and what was not. A very feeble Wilson died in retirement at their home on S Street in Washington in 1924. Edith joined him in the Washington Cathedral thirty-seven years later, in 1961, at the age of eighty-nine. As a woman of sixty-seven, in 1939, she published *My Memoir*, which was edited by the acclaimed biographer Marquis James. He did not urge her to profundity or maybe gave up after trying. In spite of his efforts to guide her elsewhere, she produced a perfect portrait of herself.

Alvey Adee never retired. He remained at work at the Department of State. His routine never changed much. A State Department car called for him every morning, unless he telephoned that he preferred to walk. Carrying his slice of apple pie in a basket, he arrived at an office and desk that remained the same, one doorway removed from the office of the secretary of state. In the last group picture of the office in which he appeared, about forty men and women stand on the broad granite steps of the State, War, and Navy Building. Adee is front row center, bent and tottering, smiling through a trim white beard; two colleagues stand close, apparently holding him up. Death came after two months' decline at the age of eighty-two, on the Fourth of July 1924, in the same Fifteenth Street house where he lived with his niece Lucy and their servants. News stories and commentaries were many, chronicling his distinguished career and relative anonymity. He too was buried in Oak Hill Cemetery, and the *Washington Post* reported that at graveside on that day, brilliant sunshine broke through the clouds of a summer storm.[5]

We don't know everything about Adee. In the National Archives we can seek his many memoranda, his treaties, the speeches he wrote for presidents; we can read his short stories, poems, and commentaries on Shakespeare's plays; "Life's Magnet," the suspense story he wrote with John Hay in Spain, is called a "classic of horror" and is available on the web. We know little about him but also a lot. No other character spanned the period of this book quite as completely as Alvey Adee, who stood in full view of nearly everything that happened in Washington in the fleeting quarter century of the Imperial Season.

APPENDIX
Seating by Rank at Table in Official Washington

Alvey A. Adee, ca. 1904

Memorandum of precedence at a dinner in the house of a private American citizen who has no connection with the public service of the United States or of a State in the Union, or of any foreign Govt, and when the dinner is not given in honor of any particular individual or of any corps or organization—

The President
The Vice President
Foreign Ambassadors accredited to the United States
The Secretary of State
Foreign Envoys Plenipotentiary
The Chief Justice
The President pro tem of the Senate
The Speaker of the House
Cabinet Secretaries other than the Secretary of State
Foreign ministers Resident
Associate Justices of the Supreme Court
The Admiral of the Navy
Senators
Governors of the States
Representatives in Congress
The Chief of Staff of the Army
Charges d'affaires

Major Generals of the Army
Rear Admirals
Foreign Secretaries of the Executive Departments
Assistant Secretaries of the Executive Departments
Judges of the Court of Claims
Secretary of the Smithsonian Institution
District Commissioners
District Court of Appeals
District Supreme Court
Brigadier Generals
Captains in the Navy
Director of the Bureau of American Republics
Army and Navy Officers below Army Brigadiers and Navy Captains
Foreign Guests in private life, untitled
American guests in private life

Notes

1. Foreign Representatives take rank among themselves in the order of their audience of credence [see State Department Foreign List, issued monthly]

2. Cabinet officers rank in the order of the creation of their respective departments [see Congressional Directory]

3. Assistant Justices rank according to Date of Commission [see Congressional Directory]

4. Senators and Representatives rank according to length of service in their respective Houses [see Congressional Directory]

5. Army and Navy Officers rank respectively according to their number in the Army and Navy lists.

6. District Commissioners rank according to date of appointment [see Congressional Directory]

7. Judges of Court of Claims rank by date of commission—Congressional Directory gives their precedence.

8. It is not possible to form an order of precedence for foreign guests who hold office or letters under their own governments—In regard to such it would be well to consult informally the diplomatic representatives of their country.

9. American guests, being in the diplomatic service of the U.S. abroad, and being at home on leave do not take precedence according to their rank, i.e., the American Ambassador to a foreign court does not rank, in an American private house, with a foreign Ambassador accredited to the U.S. He is a distinguished citizen, and may be placed according to convenience, but not above Representatives in Congress.

10. Ex-officers do not retain any right of precedence by reason of past service; but an exception is generally made in favor of an ex-President, who may be placed by courtesy, next after foreign ambassadors.

11. The wives of guests rank in the same order as their husbands. An unmarried daughter, if the actual head of her father's household, comes after married ladies of the same category—If not the head of the household she is ranked as a private citizen, after unmarried ladies.

12. If the usual arrangement of the guests, in alternate succession right and left of the host and hostess, should bring husband and wife together at table, it is customary to shift the lady to the corresponding place on the other side of the host or hostess as the case may be.

Records of the Department of State
National Archives

ENDNOTES

Prologue

1. The Japanese mission in 1860 was a temporary expedition of friendship and rightly called an "embassy." The Japanese representatives were called "ambassadors" in the press, but it was free usage of that term. They were not in actuality ambassadors speaking for their monarch.

2. Before he invented a simple presentation, Jefferson insulted the British minister with too informal a reception. The affront did not pass unnoticed. It would be odd if Jefferson had intended it, but he was never so lax again.

3. Peter Bridges, "An Appreciation of Alvey Adee," *American Diplomacy* 12, no. 4 (December 2001): 1–8. In addition to scarce secondary sources on Adee, such as Bridges's, articles on Adee occasionally appeared in newspapers throughout the country, most of them in the twentieth century, and will be noted. Extensive use has been made of the Adee Family Papers, Library of Congress, and the Records of the Department of State, Diplomatic Correspondence, at the National Archives, where many Adee papers appear over all his years of public service.

4. See R. B. Mowat, *The Life of Lord Pauncefote: First Ambassador to the United States* (Boston: Houghton Mifflin Company, 1929), 117–30, 151–59. The ceremony itself had not changed since President Thomas Jefferson created it. Nothing seems to have been added to honor the ambassadorial rank unless perhaps it was the Marine Band. But the band was usual in all White House ceremonies.

5. Three ambassadors followed Pauncefote in the same year: M. J. Patenotre, France (on April 12, 1893); Baron A. von Saurmajeltsh, Germany (on June 14, 1893); also, Baron de Fava, whose rank was increased to ambassador from Italy (on June 14, 1893). While the term *great powers* was used at this time in reference to the countries just listed, *trading nations* more formally describes them, as well as Austria-Hungary and Japan, which, with Mexico, soon also sent ambassadors.

6. *Evening Star*, Washington, April 12, 1893.

One: The Capital of the Sleeping Giant

1. It might be noted that Sir Julian took great pleasure in riding the capital's streetcars and used them frequently. Wu Tingfang, *America through the Spectacles of an Oriental Diplomat* (1914; reprint, McLean, VA: Alan R. Light, 1996), 39.

2. This is a guess for 1893. The Federal Census of 1890 was largely destroyed in a fire in the Commerce Department in 1921; the census of 1900 shows 270,000 as the capital's population, making it one of the fifteen largest cities in the country.

3. *Washington Post*, January 8, 1909; *New York Sun*, August 27, 1907; *Wall Street Daily News*, July 5, 1907. Various other clippings undated in the Adee Family Papers, Library of Congress, attest to Adee's bicycle riding.

4. Eddie Savoy went to work at the State Department in 1871 at the age of sixteen and was assigned to Adee by at least 1880, perhaps earlier. *Washington Post*, June 17, 1930. A second messenger and often monitor at Adee's office door was William Freer, an African American about whom little can be found, except that he was a resident of the city and worked for the State Department for several decades.

5. *Christian Work*, New York, December 14, 1912; various clippings from the *New York Daily Tribune*, ca. 1902–7, Adee Family Papers, Library of Congress.

6. Undated clipping from an undated issue of the *Republic*, "Celebrities at Home," ca. 1900, Adee Family Papers.

7. Reference is made here to the vast Washington, DC, photograph files in the Prints and Photographs Division, Library of Congress.

8. John Michael Valch, "From Slavery to Tenancy: African American Housing in Washington, D.C. 1790–1890," in Richard Longstreth, ed., *Housing Washington: Two Centuries of Residential Development and Planning in the National Capital Area* (Chicago: Center for American Places of Columbia College, 2010), 18–20.

9. In 1967 Constance M. Green published *The Secret City: History of Race Relations in the Nation's Capital* (Princeton, NJ: Princeton University Press, 1967), which drew attention to the subject. Invaluable for interpretation, illustration, and detail are James Borchert's three works specifically on the alleys: his unpublished PhD dissertation, "Alley Dwellings and Alley Dwellers in Washington, D.C., 1850–1970," University of Maryland, 1976; "Builders and Owners of Alley Dwellings in Washington, D.C., 1877–1892," *Records of the Columbia Historical Society* 50 (1980): 345–59; *Alley Life in Washington: Family, Community, Religion, and Folklife in the City, 1850–1970* (Urbana: University of Illinois Press, 1980).

10. My sources for the above descriptions are the photographic collections at the Library of Congress and the Historical Society of Washington, DC, as well as city directories for the 1890s and Sanborn Fire Maps for the general era, found both online and at the Library of Congress Map Division. See also James M. Goode, *Capital Losses: A Cultural History of Washington's Destroyed Buildings* (Washington, DC: Smithsonian Institution Press, 1979); and Richard Longstreth, "The Unusual Transformation of Downtown Washington in the Early Twentieth Century," *Washington History* 13, no. 2 (Fall–Winter 2001–2): 51–71.

11. Unidentified clipping, 1908, Adee Family Papers. Much was written in the press about Adee and his bicycle.

12. New York, Chicago, and Washington competed for the fair. Even the promise of a fifteen million dollar contribution by New York bankers could not compete with Chicago's munificence, and Congress, the only source of money for the capital city, was not likely to sweeten its donation to Washington. The final decision was put into the hands of Congress, which designated Chicago as the fair site on April 25, 1890. See Benjamin Truman, *History of the World's Fair: Being a Complete and Authentic Description of the Columbian Exposition from Its Inception* (Philadelphia: J. W. Kelly & Company, 1893), 1–13.

13. Albert E. Cowdrey, *A City for the Nation: The Army Corps of Engineers and the Building of Washington, D.C., 1790–1967* (Washington, DC: Historical Division, Office of Administrative

Services, Office of the Chief of Engineers, 1978), 30–34; John Y. Cole and Henry Hope Reed, eds., *The Library of Congress: The Art and Architecture of the Thomas Jefferson Building* (New York: W. W. Norton & Company, 1997), 55–63.

14. The prince, who visited in 1871, is unnamed in the State Department records.

15. The Queen Isabella Committee was the women's committee of the world's fair, named, of course, for King Ferdinand's queen, who was so instrumental in Columbus's expedition. Certainly the appeal of having Princess Eulalia at the world's fair was her position as a member of the Spanish royal family.

16. Secretary Gresham to Spanish minister Don Emilio [Edvardo] de Muruaga, Washington, May 18, 1893, and Muruaga to Gresham, Havana, May 23, 1893, Records of the Department of State, National Archives.

17. *New York Times*, May 16, 1893. The issues of the visit were covered widely in all the papers.

18. *Evening Star*, Washington, May 20 and 24, 1893; *Washington Post*, May 25, 1893.

19. *Evening Star*, Washington, May 25 and 26, 1893.

20. *Evening Star*, Washington, May 25, 1893; William Seale, *The President's House: A History* (Washington, DC: White House Historical Association, 1986), vol. 2: 209–10.

21. *Washington Star*, Washington, May 20, 1893.

Two: Men of Distinction

1. Cited in Patricia O'Toole, *The Five of Hearts: An Intimate Portrait of Henry Adams and His Friends, 1880–1918* (New York: Clarkson Potter Publishers, 1990), 143. For Richardson's drawings of the two houses as they developed in design, see James F. O'Gorman, *H. H. Richardson and His Office: A Centennial of His Move to Boston, 1874* (Cambridge, MA: Harvard College Library, 1974).

2. Michael Burlingame and John R. Turner Ettlinger, eds., *Inside Lincoln's White House: The Complete Civil War Diary of John Hay* (Carbondale: Southern Illinois University Press, 1997), 95.

3. Hay to David Gray, Madrid, July 25, 1870, John Hay Papers, Brown University Library.

4. See Tyler Dennett, *John Hay: From Poetry to Politics* (New York: Dodd, Mead & Company, 1934).

5. Hay to Adee, Cleveland, December 14, 1875, Adee Papers, Library of Congress. Hay's marriage into a life of financial ease was always recognized by everyone. In his funeral oration for Hay in 1905, Hiram Haydn observed that Hay's marriage "was more than an affair of affection between two souls going forth into life . . . it was besides, as we now see it, the opening wide [of] the door of opportunity to a freedom in work and a following of his bent, free of all concern for the ways and means of livelihood." See Hiram C. Haydn, *The Hon. John Hay: An Appreciation* (Cleveland: First Presbyterian Church, July 16, 1905), 9.

6. Henry Adams, *The Education of Henry Adams* (Boston: Houghton Mifflin Company, 1918), 364–65; see also 375–76.

7. Roosevelt to Henry Cabot Lodge, Washington, July 21, 1905, Theodore Roosevelt Papers, Library of Congress.

8. Cecil Spring-Rice to Ronald Munro Ferguson, Washington, June 9, 1894, quoted in Stephen Gwynn, ed., *The Letters and Friendships of Sir Cecil Spring-Rice: A Record* (Boston: Houghton Mifflin Company, 1929), 156–57.

9. Kate Carew of the *New York World*, 1904, quoted in L. White Busbey, *Uncle Joe Cannon: The Story of a Pioneer American* (New York: Henry Holt Company, 1927), xxviii–xxix.

10. Busbey, *Uncle Joe Cannon*, xvi–xvii.

11. Ibid., Cannon's foreword, n.p.

12. *Baltimore American*, October 13, 1901.

13. Adams, *The Education of Henry Adams*, 375–76.

14. Hay to Adee, Cleveland, November 28, 1874, Hay Papers, Brown University Library.

15. A. T. Mahan, *The Influence of Sea Power Upon History, 1660–1783* (London: Sampson, Low & Marston, 1890); Barbara Tuchman, *The Proud Tower: A Portrait of the World before the War, 1890–1914* (New York: Macmillan Company, 1962), 330–34.

16. Quoted in W. D. Puleston, *Mahan: The Life and Work of Captain Alfred Thayer Mahan, U.S.N.* (London: Jonathan Cape, 1939), 298.

17. John Hay to Clara Hay, London, June 7, 1896, in William Roscoe Thayer, *The Life and Letters of John Hay*, 2 vols. (Boston: Houghton Mifflin Company, 1908), vol. 2: 143–44.

18. Hay to Clara Hay, aboard the S.S. *Teutonic*, July 31, 1896, ibid., 146–47.

19. William Jennings Bryan's "Cross of Gold" speech (*New York World*, August 13, 1896; *Harper's Weekly*, August 20, 1896) may be heard on the web through the Douglass Archives of American Address.

20. Hay to Henry Adams, aboard the *Teutonic*, August 4, 1896, in Thayer, *The Life and Letters of John Hay*, 147–49.

21. Hay to Henry Adams, Cleveland, October 4, 1896, ibid., 151–53.

22. Hay, "memorandum," January 26, 1897, ibid., 153–55.

Three: The Pivotal Year 1898

1. Charles M. Pepper, *Every-day Life in Washington: With Pen and Camera* (Berkeley: University of California, 1900), 220.

2. Antonio Rafael de la Cova, "Fernandina Filibuster Fiascos: Birth of the 1895 Cuban War of Independence, 1895," *Florida Historical Quarterly* 82, no. 1 (Summer 2003): 24.

3. Secretary of State Richard Olney, memorandum outline, April 4, 1896, Records of the Department of State, Diplomatic Correspondence, National Archives.

4. Secretary of State to Spanish minister Emilio [Edvardo] de Muruaga, Washington, April 12, 1896, Records of the Department of State, National Archives.

5. Margaret Leech, *In the Days of McKinley* (New York: Harper & Brothers, 1959), 129.

6. Seale, *The President's House*, vol. 1: 594–96.

7. *New York Journal*, February 8, 1898.

8. Roosevelt to B. J. Diblee, February 16, 1898, in Elting E. Morison and John Blum, eds., *The Letters of Theodore Roosevelt*, 8 vols. (Cambridge, MA: Harvard University Press, 1951–54), vol. 2: 775.

9. Charles S. Olcott, *William McKinley* (Boston: Houghton Mifflin Company, 1916), vol. 2: 24.

10. This and the following related quotations and discussion come from Busbey, *Uncle Joe Cannon*, 186–98.

11. Arthur Wallace Dunn, *From Harrison to Harding: A Personal Narrative, Covering a Third of a Century, 1888–1921* (Port Washington, NY: Kennikat Press, 1971), 204.

12. Arthur Wallace Dunn, *Gridiron Nights: Humorous and Satirical Views of Politics and Statesmen as Presented by the Famous Dining Club* (New York: Frederick A. Stokes Company, 1915), 72.

13. Senator Sherman's decline was fairly much general knowledge nearly a year before his resignation as secretary of state (on April 27, 1898). The *Marion Pilot*, in Ohio, wrote on August 21, 1897, "According to critics at home and abroad, Secretary of State John Sherman is in an alarming state of dotage." A few days before, on August 18, 1897, the *Metropolis*, in Jacksonville, Florida, observed: "You hear him [Sherman] discussed everywhere—on the street cars, in the clubs, hotels, and on the street corners."

14. Spanish Ministry of State, U.S. Department of State, *Spanish Diplomatic Correspondence and Documents, 1896–1900* (Washington, DC: Government Printing Office, 1905), 111.

15. *London Times*, April 7, 1898; Mowat, *Life of Lord Pauncefote*, 213–21.

16. E. T. S. Dugdale, *German Diplomatic Documents, 1817–1914* (New York: Harper & Brothers, 1930), vol. 2: 512.

17. George Bruce Cortelyou, diary, March 10, 1898, Library of Congress.

18. Peggy Samuels and Harold Samuels, *Teddy Roosevelt at San Juan: The Making of a President* (College Station: Texas A&M University Press, 1997), 22.

19. *Glasgow Daily Record*, April 8, 1898.

20. Cambon had been the French minister to Spain in 1891.

21. Hay to Clara Hay, "Tuesday," n.d. (summer 1898 implied in text), John Hay Papers among the James Wolcott Wadsworth Jr. Papers, Library of Congress.

22. William Day made notes of the meeting, in which this remark appears. He gave the notes to McKinley, and they are now in the William McKinley Papers, August 11, 14, 18, 19, 1898, Library of Congress.

23. Adams, *The Education of Henry Adams*, 323–24.

Four: World Capital

1. Although the name "Spanish War" remained in common usage before World War I, after which it died out, "Spanish-American War" came to be in creating the documents at the protocol meeting in August 1898, a delicacy apparently introduced by the French ambassador Jules Cambon.

2. Charles Moore, *The Life and Times of Charles Follen McKim* (Boston: Houghton Mifflin Company, 1929), 182–203; Glenn Brown, *Memories: 1860–1930* (Washington, DC: W. F. Roberts Company, 1931), 52–145; Seale, *The President's House*, 678–79 and 642–45; the Theodore Bingham Papers and the Charles Moore Papers, both in Library of Congress.

3. See the Theodore Bingham Papers, Library of Congress; and the Records of the Officer in Charge of Public Buildings, National Archives.

4. At this writing, many of the drawings reside in the Records of the Commission of Fine Arts, National Archives; the model is in the collections of the Smithsonian Institution and was unpacked and displayed in the Smithsonian Castle in the 1970s.

5. McKim to Charles Moore, New York, April 17, 1902, quoted in Moore, *The Life and Times of Charles Follen McKim*, 206.

6. Thomas Hines, "The Imperial Mall: The City Beautiful Movement and the Washington Plan of 1901–1902," in Richard Longstreth, ed., *The Mall in Washington: 1791–1991* (New Haven, CT: Yale University Press, 1991), 79–99; and in the same volume, Jon A. Peterson, "The Mall, the McMillan Plan, and the Origins of American City Planning," 101–15.

7. A set of the Blue Books can be found in the Records of the Officer in Charge of Public Buildings, National Archives. Colonel Bingham's papers yield a few notes, possibly taken at the meetings

over the rules, but this is not certain. His awareness of European diplomatic forms made him very useful to the small group of four.

8. Hay to Clara Hay, Washington, October 17 [1903], James Wolcott Wadsworth Jr. Papers, Library of Congress. Edward Harriman and Roosevelt were at that time in a heated dispute over regulations and trusts involving the railroads.

9. *Collier's Weekly*, April 12, 1904.

10. The Social Files, Record Group 42, National Archives, document the social activities, customs, and innovations in White House entertaining during the first two decades of the twentieth century, including contracts, sample invitations, and newspaper clippings.

11. Hines, "The Imperial Mall," 80–92; Charles Moore, *Daniel H. Burnham: Architect and Planner of Cities*, 2 vols. (Boston: Houghton Mifflin Company, 1921), vol. 2: 129–73; see also Charles Moore, ed., *The Improvement of the Park System of the District of Columbia, 1902*, Senate Report, 57th Congress, 1st session, 1902; and Rachel Cooper, *Union Station in Washington, D.C.* (Mt. Pleasant, SC: Acadia Publishing Company, 2011), illustrated history.

Five: Diplomats

1. Cassini to Adee, Washington, January 11, 1903, Records of the State Department, National Archives.

2. The Congress of Vienna was followed seven years later by the Congress of Verona, where further details of diplomatic procedure were settled.

3. Not that Europe was unaware of the rise of America; it fully realized that America and Russia, so large in scale, would become major players in the future. Indeed Napoleon III in 1866, having observed the Union's power in the Civil War, had espoused a European alliance against the United States, and Wilhelm II proposed a similar arrangement in 1895, well within the period of this book.

4. John W. Foster, *The Practice of Diplomacy: As Illustrated in the Foreign Relations of the United States* (Boston: Houghton Mifflin Company, 1906), 131–32.

5. Public Law 100, 52nd Congress, 2nd session, March 1, 1893, 497.

6. The reception of the duke was in the Blue Room and followed the usual diplomatic form, but unlike that of Sir Julian Pauncefote and those after him, it attracted large crowds on Pennsylvania Avenue. The occasion offered plenty of diplomatic glitter, from the diamonds and plumes of the uniforms to the flowery, very carefully worded speeches of ambassador and president. Fully covered in the *New York Times*, June 4, 1899.

7. A diplomat was accused of raping a female tavern employee in the 1818 case and attempted to stay on in the United States, but public opinion was so opposed to him that at last he literally fled, fearing visitation by a mob.

8. *New York Times*, Saturday Review of Books section, January 17, 1903.

9. M. A. De Wolfe Howe, *George von Lengerke Meyer: His Life and Public Service* (New York: Dodd, Mead and Company, 1920), 136–37.

10. Records of the Department of State, National Archives, have abundant documentation of how dinners were to be held and how the seating was to be, both for legations and for private houses where diplomats were to be entertained.

11. Florence Marion Howe Hall, *Social Usages at Washington* (New York: Harper and Brothers, 1906), 102.

12. The best personal account by an American diplomat of court practices in Germany is James W. Gerard, *My Four Years in Germany* (New York: George H. Doran Company, 1917), 111–42.

13. The president was not required (before Truman in 1946) to account for his allowance. This was to cover the extras that might appear from living in the White House. Since it was so small an amount as to be nearly useless, money was secured from the various departments for household salaries and some other costs. Formal dinners wherever possible were called "state" or "official" events, so the costs could be ascribed to the Department of State. Congress was ever mindful of curbing "high living" at the White House.

14. Mowat, *The Life of Lord Pauncefote*, 23–28.

15. Beckles Willson, *Friendly Relations: A Narrative of Britain's Ministers and Ambassadors to America, 1791–1930* (London: Lovat Dickson & Thompson Limited, 1934), 236, 226–40.

16. Goode, *Capital Losses*, 231–33.

17. Pepper, *Every-day Life in Washington*, 221.

18. In the appendix to this book, an example of Adee's social directives is quoted in its entirety, specifying seating by rank.

19. Mrs. John A. [Mary Simmerson] Logan, *Thirty Years in Washington* (Hartford, CT: A. D. Worthington and Company, 1901), 504–8 and passim.

20. While the custom of the hosts sitting across from one another was more common in Washington than elsewhere, the Russian-style table service, in which the dishes are brought in separately and sequentially, compared with the French style, in which all the food is brought in at once, some is served, and some is passed along the table, was universally practiced in Washington in formal situations.

21. Julia Bundy Foraker, *I Would Live It Again: Memories of a Vivid Life* (New York: Harper and Brothers, 1932), 195–99; Kathryn Allamong Jacob, *Capital Elites: High Society in Washington, D.C., after the Civil War* (Washington, DC: Smithsonian Institution Press, 1995), 140–97.

22. *New York Sun*, August 27, 1907.

23. Mowat, *The Life of Lord Pauncefote*, 256–59.

24. Adams, *The Education of Henry Adams*, 374.

25. Mowat, *The Life of Lord Pauncefote*, 284–87.

26. Walter Fawcett, "Envoys at Washington," *Cosmopolitan*, May 1901, 381–92; Pepper, *Every-day Life in Washington*, 222–56; Nelson Manfred Blake, "Ambassadors at the Court of Theodore Roosevelt," *Mississippi Valley Historical Review* 42 (September 1955): 179–206.

27. Foraker, *I Would Live It Again*, 196.

28. Ibid., 199.

29. Cecil Spring-Rice to Daisy [White], n.p., September 6, 1887, quoted in Gwynn, ed., *The Letters and Friendships of Sir Cecil Spring-Rice*, vol. 1: 74–75.

30. Willson, *Friendly Relations*, 283.

31. Roosevelt to Henry White, Washington, DC, December 27, 1904, quoted in Morison and Blum, eds., *The Letters of Theodore Roosevelt*, vol. 4: 1082.

32. Marguerite Cassini, *Never a Dull Moment: The Memoirs of Countess Marguerite Cassini* (New York: Harper & Brothers, 1956), 94–102.

33. George Meyer, ambassador to Russia, to Judge Francis C. Lowell, St. Petersburg, February 19, 1906, quoted in Howe, *George von Lengerke Meyer*, 258–59.

34. Quoted in Gwynn, *The Letters and Friendships of Cecil Spring-Rice*, vol. 1: 470.

Six: Progress in Marble

1. William Bushong, "A Gateway Restored," *National Building Museum Blueprints* 6, no. 3 (Summer 1988): 5.
2. Moore, *Daniel P. Burnham*, vol. 1: 167–77, vol. 2: 5–13.
3. Moore, *The Life and Times of Charles Follen McKim*, 278–79; see also Christina K. Hough, "The Army War College in Washington, D.C.: Patriotic and Political Ideals in Architecture by McKim, Mead and White," MA thesis, University of Virginia, 1991.
4. Chauncey Depew, *My Memories of Eighty Years* (New York: Charles Scribner's Sons, 1924), 198–99.
5. While Presidents Roosevelt and Taft participated in diplomacy as no presidents had before, it would be Woodrow Wilson who would significantly bypass the State Department and venture into diplomacy on his own.
6. Roosevelt to White, Washington, April 4, 1902, Henry White Papers, Library of Congress.
7. Douglas MacArthur, *Reminiscences of Douglas MacArthur* (New York: McGraw-Hill, 1964), 33.
8. Busbey, *Uncle Joe Cannon*, xxv.
9. Ibid., 208–10.
10. Henderson and Pelz, folio of drawings for a new presidential mansion, Washington, D.C., privately published by Mrs. Henderson, 1903, Office of the Curator of the White House; see also Henderson Family Papers, Smithsonian Institution Archives.
11. Some of these drawings can be seen at the Commission of Fine Arts in Washington, D.C., and most were published at the time in *Century* magazine.
12. James M. Goode, *Best Addresses: A Century of Washington's Distinguished Apartment Houses* (Washington, DC: Smithsonian Institution Press, 1988), 24–47.
13. Belle Hagner, unpublished memoir, ca. 1930, Office of the Curator of the White House.

Seven: Business and Friendship

1. Hay to Adee, Newberry, New Hampshire, August 11, 1902, Adee Family Papers, Library of Congress.
2. Hay to Clara Hay, Washington, July 13 [1903], James Wolcott Wadsworth Jr. Papers, Library of Congress.
3. Hay to Adams, Washington, June 30, 1901, in Thayer, *The Life and Letters of John Hay*, vol. 2: 263.
4. Hay to Adams, New Hampshire, August 9, 1901, ibid., 265; see also Hay to Whitelaw Reid, New Hampshire, July 22, 1901, ibid., 264; also see various articles on Delbert Hay's death in the *New York Times*, June 24, 25, and 26, 1901.
5. Adee to Hay, Washington, August 18, 1902, Adee Family Papers, Library of Congress.
6. Hay to Adee, Washington, [September 6, 1902], Adee Family Papers, Library of Congress.
7. Adee to Hay, Washington, April 21, 1905, Adee Family Papers, Library of Congress.
8. Adee to Hay, Washington, September 9, 1904, Adee Family Papers, Library of Congress.
9. Adee to Hay, Washington, September 2, 1904, John Hay Papers, microfilm ed., Library of Congress.
10. Adee to Hay, Washington, December 13, 1898, August 5, 1900, and September 3, 1901, John Hay Papers, microfilm ed., Library of Congress. The idea for the "open door" is usually attributed to Alfred E. Hippisley, a British official in China who was pro-Chinese. His notes were sent to Hay

and McKinley, and these were reviewed by diplomats Henry White and W. W. Rockhill, and finally the documents were assembled and drafted for Hay by Adee, resulting in the diplomatic note called the Open Door Policy. The power of the policy lay in the implied threat the newly empowered United States made to the powers, a sort of protective warning against the arbitrary exploitation of China.

11. *Whitehall Review*, March 31, 1900.

12. Hay to Henry White, September 8, 1900, Henry White Papers, Library of Congress.

13. Adee's involvement seems to have been no secret. The *Chicago Journal*, August 11, 1900, reported: "The negotiations with China have fallen upon Second Assistant Alvey A. Adee."

14. Adee to Hay, Washingon, August 18, 1902, John Hay Papers, microfilm ed., Library of Congress.

15. Adee, "first sketch of the canal convention," Washington, April 8, 1901, Adee Family Papers, Library of Congress.

16. Adee to Hay, Washington, July 29, 1902, Records of the Department of State, Diplomatic Correspondence, National Archives.

17. Ibid.; see also the draft, "Roumanian Jew Instruction," by Adee; and Adee to Hay, Washington, July 29, 1902, Adee Family Papers, Library of Congress. Hay, so pleased with Adee's work in this matter, wrote to Adee, "Now, you have a genius for taking in an idea, letting it soak awhile, and bringing it forth in a diplomatic note twice as good as the original idea. Even if Russia does nothing we shall have a good note to present next winter." Hay to Adee, New Hampshire, August 12, 1902, Adee Family Papers, Library of Congress.

18. Adee to Hay, Washington, August 25, 1904, John Hay Papers, microfilm ed., Library of Congress.

19. J. J. Jusserand, *What Me Befell: The Reminiscences of J. J. Jusserand* (Boston: Houghton Mifflin Company, 1934), 221–22.

20. Lawrence F. Abbott, ed., *The Letters of Archie Butt: Personal Aide to President Roosevelt* (New York: Doubleday, Page & Company, 1924), 120.

21. Jusserand, *What Me Befell*, 302.

22. Howe, *George von Lengerke Meyer*, 158–59.

23. Ibid., 154–66.

24. Henry Fowles Pringle, *Theodore Roosevelt: A Biography* (New York: Harcourt, Brace & Company, 1931), 212.

25. Sidney Harcave, ed., *The Memoirs of Count Witte* (Armonk, NY: M. E. Sharpe, 1990), 434.

26. John Hay diary, June 14, 1905, John Hay Papers, Brown University Library.

27. Adee to Clara Hay, Washington, July 22, 1905, Adee Family Papers, Library of Congress.

Eight: Massachusetts Avenue

1. See Charles R. Atherton, Donald B. Myer, Jeffrey R. Carson, Lynda L. Smith, and J. L. Sibley Jennings Jr., *Massachusetts Avenue Architecture*, vols. 1 and 2 (Washington, DC: Commission of Fine Arts, 1973 and 1975); and Sue A. Kohler and Jeffrey R. Carson, *Sixteenth Street Architecture* (Washington, DC: Commission of Fine Arts, 1978). I am indebted to these excellent studies.

2. Sanborn's Fire Maps document the uses of the different buildings in this area, as in the rest of the city, 1900 and 1910, Library of Congress, Maps and Cartography Division.

3. Author in conversation with Alice Roosevelt Longworth, ca. October 1975.

4. This house was demolished in the 1960s. See Gérard Rousset-Charny, *Les palais parisiens de la Belle Époque* (Paris: Délégation à l'action artistique de la Ville de Paris, 1990).

5. *New York Times*, June 2, 1907.

6. The ins and outs of the Henry Sloane divorce and the Perry Belmont remarriage are chronicled in front-page accounts of newspapers; see, for example, the *New York Times*, April 27, 1899, for an extensive account. Belmont's brother Oliver had married Alva Smith Vanderbilt under similar but not such racy circumstances in 1895. Earlier, Belmont had in fact been married for only a year to save the reputation of a young woman who was pregnant with his child. This was little known.

7. The Leiter house, demolished in 1947, is illustrated in period photographs, Prints and Photographs Division, Library of Congress.

8. Hay to Clara Hay, aboard the *Majestic*, April 23, 1901, James W. Wolcott Jr. Papers, Library of Congress.

9. For houses built in the 1890s in Paris that very much resemble the Townsend house, see Rousset-Charny, *Les palais parisiens de la Belle Époque*, 98–99.

10. The century anniversary of Marie Antoinette's death (1893) created great interest in the ill-fated queen, to a more popular extent than the earlier revival of her taste in decor by the empress Eugénie in the 1860s. It would be difficult to describe the domestic style of the Townsend house and many others of the time without reference to Marie Antoinette.

11. *Evening Star*, May 26, 1910.

12. *Boston Enquirer*, June 12, 1897.

13. Ibid.

14. Larz Anderson journal, vol. 6, March 9, 1904, Society of Cincinnati Library, Anderson House.

15. Ibid., vol. 9, n.d. [1906].

16. John C. Stewart, *Thomas F. Walsh: Progressive Businessman and Colorado Mining Tycoon* (Boulder: University Press of Colorado, 2007), 41–71.

17. Evalyn Walsh McLean, *Father Struck It Rich*, with Boyden Sparkes (Boston: Little, Brown and Company, 1936), 119.

18. *Denver Times*, October 18, 1901; see also Stewart, *Thomas F. Walsh*, 104–5.

19. Other gold service pieces were also acquired by Walsh. One of these, a gold coffee pot with ivory ornament, made by Tiffany and Company, New York, and shown at the Paris Exposition of 1900, is now in the collections of the Smithsonian Institution.

20. Unidentified newspaper clipping, giving an account of the wedding, noted "June 27, 1888," David R. Francis Papers, Missouri Historical Society.

21. See Judith H. Lanius and Sharon C. Park, *The Wadsworth Mansion: The Gilded Age Comes to DuPont Circle* (Washington, DC: Historical Society of Washington, DC: 1995), 24–96.

22. Martha Wadsworth, photo albums, Wadsworth Family Papers, Milne Library, State University of New York, Geneseo.

23. Larz Anderson journal, vol. 6, May 13, 1904, Society of the Cincinnati Library, Anderson House.

24. *Washington Post*, April 12, 1912.

25. Washington's social affairs were often reported in the press, such as Henry Loomis Nelson, "The Capital of Our Democracy," *Century Magazine*, May 1902; books on etiquette did exist, but they were rare, mainly for visitors to town who had no contact with officials who might inform them. Such a book was Madeleine Vinton Dahlgren, *Etiquette of Social Life in Washington* (Philadelphia: J. B. Lippincott & Company, 1881). It appeared in many editions.

26. Cassini, *Never a Dull Moment*, 118–19.

27. Larz Anderson journal, vol. 1, 1921, Society of Cincinnati Library, Anderson House. No female servants were seen by guests. Formal entertainments of this elegant character used only male servants in the public rooms.

28. Abbott, ed., *The Letters of Archie Butt*, 49. Butt was particularly referring to Minnie Townsend but expressed it also as a general practice in Washington.

29. John Hay to Clara Hay, aboard the *Majestic*, April 23, n.d. [ca. 1901], James W. Wadsworth Jr. Papers, Library of Congress.

30. Kay Halle Papers, notes from conversations with Alice Roosevelt Longworth, John F. Kennedy Presidential Library Archives.

31. Cassini, *Never a Dull Moment*, 112. A german was a dance gathering that usually began with a dinner, followed by intricately organized dances with prescribed sets and "figures," all terminating before dawn with an elegant light supper. Germans had been popular in Washington for at least seventy years.

32. Ibid., 113–15.

33. Mrs. Roosevelt to Alice Roosevelt, Washington, n.d. [1901], Alice Roosevelt Longworth Papers, Library of Congress.

34. See Alice Roosevelt's diary, Alice Roosevelt Longworth Papers, Library of Congress. Debut parties did not need to be elaborate. Sometimes they were strikingly simple. The Roosevelts had a debutante party for their daughter Ethel in 1908 that was a dance at Christmas in the East Room, followed by a seated midnight dinner, simple fare in the ground floor corridor. Only Ethel's friends attended. No alcohol was served.

35. Cassini, *Never a Dull Moment*, 127–28.

36. Abbott, ed., *The Letters of Archie Butt*, 195.

37. Ibid., 180–82.

38. Alice Roosevelt diary, Alice Roosevelt Longworth Papers, Library of Congress.

Nine: Players

1. Isabel Anderson, *Presidents and Pies: Life in Washington, 1897–1919* (Boston: Houghton Mifflin Company, 1920), 227.

2. Isabel Anderson describes how at large dinners they apparently always had "the servants in full-dress livery, shorts and stockings, buckled shoes, and braided vests." Isabel Anderson, *Larz Anderson: Letters and Journals of a Diplomat* (New York: Fleming H. Revell Company, 1940), 558.

3. Anderson, *Presidents and Pies*, 160.

4. Ibid., 115–16. On the particular occasion Isabel describes, President Taft was a guest.

5. Cassini, *Never a Dull Moment*, 174–76.

6. Judith H. Lanius and Sharon C. Park, "Martha Wadsworth's Mansion: The Gilded Age Comes to DuPont Circle," *Washington History* 1, no. 7 (Spring–Summer 1995): 32–38.

7. See William Reider, *Walter and Matilda Gay: The Art and Life of a Charmed Couple* (New York: Harry N. Abrams, 2000).

8. *Sandow's Magazine of Physical Culture*, December 7, 1905, 46.

9. Michael Teague, *Mrs. L: Conversations with Alice Roosevelt Longworth* (New York: Doubleday & Company, 1981), 70–71. Mrs. Longworth was often quoted as making the same remark, and it was typical of women of the time.

10. *New York World*, March 20, 1904.

11. Cassini, *Never a Dull Moment*, 212–14.

12. Larz Anderson journal, vols. 6, 11, 12, Society of Cincinnati Library, Anderson House.

13. Adee to Clara Hay, Washington, March 16, 1905, James Wolcott Wadsworth Family Papers, Library of Congress.

14. Larz Anderson journal, vol. 6, May 13, 1904, Society of the Cincinnati Library, Anderson House.

15. Quoted in Ellen Childs, "Isabel Perkins Anderson," unpublished manuscript, 10–11, Society of Cincinnati Library, Anderson House.

16. Mrs. N. L. Anderson to Larz Anderson, Washington, May 12, 1904, Society of Cincinnati Library, Anderson House.

17. Cassini, *Never a Dull Moment*, 202–3.

18. Ralph G. Martin, *Cissy: The Extraordinary Life of Eleanor Medill Patterson* (New York: Simon and Schuster, 1979), 81.

19. Teague, *Mrs. L.*, 129.

20. Cassini, *Never a Dull Moment*, 225–26; Alice Roosevelt diary, January 20 and 21, 1904, Library of Congress.

21. *New York Times*, July 25, 1906.

22. McLean, *Father Struck It Rich*, 127.

23. Edward Fitzgerald Beale's Tejon Ranch was the largest private landholding in California, some 270,000 acres near Lebec. It remained intact for over 150 years, and its subdivision has begun as this book nears publication.

24. Emily Beale McLean to Carrie Walsh, Washington, September 26, 1908, Evalyn Walsh McLean Papers, Library of Congress.

25. J. R. McLean to Thomas F. Walsh, telegram, Washington, October 10, 1908, Evalyn Walsh McLean Papers, Library of Congress.

26. Emily Beale McLean to Evalyn Walsh McLean, Washington, July 16, 1908, Evalyn Walsh McLean Papers, Library of Congress.

27. Document, St. Leo's Church, Denver, Colorado, Evalyn Walsh McLean Papers, Library of Congress.

28. McLean, *Father Struck It Rich*, 198.

29. Alice Roosevelt Longworth diary, January 23, 1910, Alice Roosevelt Longworth Papers, Library of Congress.

30. Moore, *Daniel P. Burnham*, vol. 2: 47–52; Charles Henry Brent, *A Master Builder: Being the Life and Letters of Henry Yates Satterlee, First Bishop of Washington* (New York: Longmans, Green & Company, 1916), 360–93.

31. Lanius and Park, "Martha Wadsworth's Mansion," 37.

32. Moore, *Daniel P. Burnham*, vol. 2: 59–60.

33. Brent, *A Master Builder*, 396.

Ten: Commitment

1. Mabel Boardman's manuscript diaries beginning in 1883 mirror her younger years, as do her letters. Mabel Boardman Papers, Library of Congress.

2. Mrs. John A. Logan to Clara Barton, Avenel, Maryland, December 10, 1902, Clara Barton Papers, Library of Congress.

3. Clara Barton diary, June 13, 1892, Clara Barton Papers, Library of Congress.

4. H. B. Brown to Boardman, Washington, April 23, 1903, Mabel Boardman Papers, Library of Congress.

5. G. S. Scheffield to Boardman, Attleborough, Massachusetts, April 13 [1903], Mabel Boardman Papers, Library of Congress.

6. Levi Leiter to Boardman, Washington, April 15, 1903, Mabel Boardman Papers, Library of Congress.

7. H. B. Brown to Boardman, Washington, April 23, 1903, Mabel Boardman Papers, Library of Congress.

8. Taft to Boardman, Washington, December 27, 1904, Mabel Boardman Papers, Library of Congress.

9. Press release, draft, [1903], Clara Barton Papers, Library of Congress.

10. Adee to Barton, Washington, April 11, 1903, Clara Barton Papers, Library of Congress. See also the *New York Times*, March 29, 1903.

11. Adee to Barton, Washington, March 31, 1903, Records of the Department of State, Diplomatic Correspondence, National Archives.

12. Barton was offered a pension but responded "neither needed nor desired." Barton to Red Cross, Washington, March 21, 1903, Clara Barton Papers, Library of Congress.

13. Adee to Barton, Washington, April 11, 1903, Clara Barton Papers, Library of Congress.

14. Marietta Minnigerode Andrews, *My Studio Window: Sketches of the Pageant of Washington Life* (New York: E. P. Dutton & Company, 1928), 237–39.

15. H. Paul Caemmerer, *The Life of Pierre Charles L'Enfant: Planner of the City Beautiful, the City of Washington* (Washington, DC: National Republic Publishing Company, 1950), 291–303; see also Jusserand, *What Me Befell*, 286–87.

16. Moore, *Daniel P. Burnham*, vol. 2: 151–59; Moore, *The Life and Times of Charles Follen McKim*, 200–203, 301–12; construction records and correspondence relating to the Lincoln Memorial, Records of the Officer in Charge of Public Buildings and Public Parks of the National Capital, Record Group 42, National Archives.

17. Larz Anderson journal, vol. 1, February 28, 1912, Society of Cincinnati Library, Anderson House.

18. Congressman Wadsworth had been defeated in 1906 but remained with his wife in Washington part of the year, where they were joined by their son, James Jr., elected to the Senate in 1915, and his wife, Alice, John and Clara Hay's daughter, in very strong public statements opposing the vote for women. Indeed, Alice Hay Wadsworth later told the *New York Times* that she was certain the Germans had stirred up the suffrage movement to fuel pacifism and keep the United States out of the war (*Times*, November 19, 1917).

19. Linda J. Lumsden, *Inez: The Life and Times of Inez Milholland* (Bloomington: Indiana University Press, 2004), 81–91; see also *New York Times*, May 5, 1913; and *Washington Post*, March 4, 1913.

20. Ellen Maury Slayden, *Washington Wife: Journal of Ellen Maury Slayden from 1897 to 1919*, edited by Walter Prescott Webb (New York: Harper & Row, 1962), 196–97.

21. Ibid., 198.

22. *Washington Post*, March 4, 5, 1913.

23. Quoted in Willson, *Friendly Relations*, 313.

24. Eleanor Thackara was the daughter of General William T. Sherman. Both she and Thackara were literary, sharing many interests with Adee. They traveled together on many summer vacations.

25. Adee to Ellie [Thackara], Copenhagen, August 3, 1914, Adee Family Papers, Library of Congress; see also Adee to Ellie, August 6, 1914, and Esbjerg [Denmark], August 20, 1914, ibid.

26. Adee to Mrs. Thackara, Copenhagen, July 17, 1914, Adee Family Papers, Library of Congress; Peter Bridges, "Three Great Civil Servants: William Hunter, Alvey Augustus Adee, and Wilbur J. Carr," lecture, Bacon House Foundation, Washington, DC, October 11, 2005, copy in author's collection.

27. Author in conversation with Katherine Woodrow Kirkland, May 1981; see also Seale, *The President's House*, 85.

Eleven: The World at Last

1. Count Bernstorff, *My Three Years in America* (New York: Charles Scribner's Sons, 1920), 35–36.

2. Constantin Dumba, *Memoirs of a Diplomat* (Boston: Little, Brown and Company, 1932), 247–51.

3. Bernstorff, *My Three Years in America*, 36.

4. Ibid., 39.

5. Bernstorff, *My Three Years in America*, 101–26.

6. Dumba, *Memoirs of a Diplomat*, 286–87.

7. Gwynn, ed., *The Letters and Friendships of Cecil Spring-Rice*, vol. 2: 382–85.

8. Ibid., 222–27; Dumba, *Memoirs of a Diplomat*, 220–24; Bernstorff, *My Three Years in America*, 205, 257, 292–98; see also Robert W. Tucker, *Woodrow Wilson and the Great War* (Charlottesville: University of Virginia Press, 2007), 26, 39, 38, 132, 160–61.

9. Andrews, *My Studio Window*, 326.

10. Clipping, 1908, n.d. [*Washington Post*?], Adee Family Papers, Library of Congress.

11. Reed, cited in Thomas J. Knock, *To End All Wars: Woodrow Wilson and the Quest for a New World Order* (Princeton: Princeton University Press, 1992), 30.

12. Gwynn, ed., *The Letters and Friendships of Cecil Spring-Rice*, vol. 2: 191.

13. Bernstorff, *My Three Years in America*, 108.

14. The American ambassador to Britain believed otherwise. See Burton J. Hendrick, *The Life and Letters of Walter Hines Page* (New York: Doubleday Page & Company, 1926), vol. 3: 278.

15. Ibid., 238.

16. House to Wilson, London, May 11, 1915, cited in Tucker, *Woodrow Wilson and the Great War*, 109.

17. Edith Wilson to President Wilson, Washington, June 9, 1915, Edith Bolling Wilson Papers, Library of Congress.

18. Bernstorff, *My Three Years in America*, 157.

19. *New York Times*, April 4, 1917; see also *Washington Evening Star*, April 5, 1917.

20. Gwynn, *The Letters and Friendships of Cecil Spring-Rice*, vol. 2: 389.

21. Dumba, *Memoirs of a Diplomat*, 286; see also 287–89.

22. Andrews, *My Studio Window*, 266–67; also see Jean L. Kling, *Alice Pike Barney: Her Life and Art* (Washington, DC: Smithsonian Institution Press, 1994), 263–64.

23. Anderson, *Presidents and Pies*, 226–31; both the *Washington Evening Star* and the *Washington Post* faithfully describe the war years in Washington and the changes the war brought to everyday life.

24. Wilson, *My Memoir*, 135.

25. Anderson, *Presidents and Pies*, 161.

26. Alice Roosevelt Longworth, *Crowded Hours: The Reminiscences of Alice Roosevelt Longworth* (New York: Charles Scribner's Sons, 1933), 245; see also 246–47.

Conclusion: Ember Days

1. Eulalia, the Infanta of Spain, *Court Life from Within* (New York: Dodd, Mead and Company, 1916), i–ii.

2. William Roscoe Thayer, ed., *The Life and Letters of John Hay* (Boston: Houghton Mifflin Company, 1915), vol. 1: viii–ix. In his introduction Thayer notes that Clara Hay had edited the letters "scrupulously."

3. Meredith Galleries, *Estate of Evalyn Walsh McLean*, auction catalog, May 17, 1948, 6.

4. *Washington Daily News*, November 27, 1947.

5. *Washington Post*, July 9, 1924.

SELECTED BIBLIOGRAPHY

Published Sources

Abbott, Lawrence F., ed. *The Letters of Archie Butt: Personal Aide to President Roosevelt*. New York: Doubleday, Page & Company, 1924.

Abbott, Lyman. *Silhouettes of My Contemporaries*. Garden City: Doubleday, Page & Company, 1922.

Adams, Henry. *The Education of Henry Adams*. Boston: Houghton Mifflin Company, 1918.

Albrecht-Carrie, Rene. *A Diplomatic History of Europe since the Congress of Vienna*. New York: Harper & Row, 1973.

Anderson, Isabel, ed. *Larz Anderson: Letters and Journals of a Diplomat*. New York: Fleming H. Revell Company, 1940.

———. *Presidents and Pies: Life in Washington, 1897–1919*. Boston: Houghton Mifflin Company, 1920.

Andrews, Marietta Minnigerode. *My Studio Window: Sketches of the Pageant of Washington Life*. New York: E. P. Dutton, 1928.

Barney, Alice Pike. *Portraits in Oil and Pastel*. Washington, DC: National Collection of Fine Arts, Smithsonian Institution, 1957.

Barry, David S. *Forty Years in Washington*. Boston: Houghton Mifflin Company, 1924.

Beale, Howard K. *Theodore Roosevelt and the Rise of America to World Power*. Baltimore, MD: Johns Hopkins University Press, 1956.

Beer, Thomas. *Hanna, Crane, and the Mauve Decade*. New York: Alfred A. Knopf, 1941.

Bernstorff, Count [Johann Heinrich von Bernstorff]. *My Three Years in America*. New York: Charles Scribner's Sons, 1920.

Bianchi, Lily Urdinola de, et al. *Embassy Residences in Washington, D.C.* Bogota, Colombia: Villegas Editores, 2003.

Blake, Nelson Manford. "Ambassadors at the Court of Theodore Roosevelt." *Mississippi Valley Historical Review* 42 (September 1955): 179–206.

Boardman, Mabel T. *Under the Red Cross Flag: At Home and Abroad*. Philadelphia: J. B. Lippincott, 1915.

Bolles, Blair. *Tyrant from Illinois: Uncle Joe Cannon's Experiment with Personal Power*. New York: W. W. Norton & Company, 1951.

Borchert, James. *Alley Life in Washington: Family, Community, Religion and Folk Life in the City, 1850–1970*. Urbana: University of Illinois Press, 1980.

Boudoir Mirrors of Washington. Philadelphia: John C. Winston Company, 1923.

Brandon, Ruth. *The Dollar Princesses: Sagas of Upward Nobility, 1870–1914*. New York: Alfred A. Knopf, 1980.

Breen, William J. *Uncle Sam at Home: Civilian Mobilization, Wartime Federation and the Council of National Defense, 1917–1919*. Westport, CT: Greenwood Press, 1984.

Brent, Charles Henry. *A Master Builder: Being the Life and Letters of Henry Yates Satterlee, First Bishop of Washington*. New York: Longmans Green & Company, 1916.

Brice, James. *The Nation's Capital*. Edited by Glenn Brown. Washington, DC: B. S. Adams, 1913.

Bridges, Peter. "An Appreciation of Alvey Adee." *American Diplomacy* 12, no. 4 (December 2001): 1–8.

Broderick, Mosette. *Triumvirate: McKim, Mead & White: Architecture, Scandal, and Class in America's Gilded Age*. New York: Alfred A. Knopf, 2010.

Brook-Shepherd, Gordon. *Royal Sunset: The European Dynasties and the Great War*. New York: Doubleday & Company, 1987.

Brown, Glenn. *Memories: 1860–1930*. Washingon, DC: W. F. Roberts Company, 1931.

Browne, Charles Florence Meline. *A Short History of the British Embassy at Washington, D.C., U.S.A. or Forty Years in a School of Diplomacy*. Washington, DC: Gibson Brothers Printers, 1930.

Bruner, Robert F., and Sean D. Carr. *The Panic of 1907*. New York: John Wiley & Sons, 2007.

Burton, David H. *Cecil Spring Rice: A Diplomat's Life*. London: Associated University Presses, 1990.

Busbey, L. White. *Uncle Joe Cannon: The Story of a Pioneer American*. New York: Henry Holt and Company, 1927.

Butt, Archibald. *Taft and Roosevelt: The Intimate Letters of Archie Butt, Military Aide*. 2 vols. New York: Doubleday, Doran & Company, 1930.

Caemmerer, H. Paul. *The Life of Pierre Charles L'Enfant: Planner of the City Beautiful, the City of Washington*. Washington, DC: National Republic Publishing Company, 1950.

Calhoun, Charles W. *The Gilded Age: Perspectives on the Origins of Modern America*. Lanham, MD: Rowman & Littlefield Publishers, 2007.

Cassini, Marguerite. *Never a Dull Moment: The Memoirs of Countess Marguerite Cassini*. New York: Harper & Brothers, 1956.

Cecil, Lamar. *Wilhelm II:Prince and Emperor, 1859–1900*. 2 vols. Chapel Hill: University of North Carolina Press, 1989–96.

Charlick, Carl. *The Metropolitan Club of Washington: The Story of Its Men and Its Place in City and Country*. Washington, DC: Metropolitan Club, 1964.

Chernow, Ron. *The House of Morgan: An American Banking Dynasty and the Rise of Modern Finance*. New York: Touchstone Books, 1990.

Cherny, Robert W. *A Righteous Cause: The Life of William Jennings Bryan*. Norman: University of Oklahoma Press, 1994.

Cigliano, Jan, and Sarah Bradford Landau. *The Grand American Avenue: 1850–1920*. San Francisco: Pomegranite Art Books, 1994.

Clark-Lewis, Elizabeth. *Living In, Living Out: African American Domestics in Washington, D.C. 1910–1940*. Washington, DC: Smithsonian Institution Press, 1994.

Clymer, Kenton J. *John Hay: The Gentleman as Diplomat*. Ann Arbor: University of Michigan Press, 1975.

Cole, John Y., and Henry Hope Reed, eds. *The Library of Congress: The Art and Architecture of the Thomas Jefferson Building*. New York: W. W. Norton & Company, 1997.

Commission of Fine Arts. *Massachusetts Avenue Architecture: Northwest Washington, District of Columbia*. 2 vols. Washington, DC: Commission of Fine Arts, 1973–75.

———. *Sixteenth Street Architecture*, vol. 1. Washington, DC: Commission of Fine Arts, 1978.

Cooper, John M., Jr., ed. *Causes and Consequences of World War I*. New York: Quadrangle Books, 1972.

———, ed. *Reconsidering Woodrow Wilson: Progressivism, Internationalism, War and Peace*, Baltimore: Johns Hopkins University Press, 2008.

———. *Woodrow Wilson: A Biography*. New York: Alfred A. Knopf, 2010.

Cooper, Rachel. *Union Station in Washington, D.C.* Mt. Pleasant, SC: Acadia Press, 2011.

Cosentino, Andrew J., and Henry H. Glassie. *The Capital Image: Painters in Washington, 1800–1915*. Washington, DC: Smithsonian Institution Press, 1983.

Cowdrey, Albert E. *A City for the Nation: The Army Corps of Engineers and the Building of Washington, D.C., 1790–1967*. Washington, DC: Historical Division, Office of Administrative Services, Office of the Chief of Engineers, 1978.

Cox, Henry Bartholomew. "The Protocol Function as an Aspect of Executive Responsibility." Paper presented at George Washington University Law Center, April 30, 1975.

Crane, Katharine. *Mr. Carr of State: Forty-Seven Years in the Department of State*. New York: St. Martin's Press, 1960.

Croly, Herbert. *Marcus Alonzo Hanna*. Hamden, CT: Archon Books, 1965.

Curtis, William Eleroy. *The United States and Foreign Powers*. Meadville, PA: Flood and Vincent and the Chautauqua-Century Press, 1892.

Dahlgren, Madeleine Vinton. *Etiquette of Social Life in Washington*. Philadelphia: J. B. Lippincott, 1881.

Dawes, Charles G. *A Journal of the McKinley Years*. Chicago: Lakeside Press, 1950.

De Koven, Anna Farwell. *A Musician and His Wife*. New York: Harper & Brothers, 1926.

de la Cova, Antonio Rafael. "Fernandina Filibuster Fiascos: Birth of the 1895 Cuban War of Independence, 1895." *Florida Historical Quarterly* 82, no. 1 (Summer 2003).

Dennis, Alfred L. P. *Adventures in American Diplomacy 1896–1906*. New York: E. P. Dutton, 1928.

De Novo, John A. "The Enigmatic Alvey A. Adee and American Foreign Relations, 1870–1924." *Prologue: Journal of the National Archives* 7, no. 2 (Summer 1975): 69–80.

Depew, Chauncey M. *My Memories of Eighty Years*. New York: Charles Scribner's Sons, 1924.

Dierks, Jack. *A Leap to Arms: The Cuban Campaign of 1898*. Philadelphia: J. B. Lippincott, 1970.

Doerries, Reinhard R. *Imperial Challenge: Ambassador Count Bernstorff and German-American Relations 1908–1917*. Translated by Christa D. Shannon. Chapel Hill: University of North Carolina Press, 1989.

Dos Passos, John. *Mr. Wilson's War*. New York: Doubleday & Company, 1962.

Dumba, Constantin. *Memoirs of a Diplomat*. Boston: Little, Brown and Company, 1932.

Dunn, Arthur Wallace. *From Harrison to Harding: A Personal Narrative, Covering a Third of a Century, 1888–1921*. Port Washington, NY: Kennikat Press, 1971.

———. *Gridiron Nights: Humorous and Satirical Views of Politics and Statesmen as Presented by the Famous Dining Club*. New York: Frederick A. Stokes Company, Publishers, 1915.

Emerson, Edwin, Jr., and Marion M. Miller, eds. *The Nineteenth Century and After*. New York: P. F. Collier & Son, 1906. (Maud Pauncefote's memoir included.)

Eulalia, Infanta of Spain. *Court Life from Within*. New York: Dodd, Mead & Company, 1916.

Evans, Mrs. Jessie Fant, ed. *The Olivia Letters of Emily Edson Briggs, 1831–1910*. Washington, DC: Evening Star, 1952.

Farwell, Byron. *Over There: The United States in the Great War, 1917–1918*. New York: W. W. Norton & Company, 1999.

Fawcett, Walter. "Envoys at Washington." *Cosmopolitan*, May 1901.

Feller, Richard T., and Marshall W. Fishwick. *For Thy Great Glory*. Culpeper, VA: Community Press, 1965.

Ferrell, Robert H. *American Diplomacy: A History*. New York: W. W. Norton & Company, 1959.

Field, Cynthia R., and Jeffrey T. Tilman. "Creating a Model for the National Mall." *Journal of the Society of Architectural Historians* 63, no. 1 (March 2004): 52–73.

Flexner, Eleanor. *Century of Struggle: The Woman's Rights Movement in the United States*. Cambridge, MA: Harvard University Press, 1996.

Foraker, Joseph Benson. *Notes of a Busy Life*. 2 vols. Cincinnati: Stewart & Kidd Company, 1916.

Foraker, Julia Bundy. *I Would Live It Again: Memories of a Vivid Life*. New York: Harper & Brothers, 1932.

Forbes-Lindsay, C. H. *Washington: The City and the Seat of the Government*. Philadelphia: John C. Winston Publishers, 1908.

Foster, John W. *The Practice of Diplomacy: As Illustrated in the Foreign Relations of the United States*. Boston: Houghton Mifflin Company, 1906.

Freidel, Frank. *The Splendid Little War*. Boston: Little, Brown and Company, 1958.

General Services Administration [Don J. Lehman]. *Executive Office Building*. Washington, DC: Government Printing Office, 1970.

Gerard, James W. *My Four Years in Germany*. New York: George H. Doran Company, 1917.

Gilbert, Felix, and David Clay Large. *The End of the European Era, 1890 to the Present*. New York: W. W. Norton & Company, 1991.

Glad, Paul W. *McKinley, Bryan, and the People*. New York: J. B. Lippincott, 1964.

Goode, James M. *Best Addresses: A Century of Washington's Distinguished Apartment Houses*. Washington, DC: Smithsonian Institution Press, 1988.

———. *Capital Losses: A Cultural History of Washington's Destroyed Buildings*. Washington, DC: Smithsonian Institution Press, 1979.

———. *The Outdoor Sculpture of Washington, D.C.* Washington, DC: Smithsonian Institution Press, 1974.

Gould, Lewis L. *The Presidency of Theodore Roosevelt*. Lawrence: University of Kansas Press, 1991.

Grayson, Cary T. *Woodrow Wilson: An Intimate Memoir*. Washington, DC: Potomac Publishers, 1960.

Green, Constance. *The Secret City: A History of Race Relations in the Nation's Capital*. Princeton, NJ: Princeton University Press, 1967.

———. *Washington: Capital City, 1879–1950*. Princeton, NJ: Princeton University Press, 1963.

Green, Edward S. *National Capital Code of Etiquette*. Washington, DC: Austin Jenkins Company, 1920.

Gresham, Matilda. *The Life of Walter Quintin Gresham*. Chicago: Rand McNally & Company, 1919.

Grew, Joseph. *Turbulent Era: A Diplomatic Record of Forty Years*. 2 vols. Edited by Walter Johnson. Boston: Houghton Mifflin Company, 1952.

Gwynn, Stephen, ed. *The Letters and Friendships of Sir Cecil Spring-Rice: A Record*. 2 vols. Boston: Houghton Mifflin Company, 1929.

Hall, Florence Marion Howe. *Social Usages at Washington*. New York: Harper & Brothers, 1906.

Harcave, Sidney, ed. *The Memoirs of Count Witte*. Armonk, NY: M. E. Sharpe, 1990.

Harrington, Ty. *The Last Cathedral*. Englewood Cliffs, NJ: Prentice-Hall, 1979.

Harts, William Wright. "His Story." Unpublished ms., 1954. (Courtesy of Cal Horner, York, Maine.)

Hay, John. *Letters and Extracts from His Diary*. Edited by Henry Adams, with Clara Stone Hay. Private publication, 1908.

Hazleton, George Cochrane. *The National Capital: Its Architecture, Art and History*. New York: Press of J. J. Little and Company, 1897.

Heinrichs, Waldo H., Jr. *American Ambassador: Joseph C. Grew and the Development of the U.S. Diplomatic Tradition*. Boston: Little, Brown and Company, 1966.

Hendrick, Burton J. *The Life and Letters of Walter Hines Page*, vol. 3, parts 1 and 2. New York: Doubleday, Page & Company, 1926.

Hewlett, Richard Greening. *The Foundation Stone: Henry Yates Satterlee and the Creation of Washington National Cathedral*. Rockville, MD: Montrose Press, 2007.

Highsmith, Carol M., and Ted Landphair. *Embassies of Washington*. Washington, DC: Preservation Press, 1992.

———. *Pennsylvania Avenue: America's Main Street*. Washington, DC: American Institute of Architects Press, 1988.

Hinman, Ida. *The Washington Sketchbook: A Society Souvenir*. Washington: Hartman & Cadick, Printers, 1895.

Hobsbawm, Eric. *The Age of Empire: 1876–1914*. London: George Weidenfeld and Nicolson, 1987.

Hough, Christina K. "The Army War College in Washington, D.C.: Patriotic and Political Ideals in Architecture by McKim, Mead and White." MA thesis, University of Virginia, 1991.

Howe, M. A. De Wolfe. *George von Lengerke Meyer: His Life and Public Services*. New York: Dodd, Mead & Company, 1920.

Hulen, Bertram. *Inside the Department of State*. New York: McGraw-Hill Book Company, 1939.

Hunsberger, George Sheppard. "The Diplomatic Career of Alvey Augustus Adee, with Special Reference to the Boxer Rebellion." MA thesis, American University, 1953.

Hunt, Gaillard. *The Department of State of the United States*. New Haven, CT: Yale University Press, 1914.

Jacob, Kathryn Alamong. *Capital Elites: High Society in Washington, D.C., after the Civil War*. Washington, DC: Smithsonian Institution Press, 1995.

Jessup, Philip C. *Elihu Root*. 2 vols. New York: Dodd, Mead & Company, 1938.

Jusserand, J. J. *What Me Befell: The Reminiscences of Jules Jusserand*. Boston: Houghton Mifflin Company, 1934.

———. *With Americans of Past and Present Days*. New York: Charles Scribner's Sons, 1916.

Kazin, Michael. *A Godly Hero: The Life of William Jennings Bryan*. New York: Alfred A. Knopf, 2006.

Keim, Randolph de Benneville. *Handbook of Official and Social Etiquette and Public Ceremonials at Washington*. Washington, DC: Randolph D. Keim, 1889.

Kennan, George F. *The Decision to Intervene*. Princeton, NJ: Princeton University Press, 1958.

Kennedy, David M. *Over Here: The First World War and American Society*. New York: Oxford University Press, 2004.

Kling, Jean L. *Alice Pike Barney: Her Life and Art*. Washington, DC: Smithsonian Institution Press, 1994.

Knock, Thomas J. *To End All Wars: Woodrow Wilson and the Quest for a New World Order*. Princeton: Princeton University Press, 1992.

Kohler, Sue A. *The Commission of Fine Arts: A Brief History*. Washington, DC: Government Printing Office, n.d.

Langer, William. *The Diplomacy of Imperialism, 1890–1902*. New York: Alfred A. Knopf, 1951.

Lanius, Judith, and Sharon C. Park. "Martha Wadsworth's Mansion: The Gilded Age Comes to DuPont Circle." *Washington History* 7, no. 1 (Spring–Summer 1995): 24–96.

Lansing, Robert. *War Memoirs of Robert Lansing*. Indianapolis: Bobbs-Merrill Publishers, 1935.

Latane, John Halladay. *America as a World Power, 1897–1907*. Vol. 25 of *The American Nation: A History*. New York: Harper & Brothers, 1907.

———. *A History of American Foreign Policy*. New York: Doubleday, Doran & Company, 1927.

Leech, Margaret. *In the Days of McKinley*. New York: Harper & Brothers, 1959.

Leupp, Francis E. *Walks about Washington*. Boston: Little, Brown and Company, 1915.

Levinson, J. C., and Ernest Samuels. *The Letters of Henry Adams*. 6 vols. Cambridge, MA: Harvard University Press, 1982–88.

Lockwood, Mary S. *Historic Homes in Washington*. Washington, DC: National Publishing Company, 1899.

Logan, Mrs. John A. [Mary Simmerson Logan]. *Thirty Years in Washington*. Hartford, CT: A. D. Worthington & Company, 1901.

Longstreth, Richard, ed. *Housing Washington: Two Centuries of Residential Development and Planning in the National Capital Area*. Chicago: Center for American Places of Columbia College, 2010.

———, ed. *The Mall in Washington: 1791–1991*. New Haven, CT: Yale University Press, 1991.

———. "The Unusual Transformation of Downtown Washington in the Early Twentieth Century." *Washington History* 13, no. 2 (Fall–Winter 2001–2): 51–71.

Longworth, Alice Roosevelt. *Crowded Hours: The Reminiscences of Alice Roosevelt Longworth*. New York: Charles Scribner's Sons, 1933.

Lowry, Edward G. *Washington Close-Ups: Intimate Views of Some Public Figures*. Boston: Houghton Mifflin Company, 1921.

Mahan, A. T. *The Influence of Sea Power Upon History, 1660–1783*. London: Sampson, Low & Marston, 1890.

Martin, Ralph G. *Cissy: The Extraordinary Life of Eleanor Medill Patterson*. New York: Simon & Schuster, 1979.

Matikainen, Satu. "Great Britain, British Jews, and the International Protection of Romanian Jews, 1900–1914." Jyvaskylan Studies in Humanities no. 56. PhD dissertation, University of Jyvaskyla, Finland, 2006.

May, Ernest R. *Imperial Democracy in the Emergence of America as a Great Power*. New York: Harcourt Brace & World, 1961.

———. *The World War and American Isolation, 1914–1917*. Cambridge, MA: Harvard University Press, 1959.

Mayan, Alfred Thayer. *Letters and Papers of Alfred Thayer Mahan*. Edited by Robert Seager and Doris Maguire. Annapolis, MD: Naval Institute Press, 1975.

McElroy, Robert. *Grover Cleveland: The Man and the Statesman*. 2 vols. New York: Harper & Brothers, 1923.

McLean, Evalyn Walsh. *Father Struck It Rich*. With Boyden Sparkes. Boston: Little, Brown and Company, 1936.

Michael, William H. *History of the Department of State, Its Functional Duties together with Biographies of Its Present Officers*. Washington, DC: Government Printing Office, 1901.

Moen, Jon, and Ellis W. Tallman. "The Bank Panic of 1907: The Role of the Trust Companies." *Journal of Economic History* 52 (September 1992): 611–30.

Moore, Charles. *Daniel P. Burnham: Architect and Planner of Cities*. 2 vols. Boston: Houghton Mifflin Company, 1921.

———, ed. *The Improvement of the Park System of the District of Columbia, 1902*. Senate Report, 57th Congress, 1st session. Washington, DC, 1902.

———. *The Life and Times of Charles Follen McKim*. Boston: Houghton Mifflin Company, 1929.

Morison, Elting E., and John Blum, eds. *The Letters of Theodore Roosevelt*. 8 vols. Cambridge, MA: Harvard University Press, 1951–54.

Morris, Edmund. *The Rise of Theodore Roosevelt*, New York: Coward, McCann & Geoghean, 1979.

———. *Theodore Rex*. New York: Random House, 2001.

Morris, Sylvia Jukes. *Edith Kermit Roosevelt: Portrait of a First Lady*. New York: Coward, McCann & Geoghean, 1980.

Mowat, R. B. *The Life of Lord Pauncefote, First Ambassador to the United States*. Boston: Houghton Mifflin Company, 1929.

Mowry, George E. *The Era of Theodore Roosevelt, 1900–1912*. New York: Harper & Row, 1958.

Musicant, Ivan. *Empire by Default: The Spanish-American War and the Dawn of the American Century*. New York: Henry Holt, 1997.

Nevins, Allan. *Henry White: Thirty Years of American Diplomacy*. New York: Harper & Brothers, 1930.

Nicholson, Nigel. *Mary Curzon*. London: Weidenfeld and Nicolson, 1977.

Nolen, John, Jr. "Some Aspects of Washington's Nineteenth Century Economic Development." *Records of the Columbia Historical Society* 49 (1973–74): 524–31.

Olcott, Charles S. *William McKinley*. Boston: Houghton Mifflin Company, 1916.

Olszewski, George J. *DuPont Circle, Washington, D.C.* Washington, DC: Division of History Office of Archaeology and Historic Preservation, 1967.

O'Malley, Frank Ward. *The War-Whirl in Washington*. New York: Century Company, 1918.

Oppel, Frank, and Tony Meisel. *Washington, D.C., a Turn of the Century Treasury*. Syracuse, NY: Castle Publishers, 1987.

O'Toole, Patricia. *The Five of Hearts: An Intimate Portrait of Henry Adams and His Friends, 1880–1918*. New York: Clarkson Potter Publishers, 1990.

Otto, Louis Hein. *Memories of Long Ago*. New York: G. P. Putnam's Sons, 1925.

Pace, Aida de, and David Donald, eds. *Abroad in America: Visitors to the New Nation, 1776–1914*. Washington, DC: Smithsonian Institution and Addison-Wesley Publishing Company, 1976.

Patler, Nicholas. *Jim Crow and the Wilson Administration: Protesting Federal Segregation in the Early Twentieth Century*. Boulder: University Press of Colorado, 2004.

Pepper, Charles M. *Every-day Life in Washington: With Pen and Camera*. Berkley: University of California, 1900.

Peterson, Jon A. *The Birth of City Planning in the United States*. Baltimore: Johns-Hopkins University Press, 2003.

———. "The Nation's First Comprehensive City Plan: A Political Analysis of the McMillan Plan, 1900–1902." *Journal of the American Planning Association* 51 (Spring 1985): 134–50.

Pettigrew, William Franklin. *Imperial Washington: American Public Life 1870–1920*. Chicago: Charles H. Kerr & Company, 1922.

Pringle, Henry F. *The Life and Times of William Howard Taft*. New York: Holt, Rinehart and Winston, 1939.

———. *Theodore Roosevelt: A Biography*. New York: Harcourt, Brace & Company, 1931.

Puleston, W. D. *Mahan: The Life and Work of Captain Alfred Thayer Mahan, U.S.N.* London: Jonathan Cape, 1939.

Reps, John W. *Monumental Washington: The Planning and Development of the Capitol Center*. Princeton, NJ: Princeton University Press, 1967.

Reynolds, Charles Bingham. *Washington: The City Beautiful*. Washington, DC: B. S. Reynolds Company, 1918.

Roper, Daniel C. *Fifty Years of Public Life*. With Frank H. Lovette. Durham, NC: Duke University Press, 1941.

Rousset-Charny, Gérard. "Ernest et Maurice Sanson, une resurgence du classicism, 1863–1914." *Bulletin de la Société de l'histoire de Paris et de l'Île-de-France, 115 année*. Paris: Société de l'histoire de Paris et de l'Île-de-France, 1988–89.

———. *Les palais parisiens de la Belle Époque*. Paris: Délégation à l'action artistique de la Ville de Paris, 1990.

Scott, Pamela, and Antoinette J. Lee. *Buildings of the District of Columbia*. New York: Oxford University Press, 1993.

Seale, William. *The President's House: A History*. 2 vols. Washington, DC: White House Historical Association, 1986.

Seymour, Charles, ed. *The Intimate Papers of Colonel House*. 4 vols. New York: Houghton Mifflin Company, 1925–28.

Shoenfeld, Andrea F. "Restoration of the Ballroom." *Cosmos Bulletin* 66, no. 3 (March 2012): 3–5.

Siegfried, Andre. *America Comes of Age: A French Analysis*. London: Johathan Cape, 1927.

Slayden, Ellen Maury. *Washington Wife: Journal of Ellen Maury Slayden from 1897 to 1919*. Edited by Walter Prescott Webb. New York: Harper & Row, 1962.

Steffens, Lincoln. *The Autobiography of Lincoln Steffens*. New York: Harcourt, Brace and Company, 1931.

Stewart, John C. *Thomas F. Walsh: Progressive Businessman and Colorado Mining Tycoon*. Boulder: University Press of Colorado, 2007.

Stoddard, Henry L. *As I Knew Them: Presidents and Politics from Grant to Coolidge*. New York: Harper & Brothers, 1927.

Stuart, Graham M. *The Department of State: A History of Its Organization, Procedure, and Personnel*. New York: Macmillan Company, 1949.

Sykes, Percy Molesworth. *The Right Honorable Sir Mortimer Durand: A Biography*. London: Cassell Publishers, 1926.

Tabouis, Genevieve R. *The Life of Jules Cambon*. London: Jonathan Cape, 1938.

Taft, Mrs. William Howard [Helen Herron]. *Recollections of Full Years*. New York: Dodd, Mead & Company, 1914.

Tarbell, Ida M. *All in a Day's Work: An Autobiography*. New York: Macmillan Company 1939.

Taylor, A. J. P. *The Struggle for Mastery in Europe 1848–1918*. Oxford: Oxford University Press, 1954.

Teague, Michael. *Mrs. L.: Conversations with Alice Roosevelt Longworth*. New York: Doubleday & Company, 1981.

Thayer, William Roscoe. *The Life and Letters of John Hay*. 2 vols. Boston: Houghton Mifflin Company, 1915.

Trask, David F. "A Short History of the Department of State, 1781–1981." *Department of State Bulletin* 2046 (1981): 515–22.

Truman, Benjamin. *History of the World's Fair: Being a Complete and Authentic Description of the Columbian Exposition from Its Inception*. Philadelphia: J. W. Kelly & Company, 1893.

Tuchman, Barbara W. *The Proud Tower: A Portrait of the World before the War, 1890–1914*. New York: Macmillan Company, 1962.

Tucker, Robert W. *Woodrow Wilson and the Great War*. Charlottesville: University of Virginia Press, 2007.

Tyler, Dennett. *John Hay: From Poetry to Politics*. New York: Dodd, Mead & Company, 1933.

Tyler, Frederick S. *Fifty Years of Yesterday, 1882–1932*. Harrisburg, PA: Evangelical Press, 1932.

U.S. Senate. *Report of Hearings before a Subcommittee of the Senate District of Columbia Committee on the Conduct of the Metropolitan Police at the Suffrage Parade, March 4, 1913*. U.S. Senate, 63rd Congress, special 1st session, Resolution 499. Washington, DC: Government Printing Office, 1913.

Weatherford, Doris. *A History of the American Suffragist Movement*. Santa Barbara, CA: ABC/Clio, 1998.

Weller, Charles Frederick. *Neglected Neighbors: Stories of Life in the Alley Tenements and Shanties of the National Capital*. Philadelphia: J. C. Winston Company, 1909.

Welles, Benjamin. *Sumner Welles: FDR's Global Strategist*. New York: St. Martin's Press, 1997.

Wharton, Edith. *A Backward Glance*. New York: Appleton-Century Company, 1913.

White, William Allen. *The Autobiography of William Allen White*. New York: Macmillan Company, 1946.

———. *Masks in a Pageant*. New York: Macmillan Company, 1930.

Wiebe, Robert H. *The Search for Order, 1877–1920*. New York: Hill and Wang, 1967.

Willson, Beckles. *America's Ambassadors to England 1785–1928*. London: John Murray, 1928.

———. *Friendly Relations: A Narrative of Britain's Ministers and Ambassadors to America, 1791–1930*. London: Lovat Dickson & Thompson Limited, 1934.

Wilson, Edith Bolling. *My Memoir*. Indianapolis: Bobbs-Merrill Company, 1938.

Wilson, Rufus Rockwell. *Washington, the Capital City*. 2 vols., Philadelphia: J. B. Lippincott, 1902.

Wright, Leigh. *Julian Pauncefote and British Imperial Policy, 1855–1889*. Oxford: University Press of America, 2002.

Wu Tingfang. *America through the Spectacles of an Oriental Diplomat*. 1914; reprint, McLean, VA: Alan R. Light, 1996.

Zabriskie, E. H. *American-Russian Rivalry in the Far East: A Study in Diplomacy and Power Politics, 1895–1914*. Philadelphia: Curtis Publishing Company, 1946.

Manuscript and Public Record Collections

Brown University Library
Hay, John. Papers.

Franklin D. Roosevelt Presidential Library
Townsend, Mathilde Welles. "Memoir." Typescript, December 1944.

Georgia State Archives
Butt, Archibald W. Papers.

Historical Society of Washington, D.C.
Berryman, Clifford K. Papers.
Hoxie, Richard and Vennie. Manuscripts.

John F. Kennedy Presidential Library Archives
Halle, Kay. Papers.

Library of Congress, Manuscripts Division
Adee Family Papers.
Adee, Alvey Augustus. Scrapbooks.
Baker, Ray Stannard. Papers.
Barton, Clara. Papers.
Beale Family Papers.
Beveridge, Albert. Papers.
Bingham, Theodore. Papers.
Boardman, Mabel Thorp. Papers.
Cleveland, Grover. Papers.
Corbin, Henry C. Papers.
Cortelyou, George Bruce. Papers.
Cushing, Caleb. Papers.
Daniels, Josephus. Papers.

Foulke, William Dudley. Papers.
Gilbert, Cass. Papers.
Gleaves, Albert. Papers.
Hanna-McCormick Family Papers.
Hay, John. Papers (microfilm edition, including the diaries).
Hay, John. Papers (part of the James Wolcott Wadsworth Jr. Papers).
Helms, Edith. Papers.
Hobson, Richmond Pearson. Papers.
Holmes, Oliver Wendell. Papers.
Long, Breckinridge. Papers.
Longworth, Alice Roosevelt. Papers.
MacVeagh, Franklin. Papers.
McKinley, William. Papers.
McLean, Evalyn Walsh. Papers.
Moore, Charles. Papers.
Olney, Richard. Papers.
Pinchot, Gifford. Papers.
Ramey, George Collier, Family. Papers.
Roosevelt, Theodore. Papers.
Roosevelt, Theodore. Papers (microfilm edition).
Root, Elihu. Papers.
Sherman, John. Papers.
Taft, William Howard. Papers.
Wadsworth, James Wolcott, Jr. Papers.
Wadsworth, James Wolcott, Family. Papers.
Wetmore, George Peabody. Papers.
White, Henry. Papers.
Wilson, Edith Bolling. Papers.
Wise, Charlotte Everett. Papers.

Library of Congress, Maps and Cartography Division
Sanborn Fire Maps.

Library of Congress, Prints and Photos Division
Harris and Ewing Collection.
Historic American Buildings Survey.
Frances Benjamin Johnston Collection.
Underwood and Underwood Collection.

Milne Library, State University of New York, Geneseo
Wadsworth Family Papers.

Missouri Historical Society
Francis, David R. Papers.

National Archives of the United States
Records of the Commission of Fine Arts.
Records of the Department of State, Diplomatic Correspondence.
Records of the Department of State, World War I and Its Termination, 1914–29.
Records of the National Collection of Fine Arts.
Records of the Officer in Charge of Public Buildings and Public Parks of the National Capital.
Social Files, Record Group 42.

Office of the Curator of the White House
Hagner, Belle. Unpublished memoir.

Smithsonian Institution Archives
Barney, Alice Pike. Papers.
Henderson Family Papers. 1868–1923.

Society of the Cincinnati Library, Anderson House
Anderson, Larz and Isabel. Papers.
Anderson, Larz. Journals. Unpublished typescripts. 12 vols.
Childs, Ellen. "Isabel Perkins Anderson." Unpublished biography.

INDEX